Exploring Education Research Literacy

Exploring Educational Research Literacy

Gary Shank
Launcelot Brown

Routledge
Taylor & Francis Group
New York   London

Routledge is an imprint of the
Taylor & Francis Group, an informa business

Routledge
Taylor & Francis Group
270 Madison Avenue
New York, NY 10016

Routledge
Taylor & Francis Group
2 Park Square
Milton Park, Abingdon
Oxon OX14 4RN

© 2007 by Taylor & Francis Group, LLC
Routledge is an imprint of Taylor & Francis Group, an Informa business

Printed in the United States of America on acid-free paper
10 9 8 7 6 5 4 3 2 1

International Standard Book Number-10: 0-415-95527-0 (Softcover) 0-415-95526-2 (Hardcover)
International Standard Book Number-13: 978-0-415-95527-0 (Softcover) 978-0-415-95526-3 (Hardcover)

Library of Congress Cataloging-in-Publication Data

Shank, Gary D.
    Exploring educational research literacy / Gary Shank, Launcelot Brown.
        p. cm.
    Includes bibliographical references and index.
    ISBN 0-415-95526-2 (hardback) -- ISBN 0-415-95527-0 (pbk.) 1.
    Education--Research--Methodology--Textbooks. I. Brown, Launcelot. II. Title.

LB1028.S439 2006
370.7'2--dc22   2006024986

Visit the Taylor & Francis Web site at
http://www.taylorandfrancis.com

and the Routledge Web site at
http://www.routledge-ny.com

Contents

CONTENTS

Preface

Over the years, the notion of teaching students in education to become consumers of research has taken hold in a major way. There are a number of texts that attempt to address this goal—therefore, why is there a need for yet another book in this market?

Our answer is simple. We are not trying to teach students to be consumers of research per se. We are teaching the basics of educational research literacy.

We feel that educational research literacy is a concept whose time has certainly come. There are a number of reasons for this. First of all, the notion of research literacy is a more beneficial concept than mere consumer adequacy. There is something inherently passive about the notion of being a consumer, no matter how hard one works to consume. With the notion of literacy, however, there is a more active dimension. The literate person is applying a set of basic skills, along with his or her own unique knowledge and experience base.

Second of all, the notion of research literacy suggests a beginning point for the learner. Where does a person begin to master a complex domain like educational research? We feel that such mastery begins with the art of learning how to read the fruits of such research efforts in a confident, informed, and critical way. Once a person becomes literate, then he or she can move in any number of ways. She can go on to learn such skill areas as design and evaluation and become a producer of researcher, or he can continue to hone and refine his critical skills, so that every article he reads adds to his growing and sophisticated skill base. Either way, the beginning step is literacy.

Finally, there are some very practical reasons to learn research literacy. For instance, many graduate programs in education have very tight and content-packed curricula. In many cases, research courses have to be selected carefully, because of how tight schedules can be. If we can only offer a few research courses, or perhaps only even one, which courses should we start with or provide? For all the reasons listed above, and more, it makes sense to make sure students are taught to be research literate.

In our experience, we found it helpful to create an entire new course called "Educational Research Literacy." We have crafted and fine-tuned this book through several semesters of teaching this course to our own students. However, we see no reason that this book cannot be used in a standard Introduction to Educational Research setting, particularly if such courses are already geared to a consumer orientation. We have nothing against the notion of being a consumer of research per se—we merely feel that research literacy builds upon that notion in the spirit in which it was first intended.

The development of this book has been, to paraphrase popular culture, a long and strange trip. We would like to thank a number of people who have helped this project reach fruition.

To start with, we would like to thank Stan Wakefield for helping us find such a good home for this book. We would also like to thank Catherine Bernard and Angela Chnapko, our editors at Taylor and Francis, for all their help and support. The efforts of our developmental readers were invaluable in allowing us to tighten our focus on our audience. We would especially like to thank our Educational Research Literacy students at Duquesne University for their feedback and suggestions. Any remaining errors and mistakes are, of course, no one's responsibility but ours.

Introduction

Literacy is one of the most used (and sometimes overused) concepts in today's world. It all begins, of course, with good old-fashioned literacy per se. But there are also a number of other sorts of literacy that have risen up and staked claim to public awareness. It is not enough, anymore, to be simply print literate. In order to function in society, people need to be (among other things) numerically literate, visually literate, culturally literate, and technologically literate.

Within the smaller circle of society that is concerned with the educational process, there is another sort of literacy that has been too often ignored. Those persons who have a stake in professional education, whether they be teachers, administrators, researchers, school board members, business and civic leaders, government officials, or the like, need to be able to read and understand educational research reports and findings. That is, they need to be *research literate*.

Here is the goal of this book—to help its readers become more literate as readers of research. This book will assume that its readers are completely unfamiliar with the terms, methods, assumptions, procedures, and discussions that go into the average research report in education. As a result of these assumptions, this book will start out by helping its readers become better *consumers* of educational research.

By the end of the book, however, readers should be comfortable with exploring the idea that they can become more than just consumers of research—they can become *critical* readers of research as well. True critical literacy in any field takes time and practice, so all that this book can do is to lead its readers to that horizon. It will be up to them to make the effort to gain the critical awareness that can only come over time. The important point, however, is that these readers will be prepared to make the effort in a meaningful way. All of the basics of the processes will now be under their belts, so to speak.

Since this is a book on educational research literacy, we need to get clear from the outset on what "educational research" and "educational research literacy" mean.

What Is Educational Research?

Before we can become literate in educational research, we need to understand what educational research really is. We will introduce the concept of educational research by using the time-honored process of looking at the "who, what, when, where, and why" of educational research. Before we address these questions, however, we need to address one obvious question first:

What Is Education?

This seems like a very easy question to answer. All of us know what education is. It is the thing that goes on in classrooms every day. Teachers teach, and students learn. Now and then, students take tests to make sure they have learned what they have been taught. At the end of the year, students are either held back, they advance, or they graduate. All of us know and understand the basics of this process.

But is the concept of education really this simple? Some of us (e.g., Shank, 2006) think that education is a basic human process. By that, we mean that the act of education, that is, human beings getting together and teaching and learning from each other, is as basic as any other thing that humans do. In other words, we eat, we sleep, we seek shelter and companionship, and we teach and learn from each other. If you doubt the wisdom of these words, perform a little experiment. Gather together three or more people informally. Within five minutes, it is pretty much a sure bet that these people will be engaging in some forms of educational activities.

We need to be careful to realize that education is a very broad concept and practice. All sorts of people are engaged in education in one form or another, and all kinds of activities count as education. Informal education, incidental education, continuing education, education as a force to reform and reshape society—all of these activities help form the rich natural mosaic we call education.

At the same time, for most of us, education is most clearly identified with schooling. That is why the lion's share of educational research is conducted within school settings, or on topics that are most relevant to our current understanding of schooling. As we progress through this book, we will look at both formal and informal types of education.

What Is Educational Research?

The common wisdom in the field is that educational research is "the application of some generally accepted procedures to examine the knowledge base of education" (Hittleman & Simon, 2002, p. 2). Those procedures have a number of basic properties.

First of all, educational research procedures are *public*. Everything about educational research is conducted in a public manner. Data are collected and analyzed openly, and results are shared with all interested parties. The only part of educational research that is not public is (quite often) the actual identities of most of the people who are generous enough to contribute the data we collect. They are entitled to their privacy for a variety of reasons, and researchers strive to respect that fact.

Second, educational research procedures are *systematic*. Research data is neither haphazard nor idiosyncratic. All data are collected for a reason, and all findings should be the result of processes that are not only available for public scrutiny, but which also make sense.

Third, educational research is *purposeful*. That is, all educational research is directed toward one or more goals. Most often, it is designed to answer some research question. That question might take the form of a hypothesis to be tested, a situation to explore, or an understanding that needs to be examined in some detail.

Finally, educational research should be *useful*. The results and findings need to advance our practice or understanding of education in some way. It might result in a new or refined theory, or a guideline for changes in actual practice.

Most educational researchers feel that they are following the tenets of the scientific method in their conduct of educational research (see Shank, 2006, for an exception to at least part of educational research). Within this broader frame, they define their research designs as either quantitative, qualitative, or mixed designs (e.g., Cresswell, 2002). These distinctions will be addressed in much greater detail in later chapters of this work.

Who Does Educational Research?

There are a number of constituents who conduct educational research. The largest group of researchers comes from university settings. More often than not, these research efforts are conducted by professors of education within schools or colleges of education.

Over the years, other research communities have arisen in education. Some educational researchers work for government or independent labs or think tanks. Others work for local, state, and national departments of education. Adult continuing educators and community organizers and educators have been an active research community, particularly in areas such as action research. And there has been an increasing research presence in such informal educational settings as museums, science and learning centers, and zoos.

One area of growth has been particularly interesting—classroom research conducted by working classroom teachers (Eisenhart & Borko, 1993; Gredler, 1999; Hopkins, 2002). Classroom research is changing the face of the field. As teachers become better researchers, they incorporate their research efforts into their teaching efforts. As a result, the boundaries between teaching and research become blurred.

Where Should You Conduct Educational Research?

You need to do research where the action is. Generally, there are three main "sites of action" in educational research:

The Classroom

Since most educational research looks at schooling, it should come as no surprise that much of the research is conducted in schools. Sometimes, the researchers are trying to carefully control for various factors that might interfere with what they are looking for. Other researchers are interested in going into classroom settings as they find them, and seeing what teachers and students are actually doing there.

The "Laboratory"

When researchers are looking for more abstract factors or influences, they need to control the setting more than it can be controlled in most classroom settings. In these cases, they set up carefully controlled interactions, often testing one person at a time. Once clear findings are gathered in these sorts of artificial settings, often researchers will then go back into school settings to see if the results hold up in more natural settings.

The "Library"

Sometimes, researchers work with information that has already been collected and stored for other purposes. These "libraries" of data include such things as demographic data and standardized test scores. By looking at large data sets from all over the country or even the world, researchers can find answers to questions they could not answer by looking at smaller settings or local conditions.

Informal Learning Settings

Education is often where you find it. For those less interested in formal school settings, informal settings can offer a wealth of information. Such settings can range from Adult Learning Centers to museums to zoos to training workshops, to cover just a few of the possible places researchers could investigate. Anywhere teaching and learning is occurring is a potential site for educational research.

When Should You Conduct Educational Research?

You need to do research when the time is right to do it. How can you know when the time is right? Here are a few simple guidelines to look for:

People Are Ready for a Change

Change is at the heart of all educational research. As a result of most educational research efforts, things can be changed for the better. But if people are not willing to change, then there is very little reason to expect your research to make any difference.

People Are Frustrated With the Current State of Understanding or Knowledge

Frustration is often the most powerful incitement to change in educational settings. The status quo is perceived as being inadequate, and teachers and other educational professionals are ready and eager for things to change. Educational research can direct that change toward a systematic search for new knowledge, new theoretical or practical understandings, or new directions for change itself.

Other Researchers Are Moving in Similar Directions

Research, like most human activities, is social in nature. Therefore, researchers tend to move together in certain directions. When a good idea is accepted and practiced by the field as a whole, then research and knowledge both grow at an accelerated rate.

Why Should You Conduct Educational Research?

Research needs a purpose. Fortunately, there are a large number of acceptable general reasons for conducting educational research. Here are a few of the most important of those reasons:

First of all, you could do research to *satisfy your curiosity*. There is nothing wrong with being curious. More often than not, some of the most important and even practical findings have been discovered by people simply looking to scratch some intellectual itch. This sort of research is often called basic research. While many people believe that education is an applied field, this does not mean that researchers cannot do basic research in education as well.

Second, you could do research to *test some theory or hypothesis*. In this case, you have more than a curious notion. You have the beginnings of an understanding of the topic of interest. You are well on your way to coming up with a theory to help explain why teachers or students do what they do. But that theory needs to be tested. The best way to test it is to break down your main theory into a series of testable hypotheses, and then test those hypotheses. When you start getting a clear picture from all these little tests, you can put the whole picture together. It is a bit like working a puzzle—when the pieces start to fit, then the overall picture becomes clearer.

Third, you could do research when *you want to make something better.* It is no longer just enough to understand what is going on. You want to be able to make sure that things improve as a direct result of your research. Actually, all educational research seeks to improve our understanding of the process. It is often a matter of when and where we want that improvement to begin.

By taking into account all the aspects and nuances of education and educational research, you should now be aware that you are dealing with a complex and important area of study. This awareness is the first step to research literacy. We will continue to build on it as we move through this book.

What Is Educational Research Literacy?

Now that we understand the basics of educational research, we will begin the process of developing our educational research literacy by laying out the "ground rules" for becoming a consumer of educational research. This sort of *consumer research literacy* is built around a number of basic points.

It Takes Skill to Read Educational Research Reports

You would not expect a person sitting, say, in a physician's office, to pick up a professional medical journal and effortlessly grasp the material within its pages. Why is that? First of all, the casual reader probably has little or no medical training. Many of the terms and concepts would be foreign to this reader. Second, this casual reader has little or no experience in the medical field per se and therefore would not be aware of many of the assumptions that the journal would expect its readers to make. Finally, this reader would not be aware of trends in the medical field, and so would be unable to put any given article into the proper context of understanding.

Why would things be different in the field of educational research? Educational research is a specialized field, with its own concepts, assumptions, and history. The difference, in your case, is that you know many of these concepts, assumptions, and historical trends. Education is your field of expertise.

Even though education is your field of expertise, there is a good chance that you might find the task of reading and understanding educational research to be a daunting one. There is a tendency to think of educational research as a small area of specialization. Its practitioners speak in complex and specialized ways to each other, and others in the field seem to be shut out. If this is indeed the case, then things have to change. Educational research is for the benefit of the field as a whole, not for just a handful of specialists. That is why it is important for you to improve your skills as a consumer of research.

The trick, for both medical journals and educational research, is not to "water down" either the research or the way that it is reported. That move would be harmful to society as a whole. Instead, you must begin by acknowledging that you bring in a whole set of skills that are related to education. Take a bit of time to inventory some of those skills:

- Have you received professional training to be a teacher? An administrator? A skilled professional, such as a reading consultant or counselor? If you have any or all of these experiences, then you have a solid understanding into the basic nature of education per se, along with some valuable training in how to act as an educator yourself.
- Have you taught in the public schools? In private schools? In higher education? In adult basic education? Have you conducted training on a regular basis? Any or all of these activities contribute to your professional practical experience in education.
- Have you thought about how you might improve things? Are you curious, and do you read things just because you want to know something new? Are you willing to look at something in a new and different way, if it would help make things better? Any and all of these activities contribute to your practical and personal desires and goals to learn, to grow, and to make things better. These factors are at the heart of all good educational research.

For now, do not concentrate on what you do not know. This emphasis on your weaknesses will do nothing but slow down your progress. Everyone has areas of weakness. But, at the same time, everyone has areas of strength as well. If you can build on your strengths, then you will find ways to overcome your weaknesses. This is not just true in learning how to be an educational research consumer—it is true in life as well.

To help show you how much you already understand about how to read educational research, this chapter will lay out many of the basic ideas and goals and practices in the field.

Educational Research Operates Within a Broad Foundation of Ideas

Any literate consumer of educational research understands that there is a tradition of thought that grounds and supports research. Over the years, that tradition has grown, changed, and evolved, like any other living form of human inquiry. Readers are not expected to be experts in any or all of these traditions, but they do need to understand the basics of each tradition. Currently, there are three basic traditions that need to be addressed:

Basic Quantitative Ideas

One of the goals of many kinds of educational research is the desire to do scientifically valid work. In educational research, these goals are most often addressed within the framework of quantitative thinking. Chapter 2 addresses some of the fundamental ideas of quantitative inquiry in nontechnical language.

Statistics

It is no accident that educational research and statistics have grown hand in hand. Chapter 3 addresses some of the fundamental ideas of statistics in nontechnical language. It is not a substitute for learning statistics by any means, but it can help you get your feet on the ground, so to speak.

Basic Qualitative Ideas

Over the years, we have seen the rise and growth of qualitative perspectives and methods in educational research. This form of inquiry is quite different from quantitative research. Chapter 4 addresses some of the fundamental ideas of qualitative inquiry in nontechnical language.

Literate Consumers of Research Know How Educational Research Is Created

Educational research is not created in a vacuum. In order to understand the field as a whole, you need to be aware of the motivations and practices of educational researchers.

The first and most basic source of motivation is *curiosity*. Researchers, especially basic researchers, simply want to know or understand something.

The next source is *practical need*. The researchers, or someone they know, are dealing with a practical problem. Rather than just address these problems in an ad hoc fashion as they arise, it makes sense to do some research to see if you can address these problems in a comprehensive way.

Many research efforts are *funded*. Here, researchers are addressing issues of concern to others who are willing to pay the researchers to tackle these issues. In some rare cases (that are getting rarer as time goes by), funders will give researchers money and then allow the researchers to look at whatever they want. This sort of funded basic research has been giving away to funding designed to address specific issues and tackle specific concerns, often from a specific approach or point of view. Often, but not always, researchers will mention if their research is funded, and who is funding the work.

Probably the most common source of motivation in research is the desire to address an *ongoing concern or issue*. Trends and problems arise in research, and researchers pursue those trends or problems. Part of becoming a literate consumer is being aware of those trends and issues, and learning how to track down antecedents of research so that you can understand where everyone is coming from.

A final common source is the desire of researchers to build a *consistent body of work*. It is rare for researchers to hop from one problem to another. More often, they work singly or collectively to build a consistent and coherent body of work. This is not surprising, since one research question often leads to another, then another, and then yet another. The literate reader of research understands this process, and is prepared to track down important past work in order to understand how this body of work came to take shape and what the researchers are trying to say, prove, and find.

The Article Is the Basic Form of Educational Research Writing

There are a number of formats and outlets for reporting educational research findings.

The easiest and most accessible source for many readers is the Internet. The Internet has changed the way that educational research is conducted and its finding disseminated. Like any new way of doing things, however, the use of the Internet comes with some growing pains for the field of educational research. We will look at how to use (and not abuse or be abused by) the Internet in Chapter 14.

Next, there are a number of magazines and journals that summarize or discuss research without going into depth. These sources are called secondary sources, and they are covered in depth later in this chapter.

The next sources for educational research are regional, state, or national conferences. A good rule of judgment is this—the larger the geographical spread, the more competition to get conference papers accepted. Therefore, the greater the chance that any given conference paper has had to "prove itself as worthy" in comparison to other papers that might have been accepted for presentation instead. What does this mean for us? Simply this—the more competition, the more general likelihood that the research that is accepted is of acceptable quality and addresses issues of broad interest or concern. Since research journals publish many fewer total number of articles (as compared to articles accepted for conference presentation), then we should expect only the best conference articles to find their ways into the journal literature, as well.

Educational research can also be found in private or government reports. These reports are available from a variety of sources and in a variety of formats. More often than not, they have been conducted to address particular concerns or issues that have been raised by those commissioning this research. The best of this work usually finds its way into the research journals, so it is often not necessary to go out looking for the private or government reports. Most often, it is best to wait to see if the research gets into the research literature in more traditional ways.

In one sense, educational research comes in all sorts of packages and settings. There are reports, both governmental and private. There are books that report and interpret research findings. More and more, there are Web pages and other Internet sources that allow broader access to educational research findings.

In the final analysis, however, the bulk of educational research is reported in conference and journal articles. As we have already pointed out, journal articles represent the "cream of the crop" of educational research reports. Unlike most of the secondary articles we will examine in a little bit, primary articles are written by the researchers doing the work. All the important findings are included, rather than summarized. Methods are described in great detail, to allow us to understand how the research was conducted, and to even show us how to replicate the work if we so choose. This book will concentrate upon reading primary articles for obvious reasons—if we can learn how to read primary articles, then we should be able to tackle any other source of educational research reporting.

Getting Started

So now we are ready to look at the process of reading research articles. The first place to start is by looking at some of the basics of educational research. The following list of basics is not exhaustive, by any means, but it should help ground you in the field as a whole:

Research Articles Are Written to Address Four Basic Goals

When researchers write research articles, they do so with four basic goals in mind.

The first and most important goal in writing research articles is to *create a useful public record* of their research efforts and findings. What good is it to do research, if the researchers do not share their results? Furthermore, researchers do not want their articles to be just buried away in some dusty archive where no one will pay attention to them. That is, researchers also want to make sure their articles are useful enough for others to read and hopefully incorporate into future research efforts.

Second, researchers strive to *write research articles that are as precise and accurate as possible*. To be precise and accurate, researchers need to document thoroughly and correctly any and all pertinent steps, procedures, and findings. It does no good to create a public record if that record does not document all relevant aspects of the research. Wading through complicated details or following extended threads of logic can be demanding and taxing on readers, but this level of documentation is often necessary to create a complete and accurate picture of the researcher's efforts and findings.

The third basic goal for researchers is to *create articles that are as clear as possible*. If target readers cannot understand the points and conclusions of these articles, what good is it to place them in the public record in the first place? The most diligent researchers try to insure that their articles are clear by making them as easy to read as possible. The more readable an article is, the more likely that its target readers will spend time and effort in reading it.

The best plan for meeting the goals described above is simple—researchers need to *organize their articles in as orderly a fashion as possible*. This final basic goal helps pull everything together into a meaningful whole.

Researchers Strive to Make Their Articles Well Organized and Easier to Read

There are a number of procedures that researchers often draw upon to make their articles better organized and easier to read.

The first procedure is *rhetorical*. Researchers try to use simple terms and simple grammatical constructions whenever possible. There are some rhetorical conventions that are familiar to experienced readers that are also used. The two most common conventions, particularly in quantitative research articles, are the use of the third person (e.g., "the researcher found" instead of "I found") and the use of the passive voice. Rhetorical issues of research articles will be addressed in more depth in later chapters.

The second procedure is *strategic*. Researchers primarily use two strategies to make their articles as orderly as possible. The first strategy is to draw upon conventional *structures* used in research writing, and the second strategy is to use *precedents* that are familiar to most readers. Each of these strategies will be discussed in turn.

Researchers Build Their Articles Around Basic Structures

Researchers tend to use basic *structures* that are familiar to experienced readers. Many of these basic structures are explicitly labeled in the article itself. They might include things like Abstracts, Introductions, Methods sections, Results sections, and Discussion sections.

There is another type of basic structure that is more implicit, but just as important. This is the manner in which researchers select and arrange key facts and points throughout their articles to make the articles as clear and as thorough as possible. These less obvious structures can be called *textual structures*.

The textual structure of an article consists of its "bare bones." What are the main points to be addressed? What are the main arguments to support these points? What are the main results? How should they be interpreted? What are their implications? The Abstract can point us toward the textual structure of an article, but abstracts are too short to do the whole job. You must search for textual structures within the main body of the article as well.

In a clear and orderly article, extracting the textual structure gives you the "foundation" of the article. On the other hand, if the textual structure is not clear and well organized, then there is no way that the article as a whole will be easy to follow. So it makes sense for you to learn how to "dig out" the textual structure of an article.

There are many ways to identify and document textual structures in a research article. Here are three of the most common procedures.

One of the oldest ways to chart textual structure is to *outline* the article. Lay out the key sections of the article as your main headings, and break out the main points below these headings. Seeing these main points in reduced form often helps us to consider a number of complex points at the same time.

People who are more comfortable with visual forms of representation often map out key points by making *charts and illustrations*. These charts and illustrations are mostly just visual forms of outlines, but mapping topics and arguments visually often makes complex inter-relations easier to see and understand.

Finally, many readers resort to *underlining or highlighting* key points and passages in the article itself. This allows you to reread articles in a more focused way. As you reread, the underlined or highlighted passages seem to jump out and demand your extra attention. This is an excellent way to focus on key points, and pay less attention to supporting points and evidence.

Readers do not have to take the time to document textual structures in each and every article, nor use the same process each time. These strategies are tools to use when the organization of an article is difficult to grasp. A little extra effort can often yield great increases in understanding.

Researchers Draw Upon "Precedents" to Write Orderly Articles

Researchers also draw upon the insight that no research article stands alone. Even if its topic area is brand-new, the article is still built upon a foundation of accepted procedures and time-honored assumptions. These *precedents* allow both researchers and readers to approach articles with some sense of knowing what to expect, and what sorts of practices and assumptions are acceptable or not.

There are four basic kinds of precedents that most researchers use when they conduct their work and then write their articles. These types are *rules, conventions, shared knowledge, and shared assumptions*.

Rules

Nearly every form of research has some set of explicit rules that are used to conduct research and create, analyze, and interpret findings. Specific rules will be covered in some depth at various places in later chapters. For now, here are four of the most important rules that cut across nearly every type of research article.

Use specific methods correctly.   When researchers use methods to organize and analyze their data, they must use the proper methods. For instance, if they are doing a statistical analysis, they must use the proper statistical tools. For example, they should not use a t test when an ANOVA is appropriate (we will take a brief look at these, and other, statistical concepts, in Chapter 3). And if they do use an ANOVA, they must perform it correctly. Or, to take a more qualitative example, if they are doing a grounded theory analysis, their efforts need to match the procedures laid out to do grounded theory.

Some forms of research methods have less explicit rules. In these cases, researchers need to show us how and why they used the methods they used, in the manner that they used them.

Tell us how you did your research.   Every research article needs to be laid out so that we could do it ourselves if we chose to do so. Redoing a research study is called *replication*. The only exception to this principle occurs when the research is either so unique, or so grounded in a particular time or setting, that it could not be repeated. If this is the case, then the researchers need to set out each and every key step so that we can follow the progression of the research.

Tell us every important thing you found.   Researchers are not allowed to hold back information or findings that do not match their assumptions and goals. They do not have to give us each and every trivial detail, unless that detail goes against the "grain" of the research. But in that case, the detail is no longer trivial, is it?

Treat all participants in an ethical fashion.   This is one of the most important rules for any form of social science research. More often than not, research in this field involves using other people. These people need to be protected. They need to be protected from physical harm, and they need to be protected from psychological or social harm. Their privacy must be respected and protected. If they are members of a particularly vulnerable population, such as children or people with special needs or people who are institutionalized for some reason, then they deserve to be the objects of special scrutiny.

Conventions

Conventions are "softer" than rules, but they are no less important. Think of conventions as the ways that researchers have traditionally approached a topic or area. Often, researchers will assume that readers are familiar with the conventions they use, and so the researchers might not describe these conventions explicitly in the article.

Many conventions deal with the methods that researchers employ. For instance, in education there has been a long-standing convention of using experimental or quasi-experimental methods when testing the presence or impact of some factor assumed to be significant in some educational setting. This convention assumes that the factor can be isolated and studied. Many of these studies use some form of a treatment vs. control group design. Researchers assume that their readers are familiar and comfortable with this "isolate and test" approach, and so they make little or no effort to justify its use.

Sometimes, there are shifts in convention in a research area. In the case of the experimental approach described above, a growing number of educational researchers are taking different approaches to the study of the same sorts of factors. Some for instance can follow the conventions of action research, which say that researchers become part of the process and that when the research is finished, everyone in the setting has benefited from the work of the researcher. This is not just the application of a different set of rules to a similar topic; it is employing a different set of conventions about how and why to do research in the first place.

In the case of the example above, one convention is not better than the other. Each has its own set of strengths and weaknesses. Researchers need to be aware of the values and limits of the conventions they use, and readers also need to be aware of the same things as they read and evaluate research articles. Conventions will be revisited in a number of later chapters, where their specific operations will be examined.

Shared Knowledge

Shared knowledge consists of the information base that researchers assume their readers possess. There are two broad domains of shared knowledge:

Global shared knowledge. Global shared knowledge consists of those facts and understandings that researchers assume any average informed and intelligent reader might possess. These areas can be as simple as the notion that the world is round and revolves around the sun, and as complex as a general awareness of the importance of the theories of evolution or relativity. These sorts of knowledge are rarely documented in either the literature review or the References section. Further examination of these sorts of knowledge is beyond the scope of this work, but the thoughtful reader can contemplate how such knowledge can often serve as the invisible "glue" that holds many research articles together.

Specific shared knowledge. Specific shared knowledge deals with the actual content material of the research article. Such content material consists of theoretical and factual statements and claims that are relevant to the article, as well as a history of prior research in the content area addressed by the article. Key areas of specific shared knowledge should be mentioned in the literature review within the article and documented in the References section. Later chapters will look more closely at the role of the literature review and the use of references in research articles.

Shared Assumptions

Shared assumptions are more global and more implicit than shared knowledge, but they are an important part of the research "landscape."

One of the best ways to illustrate the operation of shared assumptions is to look at some of the differences between the assumptions that quantitative researchers share, and to compare them to the shared assumptions of qualitative researchers. These two sets of assumptions are quite different from each other. The foundational ideas of both qualitative and quantitative research, including important shared assumptions within each field, will be covered in depth in following chapters.

In the End, Content Matters

Structures and precedents are useful forms. They allow researchers to work with familiar patterns and ideas. They also provide a zone of comfort for readers. Once readers become accustomed to these sorts of patterns and ideas, they basically know what to expect from an article. That is, they grasp its formal nature.

There is a much bigger side to the story, however. Ultimately, a research article has to be about something. It has to address some *content*. Just as there are rules of order for articles, there are also rules of content.

The Contents of an Article Must Not Be Deliberately False

Fifty years ago, researchers would have insisted that the contents of an article must be true. In those days, there was nearly total agreement about the nature of truth in educational research. Nowadays, there is some debate about the nature of truth. These debates will be considered in later chapters. For now, it is clear that no researchers, regardless of their stance on truth, would condone the use of deliberate falsehoods.

At Least Some of the Contents of an Article Should Be New

An article should bring some new knowledge, new theory, or some new understandings or insights to the field. If everything that an article discusses or documents has been published before, then there is no need for this particular article. Even if an article replicates the findings of an earlier article, it should still push the realm of content forward at least a little bit.

The Content of an Article Should Be Accessible to Its Target Audience

Some articles are more specialized than others. They might address a smaller, more knowledgeable subset of researchers and readers. If they do, then that audience should be identified within the article. The use of key terms and concepts in the title and abstract of the article is a common way to signal the intended target audience. If the article makes no effort to address a specific audience, then the content and its presentation should be relevant and accessible to the average reader in the field.

Educational Research Articles Can Be Tackled Part by Part

The overall game plan for becoming a literate consumer of educational research depends upon you being able to master the art and skill of reading an educational research article.

The best way to tackle any research article is to take it on, piece by piece. Most, if not all, articles are broken down into discrete and specific parts. Each part has its own nature, characteristics, and purposes. Chapters 5 through 11 will take you from the Title to the Discussion section, and all steps in between, to assist you in learning how to look at each of these parts as a literate consumer of research.

Start With What You Know

Nearly everyone struggles at first when they start reading research articles. This feeling of struggling gradually goes away as readers eventually begin to master the art of understanding the form and content of research articles.

It is much easier to read familiar content. If you do not have to struggle with the ins and outs of the content as much, then it is easier to learn how the formal properties of research articles work. Therefore, start with what you know. You may not be much of an expert in an area, but every little bit of prior knowledge and understanding helps.

It also helps if you are interested in a content area, as well. That interest can be based on personal need, personal experience, or just plain curiosity. Anything that helps you to persevere with the task of struggling through an article will eventually help you master the art of reading articles.

At the beginning, scout around a bit to see if you have other preferences as well. Do you like quantitative articles better than qualitative articles? Ethnographies better than experiments? If you are comfortable with one type of research over another, then it does no harm to concentrate on articles using that form at the outset. However, do not lose sight of the fact that you will eventually have to master the art of reading all major forms of articles. Search out familiar content areas that use less familiar forms of research, and gradually work those articles into your reading repertoire.

Above all, do not get discouraged. This book has been designed to help reduce some of the trial and error that occurs when students try to learn this process without any sort of guidance, but it still requires a great deal of effort on your part (and on the part of your instructor, if you have one). This sort of mastery is a slow and gradual process. Be patient, take your time, and you will be amazed by your progress!

Secondary Articles

Secondary Articles Are Important Starting Points for Research Literacy

When people are just starting to learn to read, they generally do not begin with such things as, say, *War and Peace* or *Finnegan's Wake*. The length and complexity of such works are beyond the abilities of most novice readers. They need to start short and simple, instead.

The same is true for educational research literacy. No one should expect you to wade in and tackle long and complex research articles from the outset. Instead, we have developed the following alternative strategy for this text. First of all, we have written a series of simplified articles that we call "training articles." These training articles allow you to see how articles are constructed by giving you very simple articles designed to illustrate key points in a clear and uncomplicated way. Each training article is then linked to a "real" article that was actually published in an educational research journal. Each real article is similar in tone and content and method to the training article linked with it. Finally, as you progress, you will be invited to find and read and evaluate actual educational research articles in fields and areas that interest you personally. In this way, if you practice and work hard, you can speed up the process of educational research literacy substantially. The steps are laid out explicitly in the chapters to follow.

Before we tackle the task of reading and understanding these linked training and real articles, however, we will spend some time first looking at a common alternative—another simple entry point into educational research areas. This is the route of the *secondary article*.

In order to understand what a secondary article is, we first have to distinguish it from what is known as a primary article. Our training articles and the real articles linked to them are examples of primary articles. A primary article has several identifying traits. First of all, it is written by the researchers who have actually conducted the research being reported. Second, a primary article presents actual research findings instead of summaries or descriptions of such findings. And finally, and most importantly, primary articles are published in peer-reviewed journals. A peer-reviewed journal operates in the following fashion. Upon receiving a manuscript for potential publication, the editor sends a blind copy (that is, a copy without any author names on it) to two or more professionals in the field with expertise in the area of the article. These reviewers evaluate the article and offer their recommendations. Sometimes they recommend publication without changes; most often, they recommend revisions or reject the article as not worthy of publication. The value of this peer review process is the fact that it helps guarantee that the quality and accuracy of published primary articles remains high.

Secondary articles are usually not peer reviewed, and summarize, describe, or reflect upon research in a variety of ways. In the following pages, you will examine a number of common types of secondary articles to learn how to read and interpret them. You will also concentrate on their strengths and weaknesses, and you will also learn when it is okay to use them and when you need to move on and tackle primary sources.

Why is it important to be able to recognize and use secondary articles? At various points, you will most likely need to tackle new areas of knowledge and research. You will have to begin reading research articles in these areas, and you will not have prior interests or knowledge to fall back upon. When you have become a skilled reader of research articles, you will be able to bring your skills to bear on this task. You will know how to find the most important articles, and read them first. You will understand how researchers often use different formal properties of their articles to explore and document content areas. Before too long, these content areas will start taking shape for you.

At the beginning you may be often overwhelmed by such situations, however. More often than not, you use trial and error as you wade through a body of research literature. While any successful process, including trial and error, can help you become a more skilled reader, some processes are more economical and less painful for beginners. This is one of the most useful purposes of secondary articles—they can allow you entry into a new area of study without wrestling with complex issues at the outset. The material has already been interpreted somewhat for you.

A Secondary Article Is a Simple Way to Access a New Research Area

If you are struggling with research articles in an unfamiliar content area, find a simpler version of these articles. That is, find some secondary articles, and read them to get a general idea of the content area. Then, you should be able to return to *primary articles* to complete your reading.

A primary article is an account of actual research findings written by the researchers doing the actual work. A secondary article, on the other hand, is the work of someone that has read primary research articles or reports and then tells us their understandings and thoughts about those research findings (occasionally, but not often, the researchers themselves might write a secondary article, in an attempt to get their ideas out to a wider audience). Secondary sources are not usually based directly on research findings. Instead, secondary articles are usually based on interpretations of primary articles. These secondary articles are often published in journals or magazines that do not employ a peer review system. Therefore, there are less checks and balances on the accuracy of the material. In addition, the writing is expected to be targeted for a less rigorous audience. In short, secondary articles help introduce complex ideas and findings to a broader audience.

Secondary articles help you understand how findings might be interpreted in a broader sense, how findings can be summarized for a lay audience, or what researchers think about their research and their findings. These articles allow casual consumers of research to get a basic sense into what is going on in a given area.

Almost always, secondary articles are easier to read. There are two main reasons for this. First of all, the goals of secondary articles are different from the goals of primary articles. Secondary articles are much more global in scope, and so they do not have to be as precise and complete. They are not required to focus on all the research efforts and findings covered in the primary research, but only on those efforts and findings that are most important and interesting to a lay audience. Finally, they are usually oriented to make one key point. It is the job of the secondary article author to interpret all the findings from the primary research sources and to find the key points to use to present these research efforts to a lay audience.

Good Secondary Articles Can Be Easily Found

There are many good sources of secondary articles that you can use to initiate access to many types of educational research findings. Here are just a few of the most common, listed in alphabetical order:

* *The Chronicle of Higher Education*
* *Educational Leadership*
* *Educational Researcher*
* *Educational Technology*
* *Instructor*
* *Learning*
* *Phi Delta Kappan*

Lists like these cover a wide range of topics and specialty areas. At the same time, there is a great deal of consistency among the formats of their articles. One of the easiest ways to master the art of reading secondary articles is to look for common formats and learn to use them in understanding how the articles were put together.

There Are a Number of Common Formats for Secondary Articles

Secondary articles are often easy to read because they use familiar formats. Here are just a few of the most common formats for secondary articles.

Lay Review

Our first example of a secondary article form is the *lay review*. A lay review is a review that is intended for a lay audience, or an audience with no specialized knowledge of the topic under consideration. A lay review usually addresses a general, or global, topic. Its goal is to give its readers an overview of the area or issues under consideration, and not a detailed account of particulars. In other words, a lay review provides *exposure* to a topic. If you are interested in learning more, then you must explore other sources to find more detailed information.

An example of a lay review might be an article on recent research on motivation in a popular journal for teachers. The author of such a review would usually gather research from a variety of sources and approaches toward motivation, and would also summarize major trends. Such articles also often contain practical hints for applying the research as well. The emphasis is not on the details of the research, but on the broad findings and potential applicability of the work.

Focused Review

Our second example of a secondary article form is the *focused review*. In the focused review, the article promises to reveal to us "what research can tell us about Topic or Issue X." The audience for a focused review is the set of people who have some interest or concern in "Topic or Issue X." More often than not, this group of people already has some degree of knowledge and understanding of the topic or issue under consideration. However, these same people usually do not have the time, or perhaps the specialized skill, to seek out information directly from the research literature. The authors of focused reviews serve as the mediators between the research literature and the people who want or need those research findings.

An example of a focused review might be an article on recent research on extrinsic motivation in classroom settings, and its impact on standardized testing. Here, the review is much more focused, and the results are presented in a bit more detail. Like the lay review, though, the focused review concentrates on collecting and synthesizing research from a variety of settings, with the aim of giving an overall picture of the topic along with suggestions for applying the research to real educational settings. While the focused review gives the appearance of being a more direct source of information about research, it is still necessary to go to the original research studies if you need to understand those studies in some detail.

Action Plan

Our third example of a secondary article form is the *action plan*. In an action plan article, research findings are brought up for the specific task of supporting or guiding some form of action or other practical consequences. In addition you usually find a plan of things to accomplish, hence the label "action plan."

An example of an action plan might be an article on improving standardized test scores in a particular school or school district. Research is often discussed and summarized, but now it is intermingled with personal experiences and specific practical suggestions. In a sense, the action plan is a combination of the focused review and the opinion piece.

Interview

Our fourth example of a secondary article form is the *interview*. The interview format usually deals with a researcher who is being asked questions relevant to his or her area of research. The researcher usually deals with his or her research in a more personal and less formal manner. Often, researchers do these sorts of interviews in order to reach a broader audience. It is not hard to identify an interview article in a popular journal.

Opinion Piece

Our fifth example of a secondary article form is the *opinion piece*. In the opinion piece, you find material that is taken from the world of experience, but is not the product of research per se. More often than not, the opinion piece is a vehicle to capture the "practical wisdom" of an expert in some area. Since the wisdom is not backed up by formal research, it is still opinion. But the opinions of experts are usually valuable, and can often point researchers toward interesting and important topics.

An example of an opinion piece might be an article on the value of recess for first graders. Usually, the author is a person who is directly involved in the lives of first graders—a teacher, a principal, or a counselor. The authors draw upon their years of experience and their concerns for the welfare of students. More than any other secondary article, the opinion piece makes a case for a particular set of actions or point of view.

An opinion piece is the hardest type of secondary source article to evaluate. On the one hand, it captures the experience and wisdom of someone who is often in a unique position to see things the rest of us simply could never see. On the other hand, by turning away from the systematic pursuit of facts, the opinion piece leaves itself open to the charge that the author is biased and might be reporting (or even perceiving!) only what the author chooses to see. If any of the secondary source types cry out for further exploration using the tools of research, it is the opinion piece.

You Need to Exercise Some Caution When Reading and Using Secondary Articles

You cannot depend on secondary articles in the same way you might trust the primary research articles they reflect. Why is this so? Writers differ in their abilities to interpret and summarize. Writers also differ in their abilities to understand and to draw conclusions and implications from their understandings. Therefore, we would expect some secondary articles to be much better than other secondary articles.

A good secondary article can put us in touch with the basic issues and findings that it addresses, but a bad article might misinterpret or misunderstand the points of the original article, or present certain claims or findings outside their original contexts. Here is a useful practical guideline—if the research cited in a secondary article seems either too good or too bad to be true, or you feel that the original research might have been oversimplified, then go back to the original source and check it for yourself. You will ultimately be returning to those sources anyway; you might as well make sure that you are not getting off to a bad start.

Never Settle for a Simple Version if You Can Master the Real Thing

If you want findings that you can really trust, then go directly to the original source. You should not trust secondary article authors to sort and interpret findings in just the same ways that you would. Also, there is a very good chance that there are findings and implications that were not reported in the secondary article. How can you be sure that these other findings and implications are not important to you?

You may start your exploration of an area with secondary articles, but you should always finish it with a solid foundation of primary research. That is why it is so important to master the art of reading primary research articles.

Learn to Take Apart an Article to Find All the Information You Need

Research articles are put together in an orderly fashion, using structures, precedents, and content. Anything that has been put together can be taken apart. The art of learning how to read a research article by taking it apart and extracting information is the art of being a *consumer* of research.

Consumer skills are extremely important for both researchers and their readers. Researchers work hard to make sure their articles provide information for their readers. Readers must also learn how to access that information and evaluate it. In later chapters, there will be many consumer skills presented for you to learn and master.

Once You Understand an Article, Engage It

The best researchers and readers go beyond being just consumers of research. They become *critical readers* of research.

The key to critical reading is *engagement*. When you engage something you are reading you are not just extracting information from it. You are engaging in a kind of dialogue with it. You look beyond findings toward implications for the present and the future. You explore assumptions that researchers make, and try to think what might happen if different assumptions were held. In short, you are reading in an active, creative fashion.

As you become more expert in your ability to read research articles, you will find your critical facilities naturally growing. You will continue to extract information, but you will seek a dialogue with researchers and their articles. When you become as skilled in critical reading as you are in consumer reading, then you will finally know that you are an expert reader of research articles. This work will help you become a better consumer of research, but it will also help you develop your critical skills as well. Critical topics will become more and more important in the later chapters.

Teaching and Learning Educational Research Literacy

This book will strive to help you understand the basics of educational research literacy. We will try to answer questions you might have at the outset, which might confuse and hinder your learning. But, in the end, there is no substitute for practice. Therefore, your success will ultimately depend on how much effort you are willing to expend in this process.

We believe in a program of guided practice. To that end, we will start with a set of chapters that describe some of the basic points you need to understand about quantitative research, statistics, and qualitative research. It may seem that we are taking our sweet time in getting to the task of reading actual articles, but it has been our experience that novice readers of educational research often stumble when they do not understand basic assumptions about methods and approaches. So please be patient as we work our way through these basics.

Once we have a suitable grounding in the basics, then we turn to reading articles. We have provided two sets of articles—training articles and real articles. Training articles are not real. They are simple versions of the kinds of articles you will find when you read refereed journals. We wrote these simple articles as a sort of primer. They should help you grasp how articles are put together, and what they seek to achieve. We recommend that you go to the Appendices and read each of these training articles. Before each article, there is a set of questions to help guide your reading. Please pay attention to these questions, and try to answer them as you read.

There are two more sets of articles. The first set consists of real articles, written by real researchers and published in real journals, which deal with the sorts of issues and methods first raised in the training articles. When you feel ready to tackle these more complex and challenging articles, we recommend you read them as well. Finally, there are two real mixed methods articles. You will read these in conjunction with Chapter 12.

After you have read the training articles, then you are ready to tackle the next phase of this course. Here, we will examine the key parts of articles from titles to conclusions. As you progress through these chapters, we suggest that you turn to the real articles and read them as soon as you feel ready. This will help you understand the points we make in the chapters, particularly those points we illustrate with excerpts from the real articles themselves.

Next, there are a few advanced topics that need to be addressed. We take a look at mixed methods articles, to see how they compare with ordinary articles and why many researchers feel they will play more and more of a role in the field. Then we take a quick look at some of the overarching issues that affect how we read and understand educational research articles, from reliability and validity to types of errors researchers need to avoid.

Finally, we ask you to think about being a critical reader and to look at some of the dynamics of criticism in educational research as well as other forms of reading. When you are done, it is our wish that you will have a well-rounded beginning toward educational research literacy, as well as an appreciation of both research and critical reading in general.

Our Emerging Literacy Orientation

There are many ways to understand the concept of educational research. This book is about educational research literacy. People who are research literate can read many types of research reports and articles, and benefit in a variety of ways from the practice. One of the basic ways to benefit is to extract information—that is, to be an effective and efficient consumer. We will begin with the process of mastering the art of being a research consumer, and then build upon these skills until we are able to read critically.

Practice Makes Perfect

It is now time to practice some of the insights and skills you have explored in this chapter:

- First of all, create your own definition of education. Are you more interested in practical issues or theoretical issues?
- Think of a possible research question in education. It can be something very simple. How might a professor go about researching this question? How might a teacher research this same question? What would be the same? What would be different?
- Where would be a good setting to search for an answer to this research question? Could you go right into a school setting or would you have to test it out first?
- Why are you interested in this research question, to begin with? How would you like the results of your research to impact the field?
- Can you create an inventory of the skills you bring into the process of becoming research literate? Are you a skilled teacher? Administrator? Are you good at math? Have you already read lots of articles? This sort of profile can serve as your personal guide to your strengths. Effective learners most often build upon their strengths, so it is good to know what they are, at the outset.
- Can you make a list of conventions, rules, shared knowledge, and shared assumptions that are important in your personal field? Compare your list with those of students in other areas. How are your lists similar? Different?
- Describe an important piece of research in your field. What questions did it attempt to address? How was it funded? How was it reported to the field? What can you learn about research in general by looking at the way this research was conducted, reported, and presented to readers such as yourself?
- Make an inventory of a research topic where you already have developed some degree of familiarity. Why is this area important to you? Have you read primary research articles on this topic? Have you read secondary research articles on this topic? Could you write a summary of this topic area for a lay audience?
- Using the list of sources provided in this chapter, find a secondary article that is of interest to you. What kind of secondary article is it? What is it about? How familiar are you with its topic? How easy is it for you to understand? Does it list any primary research articles? Can you find one of these primary articles, and scan its contents? Can you compare this primary article briefly to the secondary article? Which article is easier to read? Which is more detailed? Which article would you trust more?

Basic Quantitative Literacy

The task of mastering educational research literacy takes time and effort. We need to approach each step with patience and due preparation. Each step requires its own particular type of guidance. In the last chapter we were guided through the art and skill of reading secondary articles. Secondary articles summarize and interpret research and research findings for us. At some point, however, we need to prepare to branch out and read primary research articles for ourselves. Before we tackle primary articles directly, however, we need to be guided through a series of basic ideas that will help us grasp these articles at their most fundamental level. Tackling these basic ideas are the next steps in our process of becoming research literate.

By now, you probably know that there are two kinds of primary educational research articles—qualitative and quantitative. If asked to distinguish between these two types of articles, you might say that quantitative articles use numbers and qualitative articles do not. If pressed, you might go on to say that more often than not quantitative articles use statistical tests and procedures to deal with numbers. These claims, while not entirely wrong, are too simplistic and can actually be misleading under certain circumstances. The real difference between qualitative and quantitative articles is grounded in the different ways that these two approaches to research look at the world of experience. We will start by looking at the ways that quantitative articles look at the world, or what we will call *basic quantitative literacy*.

The ground state of any quantitative article in educational research is its desire to be taken as a scientific piece of research. In other words, a quantitative article is a scientific article. It seeks to be shaped and guided by the basic precepts of the scientific process of research. Much has been written in recent years about the basic philosophical and conceptual ideas that ground scientific inquiry, and such lively and provocative recent thinkers as, say, Feyerabend (1975), Lakatos (1976), and Latour (1999), have stimulated and challenged our thinking about just exactly what science really is. For our purposes, however, we will concentrate on a set of "tried and true" ideas that most researchers in the field of education seem to share when they talk about research being "scientific."

What Makes Research Scientific?

Our basic and ordinary idea of what constitutes scientific research in education comprises six key principles.

It Follows the Scientific Method

This is an obvious step. There are certain simple precepts that define what most people mean by the scientific method:

First of all, scientists make predictions or lay out expectations. They do not wander blindly into some study. They make hypotheses or predictions based upon prior research or even common sense. These predictions or expectations are usually reasonable and plausible. But here is the catch—are they really true? This is where scientists must turn to the world of experience for answers.

Answers from the world of experience always begin with data. That is why the next step is all about the collection of data. There can be no science without data.

This data must be collected as fairly and objectively as possible. It must be relevant to the hypotheses stated.

The next step is to see whether or not the data and the hypotheses match. If they are in agreement, then the scientists are on the right path. If they are not, then they need to change their predictions and hypotheses, and collect more data.

The scientific method is a cycle of prediction, test, change, and more prediction, testing, and change. Because science depends upon the world of experience for the ultimate answers to its questions, it is seen as being fair and objective. That is, we can say that it does not matter what scientists might *want* to be true. The scientific method is designed to force them to *accept* and *work with* what is *really true*. This power of truth over the wishes of scientists is what gives the scientific method its real power. This is also what makes it so useful in dealing with issues where there might be a great deal of controversy. Without some objective processes for us to use to help guide the way, we might fall instead into trying to establish our particular beliefs as truth.

We have just looked at a very simplified and idealized picture of the scientific method. As we will see in the last few chapters, however, things are often more complex and less clear-cut in real life. Underlying all hypotheses and predictions, at some deeper level, are sets of assumptions that point us to look in one direction over another. As you become more literate in your efforts to read and understand educational research, you will be able to appreciate the power and beauty of the scientific method in operation, while at the same time realizing that, like any tool, it is not perfect.

It Is Public

Public scrutiny is an important part of any form of scientific research. Other researchers need to know what your claims are, what steps you followed to test them, and what your data looks like. The more open your efforts, the more powerful your conclusions will be. When there is nothing to hide, other researchers can then check your procedures and results and examine your data. Because you have not concealed anything, others can eventually trust your claims and findings.

There is another dimension to the public nature of scientific research. Scientific research is always done within the context of a community of researchers. Rarely does any one study or any one direction of research stand by itself. Likewise, researchers also rarely work alone. Most research is done within a community of research. There are two broad classes of research communities. The first class occurs when a group of researchers are physically working together as a team. The second and broader class occurs when researchers draw upon the existing research literature to find new research questions and topics of exploration. Both dimensions are important parts of nearly every ongoing scientific research program, and both depend upon research being as open and public as possible.

It Is Replicable

When a piece of research is replicable, it means that you or any other reasonably skilled inquirer should be able to repeat the steps laid out in the research process and get pretty much the same results. This sense of replicability is related to the last notion that research should be conducted in a public fashion. When your steps are presented in full enough public detail, then others are free to follow your lead and see if they come up with the same sorts of results.

Another way to look at the issue of replicability is to realize that you are most likely looking at phenomena that are part of the ordinary and regular nature of things. Science is usually not about the study of unique or one-of-a-kind things. It looks at things that show up over and over again, and thereby play regular and important roles in the situations and processes that we are studying.

It Is Fallible and Correctable

Scientific researchers often present findings and then make claims. It is important that these claims can be shown to be right or wrong. At the same time, we cannot lose sight of the fact that these claims are based on those things we see and experience in the world. Sometimes, we misperceive what we see. Sometimes, we misunderstand what we perceive. Sometimes, we see patterns and think they are more general and more permanent and more important than they really are.

All of the problems listed above are merely ways of saying that the process of inquiry in the world of experience is *fallible*. That is, we can and do make mistakes. We create scientific rules and laws that are not absolute, but are at best highly probable.

We reflect this probability when we talk about creating and testing hypotheses. Hypotheses are nothing more than claims about the world of experience that we have good reason to believe are true. But claiming that they are true, and proving that they are true, are two different things. We attempt to prove hypotheses by making predictions based upon them.

At first it seems like a simple project. We make a prediction based on a hypothesis. If our prediction is wrong, then it is clear that we are on the wrong track. But what happens if our prediction is correct? Does this necessarily mean that we are on the right track? Or could it mean that something we did not expect or see or anticipate is actually validating our prediction? Or even worse, that any perceived differences was just a fluctuation or chance happening, and not really real. In other words, being wrong seems to be a clearer guide than being correct. In one way, this is very good because it allows us to *correct* our mistakes more easily. However, the notion that our predictions could be correct due to random reasons, or reasons beyond our control, is still a vexing situation.

The answer to this dilemma comes from looking at what is actually predicted. Most of the time, scientists are predicting that some process or set of conditions or factors will make a difference in some situation. Suppose we turn things around, and predict that there will be *no* differences. This prediction is at the heart of what we call the *null hypothesis*. When we have a null hypothesis, we are predicting no differences. If we can show that the probability that the null hypothesis is true is very low, then we have good reason to believe that any effect we find is probably real and not just a chance occurrence. It does not prove that our reasons for making our predictions in the first place are correct, however. This can only come about via a program of more specific and refined research. But it does show us that we are at least probably on the right path, and that we are looking at some real effects or patterns. As evidence mounts and we make more and more corrections and refinements in our claims, we are more and more confident in the truth of our claims.

It Is Generalizable

Science is not about the unique, the exceptional, or the rare. It is about the typical, the ordinary, and the day-to-day. This is not to say that science does not run into the unique, the rare, the baffling, the one-of-a-kind, or the enigmatic. Scientists are constantly being surprised by what they find. It does mean, however, that science is constantly in the business of explaining the unexplained and showing how the unusual is really something more ordinary when understood properly.

When applied to an area like educational research, this search for the ordinary leads inevitably toward the notion of generalization. Suppose you lead a team of educational researchers who are interested in (let us say) how hands on learning affects standardized test scores. When your team sets off to study this problem, you are looking to create a setting where you can examine how *typical* hands on experiences taught by *typical* teachers to *typical* kids in *typical* schools might impact standardized test scores. You want your findings to be reflective of as broad a spectrum of students and teachers and schools as possible.

One quick point about generalization in educational research needs to be addressed at the outset. More often than not, educational researchers look at a sample of students or teachers from a specific place. It is usually a place that is relatively accessible to the researchers. For example, if the researchers live and work in Kansas, then they often study students or teachers from schools in Kansas. Does this make their research less generalizable? Only if you can demonstrate that there is something so unique about the Kansas school systems, as opposed to, say, the Kentucky or the California or the Vermont schools, that you could expect to find real and major differences. Most of the time, this is simply not the case. When we are looking at fairly basic issues, students tend to be students and teachers tend to be teachers wherever you find them. If you move into specialized settings or into whole different cultural areas, then circumstances are different. These issues will be revisited when we talk about sampling in a later chapter, but for now the point is clear—unless a setting is unique, then it is usually safe to generalize from it.

It Simplifies Our Understanding of Complex Things

One of the most important insights in science came from a very unlikely source. When we think of science we usually do not think of medieval monks. But it was a 14th-century Franciscan monk by the name of William of Ockham who came up with one of the most important principles of science. Ockham was one of the founders of a school of philosophy known as nominalism. At its heart, nominalism says that complex phenomena are nothing more than aggregates and systems of simpler things. This principle of stripping away the complex to find the simple heart underneath was a fairly new idea at the time, but it serves to this day as one of the guiding lights of the scientific view of the world.

One of the most famous expressions of this worldview is captured in an aphorism known as Ockham's razor. Do not multiply causes unnecessarily, warned

Ockham. Here is another way to express this idea—given the choice between two different explanations, the simpler explanation is most likely correct. Ockham's razor says that we should only make our theories and explanations as complex as they absolutely have to be.

So we see two different roles for simplicity in science. First of all, we should look for the simple principles and actions that are used to build even the most complex phenomena. Second, we should keep our explanations as simple as possible. These two ideas form the heart of the scientific view of the world, and they guide quantitative research at its very core.

What Are Some of the Key Issues in Quantitative Research Design?

The principles of science are found in most quantitative educational research articles. But now it is time to take things a bit further, and look at matters of research design. One of the key issues in research design is the idea of variables:

Quantitative Models of Research Focus on Variables

When we do empirical research, we need to concentrate on those things we can see or measure. There are two sorts of measurable phenomena in the world—constants and variables.

Constants are easy. They are measurable things whose values never change. For all intents and purposes, your adult height is a constant.

Researchers are usually much more interested in *variables*. A variable is some thing you can measure, and whose values can be expected to change. The temperature outside is a variable, because it changes over the course of a day. If you are like me, alas, your weight can be variable. Most of us have the sense to weigh ourselves in the morning, before breakfast, rather than after a big meal. We would expect our weight to change from one situation to the next.

Researchers Often Look at the Interaction of Independent and Dependent Variables

There are two kinds of variables that are most important to quantitative researchers —independent variables and dependent variables. These variables are often the source of confusion, but they need not be. They are actually very simple.

We start with the idea that it is useful to compare variables in the same setting. Is there a relationship between these variables? If there is a relationship, that relationship can often tell us a great deal. For example, suppose you run a fast food restaurant. For some unknown reason, your customers before noon are all under twelve, and your customers after noon are all over sixty. Here, you have two variables that seem to be in some kind of relationship—the age of your customers and the time of day. Because you have observed this relationship, you might want to adjust such things as your menu and your special promotions accordingly. Note that you have no control over these variables and you have no idea why they seem to be related in the way that they are. By comparing the ages of your customer to the time of day, however, you are able to take advantage of these relationships.

If you feel a bit uncomfortable by the example above, rest assured that you are not alone. Most people would not be content with just finding such a relationship. They would want to know *why* this relationship seems to be operating. Unless you know why, you really cannot plan that efficiently. For all you know, the forces that might be behind this relationship could change at any moment, leaving you high and dry. That is why, most of the time, we do not just look at two variables and how they are related. We want to know the basis for that relationship.

One of the best ways to ground the relationship between two variables is to look to see if these variables are *independent* and *dependent* variables. In short, an independent variable is a variable that has an impact on the dependent variable, which is the target variable. So, an independent variable is an impact variable, and a dependent variable is a target variable.

Let us look at some examples of independent and dependent variables in educational research. Suppose we are concerned that elementary-age students are not as well mannered as we might want them to be. We focus on one measurable variable related to being well mannered—whether or not a child raises his or her hand before she or he speaks. This is clearly a variable, since children will either raise their hands or not raise their hands. It is measurable, because we can see with our eyes whether or not they raise their hands. Finally, it is a behavior that is clearly defined and accepted as being well mannered. This variable now becomes our target. We want it to change—in this case, we want the incidences of hand raising to increase. Since hand-raising behavior is our target, it now becomes our *dependent variable*.

Now that we have our target variable clearly identified, we now search for possible impact variables. In other words, what can we do to increase the likelihood of our target variable? What possible variables could make an impact? When we choose an impact variable, it is our *independent variable*.

A good independent variable has several characteristics. First of all, it is measurable. We must be able to identify its presence and the degree of its change. Second, it ought to be controllable to some degree. We need to be able to control its presence or absence at least, and to some degree its strength. The more control we have over its impact, the more clear our understanding of its impact will be. Finally, the impact of a good independent variable makes sense to us. That is, we can see that there are clear reasons that it has the impact that it does.

In our example, let us use reward as our impact, or independent, variable. We pick a measurable reward for elementary-age students—in this case, a smiley face sticker. Since we have all the smiley face stickers in our desk drawer, we obviously have control over whether the children get them or not. Finally, since we know that the children like getting smiley face stickers, it makes sense to use them as a reward.

Now we are ready to talk about the relationship itself—if we start giving our smiley face stickers when kids raise their hands to speak, then we can expect hand raising to increase. This is a simple example, but it illustrates how independent variables can have an impact on a targeted dependent variable.

The principles of science and the operation of variables, and especially independent and dependent variables, are at the heart of the quantitative research process in education. Together, they are the key points to the quantitative view of research.

We Need to Look at Actual Quantitative Articles in Order to Understand How They Have Been Designed

It is one thing to talk about the ideas that form the quantitative view of research. It is another thing to actually read quantitative research articles. We need to focus on actual examples of articles when we tackle the task of learning how to read them.

Our strategy for examining articles is for us to start with *training articles* and then pair each training article with a real article from the literature. We will talk about each type of article in turn.

A training article is an imaginary article written solely to provide simple and clear examples of key parts and aspects of research articles. In other words, these are not real articles per se. They were written to give beginners a simpler version of things found in "real" articles. While we had a bit of fun with these articles, we tried to choose topics that are relevant and interesting to someone learning how to read educational research articles.

Once you have read and understood these simplified training articles, the next step is to move on and apply what you have learned to actual educational research articles. As this work progresses, you will be asked to find real research articles in areas of your own personal interest. To start the process, however, we have selected a real article to pair with each of our training articles. These real articles give you an immediate opportunity to apply the simplified structure of each training article to a real article that is similar in structure and intent.

These training articles, and their paired real articles, can be found on the CD-ROM.

The four quantitative training articles are:

Paulina Picasso—"Gender and Early Career Characteristics of High School Valedictorians From Different High Schools"

Mark Cassatt—"Comparing Rates of Practice to Midterm Grades in Four Eighth Grade Magnet School Science Classrooms"

Joanne Miro—"The Effects of High Protein Snacks on Quiz Grades in Afternoon High School Math Classes"

Maria Chagall—"Critical Factors for Understanding Male Juvenile Offenders: Developing an Empirically Based Model"

The four paired real articles are, in order:

Patrick Devine-Wright, Hannah Devine-Wright, and Paul Fleming—"Situational Influences on Children's Beliefs About Global Warming and Energy"

Robert L. Williams and Lloyd Clark—"College Students' Ratings of Student Effort, Student Ability and Teacher Input as Correlates of Student Performance on Multiple-Choice Exams"

Eleni Danili and Norman Reid—"Some Strategies to Improve Performance in School Chemistry, Based on Two Cognitive Factors"

Joseph Klein—"Effectiveness of School Staff Meetings: Implications for Teacher-Training and Conduct of Meetings"

Before we look at these articles in detail, there are a few questions we raise about quantitative articles in general.

What Are the Basic Elements
That Most Quantitative Articles Share?

There is no standard form for quantitative articles in educational research, but there are a few basic elements that are present in nearly all articles. For instance, every quantitative article has a title. Every article addresses a research question or questions. Relevant variables are also linked to these research questions. Furthermore, every article describes how those questions were tackled empirically—what methods or procedures were followed. Finally, every article presents results or findings of some kind.

Beyond these basic necessities, there are elements that are almost always found. Just about every quantitative article in educational research, for instance, has an Abstract. This Abstract is useful in helping readers decide whether or not to go ahead and read the article in question. Nearly every article supports its research questions with an argument for their validity and with references to other research in order to ground this particular article within a larger context of research efforts. Nearly every article goes beyond merely presenting results and findings, toward engaging in a discussion of these results and then drawing some conclusions.

In short, you have six nearly universal parts to a quantitative research article in education: the Title, the Abstract, an Introduction which contains and develops the research question or questions, a description of Methods and Procedures, Results and Findings, and Discussions and Conclusions. This explicit structure will serve as a roadmap to guide our literacy efforts in coming chapters.

What Are Some of the Basic Categories
or Types of Quantitative Articles?

Once you get a sense of what a quantitative article in general looks like, the next step is to categorize and understand the various types of quantitative articles you might find. Each of the training articles, for example, was designed to address a common type of quantitative article. These common types, in order of increasing complexity, are:

Descriptive Article

A descriptive article is just that—it seeks to describe some process or situation in the world of experience. Most often, these processes or situations cannot be manipulated or controlled. Instead, researchers measure their presence or operation, and then make some statements or draw some conclusions.

There are a number of reasons why processes or situations cannot be manipulated or controlled. One reason is that they might be too large or complex to control. Let us consider an example. Most state school systems record standardized test scores for all the students in their districts. For most states, these data comprise thousands, if not millions of students. At the same time, many other demographic and other variables are also recorded for these students. Such a condition almost describes a natural experiment. Students can be compared across a variety of dimensions.

Could we design controlled circumstances to generate comparable sorts of data? Perhaps, but it would be highly unlikely that any such effort would work in the real world. The effort needed to create artificial situations designed to manipulate or control such vast amounts of data would be nearly impossible to sustain. That is, it would be nearly impossible to artificially create these sorts of large-scale sources of data. Instead, we are left with the choice of examining these naturally occurring sources of data instead. Once you have your data, there are a number of interesting things that can be done with these sorts of data sets. But the first and most important step in the research process is that of simply organizing and then describing the data itself.

Sometimes, a process or situation cannot be manipulated or controlled because it would be unethical to do so. For example, suppose you were interested in basic factors that might affect the standardized test scores we were talking about above. In many cases, these test scores are used to make important decisions about peoples' futures—whether they graduate from school, whether their school gets financial help from the government, or whether they get into college. It would be unethical to manipulate factors in order to see if these manipulations have an effect on the students taking them or not. Instead, you might want to look at the scores as you find them, and see how they shape up when you place them in naturally occurring categories. For instance, you might want to look at standardized test scores in large schools vs. smaller schools, to see if school size might have an overall effect on scores.

Finally, a descriptive quantitative article might be interested in studying how a poorly understood or relatively unexamined process or situation might operate in a natural, uncontrolled setting. Under those circumstances, it makes sense to go in first to explore, to observe, to document, and then draw up some parameters for future work that might be more controlled. For example, suppose you were interested in how second language learning and math scores might interact in students at the primary level. You have no real reason to suppose that these conditions would either help or hinder each other going into the research, but you suspect they might be related. A good way to approach this issue is to take a look at existing data sets to see if they might suggest a relationship between these two areas. Beginning at this descriptive level can give you clues and suggestions—should you proceed, and if you do, in what directions?

The Picasso article was written to illustrate a simple descriptive quantitative article. There is no ethical way that the data in this study could have been controlled. Valedictorians will take classes, hold offices, and participate in sports as they see fit. As researchers, we can try to examine the patterns of their choices, and compare those patterns to observed demographic and gender differences among valedictorians.

The basic question that the Picasso article raised was this—Are there meaningful patterns to be found when we examine the demographic differences and activities of valedictorians, or are any apparent patterns just coincidental? Any patterns that we find need to be explained, and they can also serve as the basis for further research.

Description is often a key part of real quantitative articles. In the related real article, Devine-Wright et al. describe the aspects of children's understanding of global warming issues. Comparisons are made in this article as well. This time, opinions and beliefs are compared across groups that differ in their environmental awareness levels. Comparisons are also made between like-minded children and adults.

Things like opinions, beliefs, and demographic information can often only be measured in terms of their likelihoods or frequency. When this is the case, we turn to descriptive methods to get a better sense of how this information can be best understood or compared across different groups.

Relation-Finding Article

The cornerstone to most empirical studies in education is this—how does one variable change in relation to another variable? Over and over again, you will see articles that are built around this idea. If we have two variables, and changes in one of those variables seems to reflect changes in the other variable, then these two variables are in *relation* to each other. The process of finding these sorts of relations is one of the key processes in quantitative research in education.

In a *relation-finding* article, you are interested in establishing that there seems to be a relationship between two variables. In its weakest form, all you can really do is say that there seems to be a relation per se. Let us consider a very simple example. Suppose you own an ice cream cone store (lucky you!). Probably the single most important variable to you is this—the number of ice cream cones you sell in a given day. This is obviously a variable, since this figure might be reasonably expected to change day by day. You expect a certain amount of fluctuation, but you would also like to be able to anticipate or predict busy days and slow days. Are there other variables you could measure that might be related? By comparing these other variables to daily ice cream consumption, can you get a picture of what you might expect?

The Cassatt article was written to illustrate a simple relation-finding quantitative article. Like the descriptive article, there is little or no overt control. Students are given problems for practice, and are asked to do them. There are no controlled conditions for such practice, no attempt to organize students into differing practice groups, or the like. Since there is no control, there are little or no direct claims that can be made. But here we have a case where we suspect that one variable plays a role in the operation of the other variable. That is, we have a situation where one variable looks like an independent variable, and the other variable looks like a dependent variable. More specifically, we can easily argue that amount of practice makes sense as an impact variable (or ultimately an independent variable), and that test scores make sense as a target variable (or ultimately a dependent variable).

The basic question that the Cassatt article raised was this—Do we have reason to suppose that rates of practice will be related to test scores? Or is any possible relationship just coincidental?

Williams and Clark examine the relation of various factors on students' performance on multiple-choice tests. In this real article, such aspects as student effort, ability, and teacher input are taken into account by comparing each of these factors to actual student performance. Williams and Clark make use of correlation coefficients as their main tool for making these comparisons and discussing these relations.

When we move from a descriptive design to a relation-finding design, we are moving from the search for patterns to a search for possible impacts. We would like to be able to say that practice leads to higher test scores, but our control over practice is too weak to allow us to do so. There are just too many other things that could have intervened to raise or lower test scores; things that we did not measure or control for. So we have to content ourselves, in these situations, with being able to say that we have found that practice and test scores are related. To make a stronger claim, we have to move into a hypothesis-testing situation, like the one found in the next article.

Hypothesis-Testing Article

Once you have established a relationship between two things, sometimes it is possible to go on and say more powerful things about that relationship. Here is where we bring in the use of hypotheses to say these sorts of more powerful things about how independent and dependent variables are related.

Hypotheses are usually developed by using a process of logical argumentation, along with empirical support via prior research findings. First of all, hypotheses must be shown to make sense. That is, they need to be plausible. Then, we need to establish that there is prior evidence to suggest that they might be true. This evidence is either used to build an indirect case for support, or to get us to a point where we need to raise and test a new hypothesis in order to move forward.

The Miro article was written to illustrate a simple hypothesis-testing quantitative article. The hypothesis in question was very simple—did it matter what kind of snack was used to help students in afternoon math classes improve their performance? In other words, was one type of snack more effective than the other snack types? Snacks are an easy sort of variable to control. We can control their size, their components, their time of delivery, and so on. This sort of control is of utmost importance, since we are trying to isolate the effect of one particular impact variable on one particular target variable.

It is relatively easy to isolate and measure a target variable. The hard part comes in isolating the effects of a particular impact variable. This is because there could be any number of other impact variables plugging away, making their impacts on the target variable.

Consider the target variable of the Miro study—grades in an afternoon math class. There are any number of possible impact variables operating in any given afternoon math class—overall ability levels of the students, skill and effectiveness of the teacher, quality of the instructional materials, specific content being taught, environmental conditions and distractions, just to name an obvious few. There is no way to identify, control, or eliminate all these potential impacts. Instead, we divide our population into groups, and make them as equivalent as possible. Then, we change the presence or levels of the impact variable across these groups, so that the only *systematic* difference among these groups is found in the differing levels of the impact variable.

In practice, the most common way to isolate the effects of the impact variable is to randomly assign people to the different treatment groups. In the Miro study, students were randomly assigned to the fruit group or the carbohydrate group or the protein group. Students within each group may vary in terms of ability level, but when we randomize we expect that ability levels across the groups will be about the same. That is, we expect each group to have about the same profile of talented and untalented students. Randomizing helps prevent any systematic differences arising, except for the systematic differences deliberately built into the design. In this way, we have isolated the impact variable, and we can trust that any differences that might emerge between the groups will be based on this systematic difference.

Danili and Reid, in their real article, are testing the possible impact of two variables on chemistry learning in high school. Drawing from the cognitive psychology literature, they isolate and test the impact of working memory space and field dependency. This sort of isolation and testing is the cornerstone of many hypothesis-driven studies in educational research.

Model-Building Article

In the descriptive article, we looked at variables in order to see what they were telling us, and to see what patterns they reveal. When we build models, we put those patterns to work. In such an article, the model is usually based around a target variable. This target variable is of particular interest to the researchers. The model comes into place when the pattern of other variables is used to say something about the target variable.

The Chagall article was written to illustrate a simple model-building quantitative article. Like most model-building articles, it attempts to use data in order to be able to understand some situation better. In this case, Chagall is looking at those factors in the lives of young male delinquents that might affect their ability to graduate. She is looking at graduation as an important predictor of whether a juvenile defender will get into trouble as an adult; those juveniles who do graduate are less likely to get into trouble. She looks at a variety of variables to see if they can be brought together to create a model to describe young male offenders in general. Furthermore, she wants to see if this model might allow her to predict graduation likelihoods for various specific offenders based on their scores on some of these other variables.

Klein, in his real article examining school staff meetings, gathers data on a number of possible areas of influence. These data are then organized, described, and compared with each other in an attempt to build a model comparing and ranking these factors as they work together to help or hinder the effectiveness of such staff meetings.

There are a number of other categories or types of articles that can be found in the quantitative research literature, but more often than not they combine or build upon our four basic categories. More often than not, primary articles will combine several categories in an attempt to create a comprehensive picture of the phenomena they are studying.

Our Emerging Literacy Orientation

We now have a basic general picture of quantitative articles in educational research. First and foremost is the notion that these articles are done scientifically. They use the scientific method, and they follow the basic principles of scientific inquiry. Most of the time, they focus on variables. Sometimes, they describe variables and look for patterns. Other times, they look for relationships between two or more variables. Many times, they focus on target variables, which are often called dependent variables. Once the target variable has been identified and isolated, then the researchers look at one or more variables that might have an impact on the target variable. These impact variables are often called independent variables. Quantitative researchers often use hypotheses and models to guide their efforts.

One of the key target virtues in quantitative research is objectivity. Quantitative researchers are looking for the truth. Sometimes, that truth is captured in their hypotheses and models. Other times, proposed hypotheses and models will fall flat on their faces when put to the test. Putting hypotheses and models to the test, and taking the chance that they will fall flat on their faces, is a necessary risk in quantitative research. It is a good way for researchers to be sure that their findings are true—If you give your ideas a legitimate chance to fail, and they succeed, then you can be that much surer that you are on the right path. This virtue is an important thing to look for, as you read and evaluate quantitative articles.

Practice Makes Perfect

It is now time to practice some of the insights and skills you have explored in this chapter:

- *Scientific method.* Can you outline the basic steps of the scientific method? Can you design an outline of a study that might follow the scientific method?
- *Scientific procedures.* Beyond the scientific method itself, there are five procedures that characterize scientific research. Can you identify them? Can you apply them to the study you outlined above?
- *Variables.* What is a variable? What is the difference between a dependent and an independent variable? Can you give examples of each?
- *Descriptive designs.* Which training article uses a descriptive design? Discuss the key points of this design briefly, using the training article as your example.
- *Relation-finding designs.* Which training article uses a relation-finding design? Discuss the key points of this design briefly, using the training article as your example.
- *Hypothesis-testing designs.* Which training article uses a hypothesis-testing design? Discuss the key points of this design briefly, using the training article as your example.
- *Model-building designs.* Which training article uses a model-building design? Discuss the key points of this design briefly, using the training article as your example.
- *Objectivity.* What is objectivity? Why is it so important in quantitative research?

Basic Statistical Literacy

As we continue to advance in our efforts to understand primary articles, we need to remind ourselves once again of the differences between primary and secondary articles. One of the key differences is the fact that secondary articles often summarize and describe research findings, while primary articles present those findings to us. When dealing with primary articles of a quantitative nature, these findings are most often rendered in statistical form. Therefore, to read many sorts of primary articles, we need to develop some basic statistical literacy.

Before talking about statistics and statistical literacy, we first need to talk about the difference between technical literacy and intuitive literacy. Technical literacy focuses on specific tools and techniques, and on knowing when and how to use them. Intuitive literacy, on the other hand, is based upon a clear and lucid global picture of "the big picture" while focusing on what is most important and most unique about that particular approach. This distinction is no more important in educational research than when it is used to talk about issues of statistics.

Most consumers of educational research are afraid they have to start with the technical aspects of statistics in order to read and understand educational research articles. This is simply not true. Basic statistical literacy begins with an intuitive understanding of what the statistical approach is trying to accomplish, and how its tools are used to accomplish those goals. This is not technical literacy, but intuitive literacy. All forms of technical literacy are built upon a foundation of intuitive literacy, and technical literacy is only as good as the intuitive literacy that supports it. Therefore, it makes perfectly good sense to focus, as we will, on the intuitive aspects of basic statistical literacy. That is what will be covered in this chapter. We will revisit the notion of technical literacy in Chapter 14, where we will be more prepared to address those issues.

In order to master the intuitive side of basic statistical literacy, there are a number of ideas that need to be presented and grasped. The following idea is perhaps the most important.

There Is a Statistical Worldview

While science can be quite complicated and its ideas can be profoundly complex, at heart science is a simple enterprise. Science is the pursuit of order and its effects in the empirical world.

The simplest and most basic idea in science is this—underneath all the details and particulars and seemingly endless factors that seem to affect those things we study, there are usually only a few simple processes at work that can explain most of the things we see and experience.

Sir Isaac Newton's vision of gravity is a perfect example. In the real world, we see many things fall at different rates. Stones fall faster than pieces of paper and feathers may fall even slower still. Newton had the genius to look past most of the details, and see that there was a common force that seemed to be operating every time that something was falling. This force, known as gravity, was actually constant for all objects. Feathers and paper fell slower because of the added effect of wind resistance. In a vacuum, they fall at the same rate as a stone.

Newton discovered two orderly processes, namely gravity and wind resistance, which could be used to explain most of the differences we might find among falling objects in the real world. This allowed Newton (and us) to ignore a whole bunch of other properties of things when we look at how things fall. We can safely ignore their colors, their molecular compositions, their surface temperatures (so long as they were solid), how long they have been in existence, and even their differing weights. As an aside, we no longer look at gravity in the same way that Newton did, but this fact does not really affect our example. This process of trying to find a few simple factors to explain complex phenomena is alive and well in science today.

Notice that Newton was not just able to describe how the forces of gravity and wind resistance interact when things fall. He went further, and created a mathematical model to describe how gravity functions in the real world. Looking at the simplest case, where things are falling in a vacuum and wind resistance is equal to zero, Newton offered the following model:

$$d = (1/2)gt^2$$

In plain English, this model says that the distance an object falls is equal to one half some gravitational constant, which he called g, multiplied by the square of the amount of time it had been falling. Research has shown that this gravitational constant is approximately (32 feet/second^2). So if we drop something in a vacuum, it will have dropped 16 feet after the 1st second, 64 feet after the 2nd second, 144 feet after the 3rd second, and so on. From this one simple model, we can make all sorts of predictions about falling objects, and we are free to ignore just about everything except the amount of distance they fall, and the length of time that they have been falling.

The kind of model that Newton built is known as a *deterministic model*. A deterministic model says that if you know all your causes, and all your beginning conditions, then you can predict and describe all your effects precisely and exactly. This view of science and the world reached its height in the scientific practices of the late 19th century.

From the very beginning, though, scientists knew that actual observations or experimental results would most often be different from the exact predictions of deterministic formulas and models. These differences were first explained away as simple errors of observation or measurement, or the impact of contaminating factors or unforeseen effects. Scientists reasoned that ongoing improvements in our abilities to observe and measure and isolate specific effects would eventually help eliminate these variations and help bring actual observations and findings into agreement with the predictions of deterministic models.

Better measurement and better control did help our efforts to measure a great deal, but it did not bring about perfect or near-perfect results, however. Scientists began to realize that there seemed to exist a built-in degree of variability for any given individual observation or effect. At the same time, however, larger aggregates of observations and effects seemed to fall in line with earlier deterministic models. It became clear that a newer, and more sophisticated, model needed to be drawn up to replace the deterministic model.

Science had turned to the venerable field of statistics for help in explaining away errors of measurement and observation. Eventually, it became clear that probability was not just a tool for helping make better measurements and observations. It was at the heart of all empirical phenomena, in ways we will discuss in a bit.

One by one, the sciences began to give up their deterministic models in favor of probabilistic ones. Physics was the first science to fall in line with this new paradigm. The social sciences are among the last to do so, and are just now exploring the ramifications of abandoning strictly deterministic models.

What are the two main assumptions of the statistical worldview?

1. Probability is built into the very fabric of reality.
2. Within the framework of probability, there are systems of order and even stability in the world.

Because it is one of the disciplines near the end of the line in adopting a probabilistic view of its phenomena, educational research is in a bit of a state of flux regarding these matters. It is wise to remember that the statistical worldview, as it is currently understood, has only been around for less than a hundred years. Many of the basic assumptions of both probability and statistics have been the topic of both ongoing and recent debate (Salsburg, 2001). For instance, currently such alternative modes of statistical analysis as Bayesian analysis play a very small role in the overall statistical consciousness of the educational research world. We should expect these sorts of alternate and more sophisticated models to play more of a role in educational research methods and theories in the future, so we must remain open to them.

Once you get past the basics that have been laid out in this chapter, there is a wide-open territory of ongoing discussion and exploration in statistics and its application to educational research. This is not a source of worry, though. This is an indication that, as statisticians and researchers work together, they will forge richer insights and more sophisticated and powerful tools. Right now, it seems clear that the fundamental principles of statistics play a basic part in how the world is put together. As time goes by, the role of statistical principles in the educational research world should get clearer as well.

Statistics Uses Probability to Balance Order and Freedom

Statistics, as a formal branch of mathematics, has been around since at least the 17th century. The first tasks for statistics dealt with probability issues in such areas as gambling and handling actuarial data (Folks, 1981). These tasks are still being handled quite well by using statistical techniques.

What exactly is probability? Probability is the way that mathematicians and researchers study those things and events whose properties are grounded in likelihood (Salsburg, 2001). In an ideal world, researchers would like to be able to pin things down exactly. Most things in the real world, however, cannot be pinned down so precisely. For example, no one can predict that some single event will surely happen. They can only say that it is more likely or less likely to happen. When researchers do this, they are using the processes of probability.

Probability is not a weak tool, however. Through refinements over the last four centuries, researchers are able to say some fairly precise things within a probability framework. This is because probability, while dealing with merely likely things and events, is surprisingly orderly (Folks, 1981). This orderliness can then be transferred to statistics, as well.

The order found in statistics is based on moving away from the unique and the individual toward the typical and the collective. The more individual things or events you look at collectively, and the less unusual and the more ordinary the properties of those things you concentrate upon, the better you can use statistical tools to predict, control, or understand them.

Statistics Starts by Looking at Data and Distributions

Researchers using statistics soon discovered that the nature of things became clearer, and their ability to predict and control got much better, when they moved from the "few" to the "many." This is particularly true for things that are measured.

Measurement in research comes with its own language. For instance, an individual score or measurement is called a *datum*. A collection of scores or measurements is called *data*. A collection of measurements for a single event or category forms a *distribution*.

Distributions can be formed in a number of ways. For instance, if you take a single rock and weigh it many times, this collection of recorded weights becomes a distribution of measured weights for this single rock. If you measure the height of a group of people, then you have a distribution of height scores for that group of people. As you can see, you can have a distribution that is related to just one thing, or a distribution that is based on a single type of measurement of many things that are related in some way. This is an important point that has several key uses in statistics.

Sometimes, distributions are specifically created for a variety of objects and events—such as test scores for students. Other distributions seem to exist in nature, and are just waiting to be discovered—such as the heights or weights or shoe sizes for some population of people. Once a distribution has been created or discovered, it can then be studied and measured. One of the first and easiest ways to study a distribution is to see what type of distribution it is. Therefore, it makes sense to create types, or categories, of various sorts of distributions.

There Are a Number of Different Types of Distributions That Can Show Up in Research

For all intents and purposes, there are many kinds of distributions that can show up in the course of measuring and doing research. Looking at the following three types of distributions can give us a reasonable picture of some of the most important natures and properties of distributions as a whole:

The Constant Distribution

When all members of a distribution have exactly the same value, then this is an example of a *constant distribution*. If you measure how many people on earth breathe oxygen, the answer is "all of them." This is an example of a constant distribution. Researchers can locate and identify constants, and check to make sure they are still constant, but that is the extent of research that can be done with a constant distribution. This is also why we never see constant distributions in educational research. We need to understand that constant distributions do exist, however. For one thing, they make it clear that all other forms of distributions deal with variables in some fashion.

The "Blob" Distribution

Suppose you decide to measure the effect of barometric pressure on eye color of teachers. Barometric pressure will vary, and so will eye color, and so you will get a distribution of these comparisons. The only problem is this—these things are absolutely unrelated. Any distribution you get will just be a "blob" of scores. There will be no structures or orderly patterns to discover.

If you get a "blob" distribution, then odds are that you are on the wrong track. A blob distribution teaches us an important lesson—just because you can measure something and organize those measures into a distribution, this in itself is no guarantee that you have found anything meaningful. Researchers are much more interested in distributions that reflect meaningful patterns of change. These meaningful patterns of change usually reflect the kind of probabilistic order we were talking about earlier. The next distribution we will discuss is based on one of the most important ways we understand change as a meaningful but probabilistic phenomenon.

The Normal Distribution

The normal distribution is so important that it is the default distribution for most statistically based practices in educational research. Basically, a normal distribution occurs when there is a meaningful typical score for the distribution, and there is an orderly process of change that accounts for differences between this typical score and other given scores. This combination tends to create the symmetrical form that is called the "normal curve." The normal curve is nothing more than a pictorial, or graphic, representation of an idealized normal distribution.

The normal distribution is often standardized to describe probability conditions. In this process, the total probability of all possible outcomes or measures is arbitrarily set at "1." Every subset of possibilities is then computed as some fraction of 1. If you think of "1" as "100%" and, say, "0.99" and "0.52" as "99%" and "52%," respectively, you can see the practicality of this standardization.

Standardization also allows you to go right from a distribution of raw scores to a standardized picture of how the distribution of scores reflects the likelihood of each and every score. This allows researchers to see just how common or how rare various measured scores really are. When we look at actual results later on in this book, we will see how these normalized standards play a role in helping decide whether or not given results are significant or not.

Finally, the normal distribution seems to turn up everywhere. Just about any naturally occurring variable, when studied, turns out to be normally distributed. Height, weight, shoe size, IQ score, and many more measures, fall into the realm of the normal distribution.

Other Systematic Distributions

Too often, the student of statistics assumes that the normal distribution is "the only game in town" distribution-wise. This is not the case. Some distributions, like the z distribution, t distribution, F distribution, and chi-square distribution, are used to test significance values of various statistical tests. More often than not, we find tables of these values in the backs of statistics books. These tables were derived from their various distributions.

There are other distributions to describe data as well, but they are not as commonly used in educational research studies. Examples include the Cumulative Frequency distribution, the Poisson distribution, and the Joint Probability distribution.

Most of the time, however, the normal distribution or some variant of the normal distribution is being used by researchers to model their data.

Distributions Have Important Properties

Early on, statisticians discovered that normal (and other) distributions displayed a number of key properties. The two most important are *central tendency* and *dispersion*:

Central Tendency

When you put scores together to make a distribution, you usually find that these scores are not distributed in a smooth and homogeneous fashion. Instead, they tend to cluster. This clustering is what is meant by the term *central tendency*. There are three common types of central tendency:

The first type of clustering is based on the notion of *commonness*. If you make a lot of measures of the same thing, or similar things, then it makes sense that some given score might end up being more common than the others. This "most common" score is called the *mode*.

The mode stands apart from all other scores in a distribution. That is, the mode divides the distribution into two groups—the mode score and all the rest of the scores. So, in order for a score to be the mode of the distribution, it merely has to have a higher frequency of occurrence than any other individual score. How much higher a frequency of occurrence is not an issue.

The mode is only useful as a descriptive tool. That is, you cannot link the mode directly to any other sort of probability measure, other than to simply say it is the most common score. And just to further complicate matters, sometimes you have the case where more than one score has the highest frequency of occurrence. In this case, you have two or more scores that serve as the mode, and we call such distributions *multi-modal* distributions.

The second type of clustering is based on the notion of *clustering above and clustering below*. Suppose you take 100 people, and measure their heights. You can use those measurements to create a long line of people. In this line, you can put the shortest person on one end and the tallest person on the other end. As you move from the short end, the people get taller, and as you move from the tall end, the people get shorter. At some point, you will be right in the middle of that line. The height of the person in the exact middle will be the height that splits this line into two equal parts. This score, which splits a distribution into two equal-sized groups, is called the *median*.

The median is more useful than the mode. Suppose you have a group of 100 schoolchildren, and the median height is 4 feet. When you talk about this group of 100 children, you can say that 50 of them are at, or under, 4 feet, and the other 50 are over 4 feet. Another way to think of the median is to look at it as a ranking tool. If you rank these kids from the 1st tallest to the 100th tallest, then the median height is the height of the 50th tallest kid. There is no reason, however, to suppose that these rankings are uniform. In other words, there is no way to know how much taller the 51st kid is when compared to the 50th kid. She may be a quarter of an inch taller, or a foot taller. There is no way of knowing from just the ranking. All you know is that she is taller than the 50th kid and shorter than the 52nd kid. Therefore, the median is useful when just ranking is good enough, or when ranking gives us the best picture of what is happening in the distribution.

In order to make more precise claims, you need a more sophisticated measure of central tendency that focuses on the *average score*. This more sophisticated picture is called the *mean*.

The mean is one of the most familiar and most used statistical tools. It is so familiar because it is so valuable. Here are three very valuable properties of the mean:

- *It is based on the value of every item in the distribution.* If you change one score in a distribution, it is quite possible that the mode and the median will remain unchanged. This is not true of the mean. The mean is based on the average of every score, and so if you change one score you change the mean. This also allows you to perform mathematical operations using the mean that you cannot do using the mode or the median.
- *It is the balance point of the distribution.* Because the mean is the average score, it balances extreme scores in both directions. This makes it the one score in a distribution that is overall closest to the set of all other scores. If you take any other score in a distribution and compare it to all other scores, the overall distance will be greater for that other score. This property of the mean, being least distant from the set of all other scores, is used by researchers to create strategies for understanding variation within a distribution.
- *It is the best first guess of any given score in a distribution.* Suppose you know that a person is a member of a group of 100 people. You also know that this group has an average height of 6 feet. How tall is this person? Your best guess, in the absence of any other information, is 6 feet. You may not be correct, but your likelihood of being correct is better when you use the mean instead of some other height. Researchers build upon this insight in two ways. They use the mean as the basis for predicting likelihood of individual events or things within a distribution. They also refine their predictions by looking at sophisticated ways to modify the mean as the best predictor for individual scores.

Dispersion

One of the most obvious things about a distribution is the fact that there is almost always more than one score represented. When there is more than one score, then the distribution is "spread out" in some fashion. This property of distributions, to spread out, is called *dispersion*.

It is easy to see that measures of central tendency allow you to look at distributions in an orderly fashion. If you know the most common, or middle, or average score, then you can say something about the typical makeup of distribution. If a distribution was just a set of things or events that consisted of just one score, then all you would need to understand the distribution would be the value of that one score. But most distributions are made up of many different values of scores. Are those different values just out there, willy-nilly, or is there some order in their variation? The answer is that they are indeed orderly, but in a probabilistic way. That is why it is important to look at dispersion along with central tendency, when you are trying to understand a distribution.

There are several types of dispersion to consider when looking at distributions. The first type of dispersion is a measure of the simple spread of scores. When you look at a distribution, what is the highest score? What is the lowest score? How much "room" is there between the highest and the lowest score? This "room," or the simple difference between the highest and lowest score, is called the *range*.

The range is similar to the mode, in that it is mainly useful as a way to describe the distribution. But, again, in order to get a more precise and sophisticated picture of the dispersion of a distribution, you need to use more powerful tools.

The most powerful and useful measure of dispersion is the *standard deviation*. Like the mean, the standard deviation has a number of important properties. Here are three of the most important:

- *The standard deviation captures the average distance of any given score from the mean.* The mean is the average of scores. Conceptually, the standard deviation is the measure of average difference between the mean and all other scores. If you think about it, the raw measure of change between the mean and all other scores will always be zero. This is because the mean is perfectly balanced between lower scores and higher scores. These differences cancel themselves out. Therefore, difference has to be converted from "above" and "below" the mean; they become differences "away from" the mean. Any good basic statistics book can show you these steps. The end result is the same; you have a tool to look at the average variation of scores from the mean.

  You can also use the standard deviation to put individual scores in context. You can create standard scores, which tell you how far above or below the mean a given raw score is. These sorts of standard scores have enormous use in education and educational research.

- *The standard deviation is the first tool for looking at patterns of variability and probability in a distribution.* The size of the standard deviation, in relation to the mean, is a good estimate of the degree of variability in a distribution. If the standard deviation is large, then there is most likely a wide spread of scores, and less scores at or near the mean. If the standard deviation is small, then you have the opposite case. Many of the scores are at or near the mean.

  If your distribution is normal, then the standard deviation can be used to tell you things about the probable range of scores in that distribution. Roughly two thirds of all scores in a normal distribution fall in the range from one standard deviation below the mean to one standard deviation above the mean. When that range is extended to three standard deviations below the mean to three standard deviations above the mean, then over 99% of the scores are covered.

- *The standard deviation maps out areas of genuine change within a distribution.* The mathematics is too complex to go into here, but standard deviations mark important areas of change within the normal curve. If you consider the range from one standard deviation below the mean to one standard deviation above the mean, all the scores within that range conceptually "belong" to the mean. That is, any principles of change in operation are essentially the same principles that formed the mean scores. As you move away from the mean, one standard deviation at a time, you are marking different patterns of change. Not only are the events becoming less likely, but the processes creating those scores are acting less and less like the processes that shaped the scores in and around the mean.

Distributions Can Be Used to Describe Either Populations or Samples

A distribution can consist of the scores from an entire *population*, or a distribution can be a *sample* from a larger population.

When you can measure every member of some group, then you have population distribution. For instance, you can measure the height of every person who was on the roster of a major league baseball team on December 31, 1999. This distribution will have a mean and a standard deviation, and these values are called the *parameters* of the distribution.

As you might suspect, it is rare when researchers can gather data from an entire population. Most of the time, populations are too large to measure, or else they are in flux and hard to measure precisely. Consider the population of people who are alive in the United States. Not only is this a very large number, it is also a continuously shifting population. People are born and die every instant.

Because population data are rare in educational research, researchers almost always collect sample data instead. A *sample* is some subset of a population. Sample data also form distributions with means and standard deviations, and these values are called the *statistics* of the sample distribution.

Since a sample is a subset of a population, then not every member of the population has been selected to be part of the sample. How are members selected, and how are members left out? This is determined by the sampling strategy that has been used. There are four broad sampling strategies that are used in statistically based research:

Convenience Sample

In this case, those members of the population that are closest at hand form the sample. This method is the least acceptable type of sampling strategy. It can be defended to some degree if you can make a case that the members nearby are no different, really, than any other members of the population. Also, it helps if you do not use all the convenient members to form the sample, but if you pick some random subset of these convenient members instead. Generally, however, it is better to use some other method if you can.

Purposive Sample

In this case, the members of the sample are selected because of their particular characteristics or nature. In this case, you are treating this sample as if it were its own little mini-population. When you restrict your sample in this way, you limit the things you can generalize to the population as a whole. For this reason, purposeful samples are much more common in qualitative research, where there often is no attempt to generalize from the sample (Shank, 2006).

Representative Sample

In this case, every effort is made to try to make the sample a miniature replica of the population. Sometimes representative samples are also called *stratified samples*.

This is the sort of sampling that is used by, say, election forecasters and TV ratings firms. Very often, research companies use very sophisticated and proprietary sampling formulas to collect representative samples. Most private researchers do not have the resources or the sophisticated knowledge to concoct representative sampling strategies that are accurate enough to adequately mirror the target populations. Therefore, they most often resort to the fourth and final sampling strategy, discussed below.

Random Sample

In this case, members of the sample are drawn at random from the population. When a sample is truly random, then every member of a population has an equal chance to be included in the sample. The advantage of a random sample is the fact that variations in the data caused by factors that are not being studied are spread out by the randomization process. If there are some really high IQ kids in the sample, for example, there is a good chance that there will be some lower IQ kids chosen as well. That is, other sources of variation will tend to average out. Since many of those sources of variation, like IQ, cannot be controlled, the next best thing is to spread them out in an unsystematic (or random) fashion. For most statistical research, random sampling is the sampling strategy of choice.

Normally Distributed Samples Can Be Measured or Compared to Each Other

There are two basic strategies that researchers often use when dealing with samples.

The first strategy is to use normally distributed samples to understand the nature of the population. By normally distributed sample, we mean that the shape of the sample distribution is a normal distribution, the same as the population distribution. In real life, sample distributions do not have to be that close to being perfectly normal. As long as the distribution is not glaringly non-normal, the approximation is usually okay.

In some cases, a researcher will know the parameters of a population. For instance, a manufactured product is supposed to weigh so many ounces. Researchers can collect samples of these products as they come off the conveyor belt, and weigh them. Enough samples are taken to make up a reasonable sampling distribution. Ideally, the mean weight of a sampling distribution should be the same as the intended product weight. Since intended product weight is supposed to be a constant distribution (every example of the product is supposed to weigh the same), the standard deviation of the samples should be as close to zero as possible. This use of sampling for *quality control* is an accepted part of the manufacturing process.

In many cases, however, population parameters are unknown. In educational research in particular, researchers rarely have clear-cut population parameters to work with. In this situation, researchers collect a number of samples from some population, and compare those different sampling distributions to come up with an *estimation* of what the population is like. The more samples taken, and the more sampling distributions created, the closer the combined results are to the true population mean. In a way, this process is like the quality control process described above, except for the fact that the actual parameters of the population are not known.

The other strategy for using samples in research is to compare samples to each other. Do these samples belong to the same population, or are they samples from different populations? This question is the basis for many statistical tests. Because this use of samples is so important and central to the use of statistics in educational research, it will be covered in depth in the next point.

Every Statistical Test Is Designed to Tell You Something

The use of statistics to test assumptions and hypotheses is called *inferential statistics*. Inferential statistics is built around the notion that probability can be used to test certain claims about populations and samples. Most inferential tests are designed to give probability based "yes" or "no" answers. That is, they can tell us if two or more things are more likely to be the same or if one or more are more likely to be different. We use different tests when we want to get at various and more complex versions of "yes" and "no."

There are literally hundreds, if not thousands, of different sorts of statistical tests that have been discovered and refined for researchers to use. Let us go back to the issue of technical vs. intuitive literacy for a second. As we become more and more technically literate, we get better and better at understanding and using most of the more common and familiar tests, and we learn and understand more and more new and more sophisticated tests. There is no substitute for time and practice in this process. However, in order to gain intuitive literacy, it is enough for now to start with learning and understanding a handful of common and basic statistical tests. We see this in the quantitative training articles. Each article illustrates one or more of these basic statistical tests in operation:

Correlation

The first common statistical test we will consider is the correlation coefficient. The idea behind the correlation coefficient is to determine the probability that two variables are related. The most common type of correlation coefficient is the Pearson product moment correlation coefficient, which is symbolized as r_{xy}. The x and the y in the subscript stand for each of the two variables being compared, respectively.

How does a correlation coefficient work? It is really quite simple, conceptually. First of all, the researchers gather pairs of scores for each person in their study. That is, each person in the study has a score for both of the variables in the study. These scores are then compared, and an overall comparison is made. The "yes-no" question in a correlational study is this—is the relationship between these two variables different from zero? If the answer is "no" then it is highly likely that we were unable to find a relationship, or there is in fact no relationship. If the answer is "yes," then it is highly likely that there is indeed a relationship between these two variables.

Let us illustrate this process with a quick example. Suppose we are in an imaginary town called, let us say, Keebler. Keebler is famous as the fudge capital of Europe. People in Keebler eat more fudge per capita than anywhere else in Europe. We have also noted that the fudgy people of Keebler are also a bit pudgy. We wonder if there is a relationship between fudge eating and weight—do people who eat more fudge also weigh more?

Since people in Keebler pride themselves in their dedication to the furthering of science, all the kind people of the town volunteer to take part in our study. As it happens, there are exactly 1,000 people of fudge-eating age in Keebler. We ask them to keep a diary to record how many kilograms of fudge they eat in a month's time. At the same time we collect the diaries, we also weigh each Keeblerite. Now, each person in the study has two measures: x = the number of kilograms of fudge consumed in a month, and y = their individual weight in kilograms. Both of these measures are used, pair by pair, to come up with a general index of comparison, or the correlation coefficient.

The correlation coefficient is an index of comparison, as we stated earlier. As such, it ranges from +1.00 to –1.00. When we have r_{xy} = +1.00, then we have a perfect index of direct comparison. That is, when one variable changes to some degree, the other variable changes in the same direction to the exact same relative degree. Suppose we found out that all the biggest fudge eaters were also the heaviest persons, and all the skimpiest fudge eaters were also the lightest persons. Then we have r_{xy} somewhere close to, or equal to, +1.00.

If we have r_{xy} = –1.00 then we have the exact opposite situation. All the skimpiest fudge eaters are really heavy, and all the big time fudge eaters are also the light-weights. Note that this relationship is just as strong as the first one—it is just an inverse relationship instead of a direct one. It is only when r_{xy} = 0.00 that we have no relationship. In that case, if we plotted the data, we would end up with a "blob" distribution—neither variable would be related to the other.

If we look at the Cassatt article, we see the researchers using a Pearson correlation coefficient as their main test. They are correlating the number of practice problems with students' midterm grades. In this article, r_{xy} = +0.699. Is this a direct relationship or an inverse relationship? The + sign tells us that it is a direct relationship.

Our value of +0.699 looks really good on the surface. But how can we be sure that it is really different from no relationship? We can imagine situations when our sample size is small where one or two measurements then coincidentally fall into place and give the impression that there is a relationship where there really is none. To guard against this, we do a probability test on the actual correlation coefficient that we get. In effect, we are trying to test the likelihood that our actual coefficient is not one of those cases where "no relationship" ends up looking like a relationship. When we do this test, we see that there is greater than a 95% chance that the correlation coefficient we calculated is actually greater than zero. This test is sensitive to sample size—the larger the sample, the smaller the correlation coefficient has to be in order to pass the probability test of being greater than zero.

So now we can look at the correlation coefficient as it is usually reported: r_{xy} = +0.699, $p < .05$. The ($p < .05$) is our way of saying that we have done a probability test, and there is less than a 5% chance that this correlation is actually zero.

We have spent a lot of time on the correlation coefficient, but we will see the logic of testing is similar for our other common examples.

t test

When we are looking beyond relation to try to see if there are causal relations, our simplest testing tool is the t test. When we have a t test, we have a comparison between two means. More often than not, we have a target variable (or the dependent variable) under two different conditions. Let us go back to the fudgilious town of Keebler. Suppose we found that there was a strong direct relationship between fudge consumption and being overweight. Notice that, when we do a correlational study, we can make no claims about whether or not increased fudge consumption *causes* excess weight gain. We just know that they are related. For all we know, it could be the case that heavy people naturally eat more fudge, or that heavier people eat more total food in general, or that there is something else causing both increased fudge consumption and increased weight.

In order to see if fudge contributes to being overweight, we need a more controlled study. First of all, we need a target variable (or dependent variable). In this case, we are interested in weight gain. So we set up a little study. We get a bunch of volunteers, and then create two groups.

The first group is our control group. This group gets 2,500 calories a day, but none of those calories come from fudge. After a month, we measure weight gain (or loss) for all the people in this group. We now have a distribution of weight-gain scores for this sample, with a mean and a standard deviation.

The second group is our treatment group. This group also gets 2,500 calories a day, but these people get 1,000 calories, or 40% of their calorie intake, from fudge. Notice that we are trying to control for any differences between these two groups, except for the presence or absence of a substantial daily amount of fudge. Weight-gain scores after one month are collected, and a group mean and standard deviation are calculated.

Now comes the payoff. The two means are compared. If the fudge group has gained more weight on the average, then we can say that fudge contributes to weight gain even when calorie intake is standardized. But, like the correlation coefficient, we do not just depend upon some raw difference between the means. We need to take into account any differences in the distributions and the size of the samples to create a probability based test. Using the same fairly standard 95% criterion, if the difference between the means is greater than we would expect, then we can say "yes"—these two means are different and therefore these two conditions are different. In this case, it means that eating fudge will really make you gain more weight. If the differences are less than we might expect, then we say "no"—these two groups are really more likely to be just two samples from the same population. In this case, it means that eating fudge does not seem to make people fatter or thinner than eating anything else.

An actual t test might look like this: $t(df = 58) = +23.33$, $p < .05$, or $t(df = 58) = -23.33$, $p < .05$. What do these numbers mean?

The equation in parentheses tells you the degrees of freedom of the t test. In this example, we had two groups—the treatment group and the control group. Each group had 30 people in it, so we have a total of 60 people. But there are always fewer degrees of freedom than there are participants—think of degrees of freedom as being a conservative adjustment of the number of people in each group. Most of the time, the degrees of freedom of a group is $(n - 1)$, or one less than the actual number of people in the group. We use degrees of freedom instead of actual head counts for technical reasons that we will not cover here, but which can be found in any good introductory statistics book. If we reduce each group total of 30 by one, and we have two groups, then we reduce the overall total from 60 to 58.

Once we have the degrees of freedom, we have the actual t value, or the difference between the two conditions. This difference is not a raw difference between means, but the difference has been standardized by taking into account the amount of variation in the distributions of the two groups. This allows us to use tables of standard differences in order to do our probability tests. In this case, like the correlation example, there is less than a 5% chance that this standardized mean difference is actually zero. Why are some *t* scores positive and others negative? It is simply a matter of which mean is subtracted from which mean. In this case, the signs do not really mean anything important—it is the magnitude of the differences that is important.

When we use a treatment group and a control group, then we are testing their differences with an *independent t test*. Sometimes, we want to use the same group as its own control group. This is also called a pretest-posttest design. We take a group and give it a pretest. We then give our treatment, and test again to see if the treatment has boosted performance. We use a slightly different version of the *t* test in this case, called the *dependent t test*. There are two things we need to remember about the dependent *t* test. First, it looks at pairs of data. Each pretest and each posttest score must come from the same person. Second, because the data come from the same person in a pairwise form, there are fewer degrees of freedom in a dependent *t* test.

There is no actual *t*-test example among the training articles per se. The Chagall article uses *t* tests to look at whether or not each item in the predictor equation is contributing significantly to the process, though. These *t*-test values, taken with other findings, allow us to decide whether or not to include these items in the final equation or not.

ANOVA

When we have more than two variables to compare, then we often use an ANalysis Of VAriance, or ANOVA for short. Conceptually, the idea behind ANOVA is very simple. Remember that a *t* test allows us to compare two groups to see if they are different from each other. Suppose we have more than two groups. Then, instead of using a *t* test, we use an ANOVA.

Procedurally, however, things can become a bit more complex when we move from the *t* test to an ANOVA. When we perform a *t* test, more often than not we are comparing two means. This is because the mean is often the best indicator of any given score within a group. Remember that our comparisons are based on looking at the variation we find, and looking at the odds that this variation is beyond the range of normal variability we might expect to find. For instance, if we took two samples from a single population, we would not be surprised to find that the means of those two samples might be slightly different from each other. At some point, however, we cannot merely shrug away differences if they grow to be too large. That is, we are comparing the differences we find to the probability that those differences are real. When we do this, we are examining all the differences we find to one standard of probability.

In the *t* test, we have a simple situation—we have one difference to examine and one standard of probability to use (in most cases, whether or not that difference is less than 5% likely to have arisen by chance). Therefore, we can use the differences between the two means as our one and only measure of difference.

When we move to the ANOVA, we still have only one overall standard of probability to use, since we have only one overall set of data. But, unlike the *t*-test situation, we have more than one group. If, for example, we have three groups, then it is very risky to compare each mean to each other mean. When we do this, we go from making one comparison as we did in the *t* test, to making three comparisons—mean 1 to mean 2, mean 2 to mean 3, and mean 1 to mean 3.

When we make more than one comparison against a probability standard, then we run the risk of finding significance that just is not there. The best way to see this is with an extreme example. Suppose you use the standard of $p < .05$. What this means is the following—if you took this sample 20 times, then you would only expect to get such an extreme score less than one time. But suppose you did sample 20 times, and one of your scores was significant at $p < .05$? Could you trust that one score? Not really, since it is within the realm of possibility for one of your sample scores to be in that range.

The same argument holds when you are comparing scores across more than two groups. If for example you have seven groups, then you would need to do 21 *t* tests to compare each mean to every other mean (check out the math if you do not believe me). If you are testing each mean at the $p < .05$ level, then it would be no surprise at all if one of those comparisons was significant. This would be well within the likelihood of the actual probability situation. The actual probability values are not created by simply multiplying by the number of groups to be compared, but it does go up in the direction you might expect. Rather than dealing with the technical aspects, it is sufficient for us to realize that we need to make sure that our overall probability value is well understood and respected by our techniques.

Even if we were to partition our probability level across all 21 comparisons, making each comparison some fraction of $p < .05$, we still run into the problem of redundancy. In order to make sure we have a clean picture of the contributions of each mean, we can only use each mean one time. This would allow us to make no more than six comparisons, since any comparison beyond six would necessarily require us to use at least one mean more than once. In fact, we can create what are called orthogonal comparisons, or patterns of comparisons of means, that can allow us to cover all the means in six comparisons, in this case. The problem with this is the fact that these comparisons, in order to use each mean once and only once, can end up looking rather strange and indirect.

More often than not, however, we want to compare the groups as intact groups. How do we do that, and still respect the overall probability values for our tests? ANOVA designs solve that problem by moving away from means and comparing sources of variation. Suppose you have three groups. Your probability statement is based on testing the odds on whether or not all your scores really belong in one big group. You have divided the scores into three smaller groups. What are your sources of variation for any given score? First of all, there is the basic source—the difference between that given score and the one big group. Then, there is a source of variation within the smaller group—if, say, you are a member of group three, then you do not expect your score to be identical to all other group three scores. This is called *within-group* variation. On the other hand, there is one final source of variation—the differences between the three groups taken as a whole. That is, we might expect group one scores to differ from group two and three scores, or group two and three scores to differ from each other. This is called *between-group* variation.

The key to ANOVA is the fact that within-group variation and between-group variation are independent of each other. If you think about it, you can see why this is so. Within-group variation ought to be nothing more than the ordinary and unsystematic variation you might find when you measure any given group of people. You would not expect their scores to all be exactly the same. Between-group variation, however, is based on the differences between those groups. More often than not, these differences are systematic. Usually, these differences are due to treatments or conditions that the researchers have identified or manipulated.

Since these two sources of variation are independent, their sum is the value for the total variation. These two sources of variation can then be compared, and that comparison can be evaluated in terms of the overall probability statement. In this fashion, we are able to make the clean and simple sorts of comparisons we want to make even though we have more than two groups.

How does this work in practice? When we do an ANOVA, we are looking at an adjusted ratio of between-group variance and within-group variance. We will not go into the adjustment details here—suffice to say, the adjustment allows us to look at these two sources of variance as a ratio. This ratio is called the F ratio, in honor of Sir Ronald Fisher, an early pioneer of statistics. The greater the numerical value of the F ratio, the higher the likelihood that the between groups variance is greater than the within groups variance. This is indeed the finding that we want, since differences between groups are systematic and differences within groups are not systematic. On the other hand, if the F ratio is not significant, we cannot say that this proves that our groups are equal. All that it says is that most of the variation we found is unsystematic—therefore, we really cannot say anything much about our findings.

What can we say if the F ratio is significant? We can conclude that at least one of our groups is different from the rest of the groups. When we have three groups, we can now say that at least one of the groups is different from the other two. More often than not, we want more precise and detailed findings. To get these, we often use *post hoc* tests. Most post hoc tests allow us to compare means directly. We are now on safer ground to make these comparisons, since we have already established that there is an overall significant difference among these groups. There are many different sorts of post hoc tests that are used. Each has its own strengths and weaknesses. It is not unreasonable for readers to expect some justification by the researchers regarding which post hoc tests are used, and why.

When we looked at t tests, we saw that there were variations of the t test for treatment-control designs and pretest-posttest designs. The same is true for ANOVA designs. Most often, ANOVA designs that use some version of a pretest-posttest model are called *Repeated Measures* designs. In a sense, they allow us to expand pretest-posttest ideas using three or more variables.

The Miro training article uses an ANOVA design to test its hypothesis. Three snack groups were identified, and students were randomly assigned to one of the three groups. Basic characteristics of the snacks were standardized as much as possible, in order to eliminate potential sources of variation. Once overall significance was established, a post hoc test was used to help refine the analysis of the findings.

Chi-Square

All of the tests above depend on scores that are normally distributed. They also deal with variables that are present in greater or lesser degree. For example, people tend to be taller or shorter, or heavier or lighter. What about studies where we are merely looking at the presence or absence of something, and we are studying the relative frequencies of these sorts of things?

For instance, a U.S. senator is (among other things) either a man or a woman. How can we look for patterns in the frequency of men and women in the U.S. Senate, for example? If men and women are equally likely to be senators, then we would expect 50 senators to be men and 50 senators to be women. Is this indeed what we find? And how close to 50-50 should we count as being more or less the same. Is 49-51 close enough? How about 40-60? What about 30-70, or 20-80, or 10-90, or less?

The essence of a chi-square design is this—do the frequencies we observe in the world match those we might expect, or is something different going on? We often find chi-square designs where no manipulation of data is possible, and so all we can measure are frequencies. We also need to have data that can be assigned to independent categories—for instance, a senator can be a man or a woman, but not both at the same time.

The Picasso training article uses a chi-square design to address its research questions. Its variables are sortable into exclusive descriptive—either you are in an Advanced Placement class or not, either you hold an office or not, either you earned a sports letter or not. These variables are also independent of each other as well. Whether or not you have a sports letter has no bearing on whether you take Advanced Placement classes, given that you are a valedictorian to begin with. In fact, even non-valedictorian athletes take Advanced Placement classes—cultural stereotypes aside. The essence of this study is to use actual findings to create a possible pattern of expectations, and then see how actual findings fit within those expectations. This sort of pattern is at the heart of most chi-square designs.

We have looked at only a handful of statistical tests, but more often than not their ideas can be found at the heart of most advanced testing strategies. That is, if we pay attention to the logic of the testing that has been described here, then we have an important conceptual tool to use when we read and grapple with more complex examples.

Statistics Can Also Be Used to Model the World

Researchers often have theories about how the world works. In many cases, these theories can be developed, refined, and tested using statistical models. More often than not, these models can be very complicated and even complex.

In the days before computers, it was virtually impossible to do the computations needed to create and support many of these statistical models. Nowadays, most laptop computers running standard statistical packages can generate the volume of computations needed to support many of these models. Therefore, these sorts of models are showing up more and more in the educational research literature, and so you need to at least understand their basic structures and operations.

One of the most basic statistical modeling tools is the use of *multiple regression* equations. A multiple regression equation allows the researcher to predict or explain changes in one variable by looking at measures in a number of theoretically related variables. A multiple regression equation is a simple model of the world, based on the interaction of variables. In essence, a target variable is identified. Then, other variables that may be deemed useful in predicting or explaining any changes in that target variable are measured. These predictor or explanatory variables are then examined to see if they should be added or deleted from any final predictor or explanatory equation. We often find predictor or explanatory variables ranked in terms of their predictive or explanatory power as well. This makes sense, because we want to make sure we pay attention to the best indicators when we apply the findings of this sort of research.

The Klein article is an example of the use of multiple regression procedures to build a model to predict effective staff meetings.

As researchers look at more complex relations of variables to each other and to some expected outcome or situation, the models grow more complex. If the researcher is interested in creating a network of correlations that can be used to show how various variables impact each other, she can create a *path analysis* model. If the researcher is interested in seeing if intercorrelations among many variables contain patterns or factors that link certain variables to each other, then he can do a *factor analysis*. The Chagall article uses factor analysis to build its model. If the researcher is interested in the presence and impact of latent variables that cannot be measured directly but can only be inferred from the interactions of other variables, then she can develop a *structural equation model* to address those issues.

These are only a few of many such modeling procedures that are used in educational research. Before you throw up your hands in despair in the presence of such models, you need to remember that it is the researcher's job to translate the findings of the statistical modeling procedures into ordinary theoretical language. Such statistical procedures are only used to *support* the creation of theory; they do not *replace* the efforts of researchers to create theory.

There Are a Variety of Places to Turn to Build Upon Your Basic Understanding of Statistics

Where do you turn for more information on statistics? There are literally hundreds of introductory textbooks in statistics that are targeted toward the educational audience. Each has its own approach to the topic. At one extreme, there are books that are thorough and exhaustive (Kirk, 1984, is an excellent example of this sort of text). More often, authors try to make the material straightforward (Evans, 1997) or intuitive (Weinberg & Schumaker, 1997). Minium, Clarke, and Coladarci (1999) try to combine basic coverage with an emphasis on reasoning.

There are also books that deal with the ideas of statistics. Folks (1981) is a classic, and Salsburg (2001) is a recent and highly readable and provocative look at the field. Some books on statistical reasoning have been around for some time. Phillips's (2000) classic text on thinking about statistics is now in its sixth edition, and Williams and Monge's (2001) approach toward reasoning about statistics is in its fifth. Both are well worth reading.

For those who are "terrified" of statistics, there is Kranzler (2003). More advanced students who are looking to expand their practical wisdom might want to read van Belle (2002). As you might guess, this list barely scratches the surface.

Our Emerging Literacy Orientation

Statistics is an integral part of the quantitative research landscape, and so it is necessary for us to confront the basic worldviews and logic of the statistical approach. We have seen that statistics is a way to address complex forms of order that play a key part in the everyday world. Probability is a powerful tool to help us uncover and understand those forms of order. Statistics can help create a descriptive picture of some phenomenon or process, and statistical tests can be used to answer questions and test hypotheses. Statistics can also be used to model processes in operation in the world.

Once we have developed an intuitive and logical grasp of some of the fundamental insights and perspectives of statistics, we can then be more confident in our efforts to tackle more and more advanced and complex uses of this fascinating process. It is surprising how often even the most complex statistical analyses are ultimately built around the simple key logical and intuitive principles we have covered in this chapter.

Practice Makes Perfect

It is now time to practice some of the insights and skills you have explored in this chapter:

- *Normal distributions.* Here are a few distributions: (a) the height of all people in North America; (b) IQ scores in a large school district; and (c) number of potatoes consumed per year in American households. Why would you expect these distributions to be normal? Consider the distribution of the ages of Americans who die from heart attacks. Why would you not expect this distribution to be normal? Can you give another example of a large, naturally occurring distribution that is not normal?

- *Central tendency and dispersion.* Here are a few distributions: (a) IQ scores in a large school district; (b) number of bass, crappie, and bluegill in a farm pond, and (c) personal income for the bosses and workers in a small business. What are the best measures of central tendency and dispersion for each distribution? Why?

- *Sampling strategies.* Pick a research topic where you feel you have some degree of interest and familiarity. Assuming that you were going to use statistical procedures to answer your research questions, how would you generate a sample in order to study this topic? What would be some reasons to eliminate the other three basic sampling strategies?

- *Correlation.* Interpret the following correlation in ordinary language:
  $r_{xy} = +0.90$, $p < .05$

- *t test.* Interpret the following t score in ordinary language:
  $t_{(df=34)} = +34.78$, $p < .05$

- *ANOVA.* Interpret the following F ratio in ordinary language:
  $F_{(2, 57)} = 21.87$, $p < .05$

- *Chi-square.* Interpret the following chi-square in ordinary language:
  chi-square $_{(df = 5)} = +24.90$, $p < .05$

Basic Qualitative Literacy

Scientific models, and quantitative and statistical perspectives, have dominated educational research for most of its brief history. In the past few decades, however, there has been a growing qualitative presence in the field. For that reason, we need to develop our *basic qualitative literacy* skills as well.

Basic qualitative ideas are actually harder to capture and characterize than basic quantitative ideas. In quantitative research, we find a universal desire to conduct research in a scientific fashion, and a nearly universal adherence to statistical views and procedures to help conduct that research. The picture is quite different in qualitative research. This is probably due to the fact that there was no one single group who introduced qualitative research, and no one single set of methods or procedures that are universally accepted as necessary for doing qualitative research. There are, however, some basic perspectives that seem to run through most qualitative studies in education.

What Makes Educational Research Qualitative?

Here are four of the most common dimensions found in qualitative research in education.

Meaning Is the Key to Understanding

If we look at the primary goal of empirical inquiry, it is the pursuit of truth. Quantitative and qualitative research, however, pursue truth in different ways.

Quantitative inquiry uses the scientific method as its basic tool. The idea behind the scientific method is this: If we use the scientific method carefully and properly, then we will find facts and laws that can stand on their own. It will not matter if anyone thinks they are true or not; if they have been gathered or formulated properly then they will be true regardless of what anyone might think or not. This is a very powerful tool, and it has rightfully led inquirers along useful and correct paths for centuries.

How does this scientific model of inquiry relate to the issue of meaning? To answer this question, we need a working model of what constitutes meaning. One very common approach is to say that meaning exists as a thing in the world. Just as researchers can discover facts, they can also discover meanings. These sorts of meanings we might call "meanings in the world." The best examples of "meanings in the world" are the laws of nature. The laws of nature are not facts per se—but they allow us to understand why, and how, certain things happen in the world of experience.

In the search for the general laws of nature, though, we also have to understand what individual things mean, as well. If we know what these individual things mean, then we can learn how the laws of nature operate within them and through them. The key to understanding the meaning of individual things is the idea that the meaning of something is not so much what it *is*, but what its *practical effects* are. This is called the principle of *operationalization*.

When we define something in terms of how it acts or reacts in the world, we are making an operational definition. A common example of this sort of definition comes from geology, in the Moh's hardness scale. The meaning of "hard" in geology is based on what substance can scratch another substance. That is, if we have one rock that can scratch another rock, but the second rock cannot scratch the first rock, then this *means* that the first rock is harder than the second rock. Moh took ten common substances and ranked them from one to ten in comparative hardness: talc, gypsum, calcite, fluorspar, apatite, feldspar, quartz, topaz, corundum, and diamond. Things that cannot scratch talc or gypsum are at the "soft" end of the scale, and things that can scratch corundum or diamond are at the "hard" end of the scale. In this way, hardness has been operationally defined. Anyone who uses the Moh scale already knows what hardness means, so there is no confusion or disagreement to get in the way of further research.

In summary, "meaning in the world" has two sides to it—there are abstract meanings in the world that we see via the laws of nature, and there is the specific meaning of individual things in the world via their operations in the world. These are the ways that meanings tend to be addressed in quantitative studies.

The nature of meaning does not stop here, though. Anyone who has ever had a meaningful conscious thought realizes that there is another side to meaning as well. People hold meanings. They either make these meanings out of their own experiences, or take them from friends, family, culture, and other sources. Let us call this sort of meaning "meaning in the person."

Researchers tend to look at meaning along a continuum. At one end of the continuum is the position that the only meaning that matters is "meaning in the world." The other end of the scale holds to the belief that the only meaning that matters is "meaning in the person." There are virtually no researchers at either extreme. Nearly every researcher agrees that both of these two types of meaning exist. They differ in the relative roles that these forms of meaning play and the relative importance these forms of meaning hold in inquiry. Let us look at each mode of inquiry in turn.

Quantitative researchers acknowledge, of course, that researchers are human beings, and as such they come from families, countries, and other cultural settings. They further acknowledge that different cultural settings play differing roles in the ways that inquirers might look at the world. The task of quantitative inquiry, however, is to create a universal set of theories and findings. If the laws of nature, as we understand them, are tilted in favor of any particular race or ethnic group, or one gender over the other, then our understanding is almost surely erroneous. The laws of nature were designed to run the universe, not to accommodate human beings or some subset of them.

For these reasons, quantitative researchers tend to be suspicious of the role that "meaning in a person" might play in inquiry. Any genuine research findings should be meaningful to all people in the same way, so long as those people have the basic scientific skills to understand those findings. "Meaning in the person" can be interesting and fascinating, but it belongs in the arts and other subjective endeavors. It should play no real role in empirical inquiry.

The qualitative picture of meaning is somewhat different. First of all, there are a relatively small number of qualitative researchers who think that the only form of meaning is "meaning in the person." Probably the most famous is von Glasersfeld (1984) and his model of radical constuctivism. Most qualitative researchers in education take a more moderate approach. They acknowledge that there are indeed facts of nature that go beyond what people might think or wish them to be. For example, we may jump off the top of a ten-story building and decide that we will not get hurt, but we had better hope there is something at the bottom to break our fall.

Most qualitative researchers, therefore, are not saying that there is only personal meaning. Instead, qualitative research looks at meaning in a fundamentally different way. When quantitative researchers use such things as operational definitions, they are striving to settle issues of meaning prior to testing hypotheses and theories. From a quantitative perspective, this makes perfectly good sense. If we are not all clear on meaning at the outset, then how can we possibly know whether our findings are true or not?

In contrast, qualitative researchers feel the whole point of research is to examine the processes and types of meanings that we might find or make in the world. If you look closely at the quantitative approach to meaning, it suggests that researchers are observers of processes that are external to them. In quite a few quantitative settings, this might as well be true. For instance, astronomers looking into the Hubble Deep Space field are examining galaxies that are billions of years old, and which almost certainly no longer exist.

When we move into the human sciences, though, we cannot escape the fact that human beings are an integral part of that reality. When we try to understand why things are the way they are, then we are going beyond the search for the laws of nature. We are looking at the roles that personal and interpersonal meanings play in shaping lived experience, and we are striving to understand those experiences on their own terms. This approach to meaning is not in conflict with the operational definitions and empirical laws of quantitative inquiry—it is simply a move in a different direction.

Research Is Best Pursued in Holistic Natural Settings

As we have discussed earlier, at the heart of the scientific method is the assumption that the simplest phenomenon, the simplest theory, the simplest law is most likely true. Simplicity has been raised as the key to uncovering and understanding order in the empirical world. Complex things are aggregates of simple things. These simple things are the *components* of complex things. These components are like the parts of a watch. When they are put together, in the right way and in the right order, then collectively they make a watch. Furthermore, a skilled artisan can take apart a watch, look at the pieces, and put them back together. In a similar fashion, researchers often look for the simpler components of complex phenomena, so that these simpler components can be isolated and examined.

From the qualitative perspective, things are much different. Qualitative researchers do not necessarily believe that the search for simplicity is the basic strategy in empirical inquiry. They are much more interested in tackling things within their natural contexts, and seeing how the various aspects and facets of that context come together to bring about the worldviews under observation. There are a couple of reasons that qualitative researchers prefer to look at natural, complex settings.

First of all, qualitative researchers believe that complex settings are not just aggregates of simple principles. That is, qualitative researchers do not subscribe to the component approach to complex settings. A complex setting is not like a watch. It is more like, say, an oatmeal raisin cookie.

How does a watch differ from an oatmeal raisin cookie? First of all, a watch is a mechanical device that consists of components. These components can be isolated, their roles can be studied, and they can be taken out and replaced at will. An oatmeal raisin cookie is a result of a *process* where *ingredients* are brought together in a skilled way.

The link between ingredients and the process of using them to create an end product is much different than the link between a mechanical device and its components. For instance, watches are constructed. No one really constructs a batch of oatmeal raisin cookies—they mix them up and bake them. The ingredients of an oatmeal raisin cookie are not components. Some ingredients maintain their identity when used, like the raisins. Most of the ingredients vanish into the final product in some way, while still making an important contribution to the end product. For example, when we add eggs to cookie batter, in one sense they vanish as eggs. Oatmeal raisin cookies that are made without eggs, however, are not at all what we expect from oatmeal raisin cookies in general. Finally, the people who put together oatmeal raisin cookies are not machinists or technicians. They are bakers. Baking is a much different skill than assembling mechanical parts. All in all, the only way to understand oatmeal raisin cookies, from batter to tasting, is to realize that all the ingredients and cooking steps interact in a holistic manner. Therefore, complex things in the environment, whether they be cookies or cultural practices, need to be studied in ways that move away from mechanical perspectives toward an inquiry that understands and respects their holistic natures.

As a second general point, qualitative research operates on the assumption that our understanding of a given setting is impoverished or incomplete, and one of the main goals of research is to get a clearer and more realistic picture of the complex dynamics in operation in that setting. Since the goal is to tackle complexity as such, it would be counterproductive to seek out only simple phenomena. The very targets of the research are most likely embedded within settings in rich and complex ways, and any attempt to simplify would probably eliminate the very things the researchers were most likely looking for.

Researchers Look for Patterns in the Search for Meaning

It does no good to simply collect evidence of meaning as we would gather mushrooms in a forest. We cannot just wander around some environment and pluck statements and observations and toss them in our baskets. Going back to the oatmeal raisin cookie example—qualitative researchers are not just interested in the ingredients per se. These researchers want to know the recipes as well. These recipes make themselves known in qualitative data as *patterns*. When we can find patterns in place, then we know that things are related to each other in meaningful ways.

One of the most common ways to look for patterns in qualitative research is to look for *themes*. Themes are best envisioned as underlying principles at work that help make any given setting coherent and intelligible. As such, it is quite possible for two researchers to take a given body of qualitative data and come up with different patterns of themes. This does not mean that either, or both, researchers have done a poor job. It is a reminder that there are many more themes inherent in data than we can extract. It is our job as qualitative researchers, therefore, to show how *our* thematic "take" on the data advances our understanding of the topic. In this way, we do not confuse themes with the laws of nature, and we do not set ourselves up for trying to find the ultimate pattern in any given qualitative data. In this example, we can also see one of the fundamental ways that qualitative and quantitative research approaches differ.

Researchers Are Not Just Observers, but Are Also Participants

As we mentioned before, quantitative researchers often adopt a stance where they are "outside looking in." There are many forms of research where this stance is of value. In qualitative research, however, it is more often the case that researchers do best when they are "inside looking out."

Participation takes on a variety of forms. At one end, we have the simple participant observer. Participant observers are on the scene, but they are usually trying to stay out of the center of action. In these cases, researchers are interviewing key people, taking notes, and doing simple things under some kind of supervision. In a sense, these researchers are novices who are trying to learn the ropes from more skilled veterans on the scene.

In the middle of the spectrum are those researchers doing autobiographical research. These researchers are generally more experienced in the settings they are studying. They are not only documenting their experiences, but they are also reflecting and meditating upon them as well. The goal in this form of research is to give a more in-depth and interpretive picture of things, framed within the researcher's life experiences and worldview.

At the far end of the spectrum are those researchers who are using the research itself to make the world a better place. This is generally known as action research. The most famous action researcher in education was Paulo Freire (1983). In his work, Freire taught poor and illiterate Brazilian peasants to read by helping empower them socially and politically. For his efforts, Freire was eventually sent into exile by the Brazilian government. We do not need to risk imprisonment or exile to do action research, but we need to realize that this degree of committed participation is powerful stuff, indeed.

What Are Some of the Basic Tools and Procedures Used to Gather Qualitative Data?

Qualitative research rarely uses complex and sophisticated data gathering and analysis tools. Instead, it depends upon the refinement and enhancement of those sorts of ordinary skills we use in our day-to-day interactions (Shank, 2006). Some of the most important of these skills and actions include:

Observations

Observation is both critical and simple. While there are many observational protocols, the basic idea is quite simple—go somewhere and pay attention. Most often, we use our eyes to guide us, but good observation involves all of our senses as we need them.

Interviews

An interview is a specialized form of conversation. When we interview someone, we are gathering information, opinions, and insights from that person. There are a variety of interview protocols in qualitative research. These forms range from highly structured interviews, to semi-structured interviews, through open-ended interviews. Kvale (1996) is one of the best introductions to the use and meaning of interviews in qualitative research.

Focus Groups

Focus groups are highly specialized group interviews. Usually, six to eight people are gathered, and are asked to comment and reflect upon issues or topics that they might share in common. The goal of a focus group is to get at information and insights in a collective fashion. Quite often, this collective format leads to a deeper exploration of issues by participants. Morgan (1998) is one of the most useful guides to the art of conducting focus groups.

Materials Analysis

Materials analysis looks at the "stuff" that cultures generate and use in day-to-day life. This stuff can range from the permanent, such as buildings and furniture and the like, to stuff as ephemeral as baseball cards and Cabbage Patch dolls. These materials are often fascinating windows into the types and roles of meanings we might find within a given culture. Hodder (2000) provides a recent introduction into this topic area.

Archive and Historical Records Analysis

Archival and records analysis is a specialized form of materials analysis. Archives include documents and records from such sources as government agencies and newspapers. These archives are often used to corroborate historical and factual aspects of participants' recollections and opinions. Hill (1993) covers the basics of archival strategies and techniques in research.

Interpretive Analysis

Interpretive analysis is a general heading for a large and complex array of qualitative methods. Some of these methods will be discussed in the next section. In general, though, the notion of interpretive analysis is this: Understanding is most often understanding within a framework. Interpretive analysis seeks to provide an explicit framework so that researchers and readers are both clear on the perspectives and frameworks being employed. A popular interpretive framework, for instance, is phenomenology (see Moustakas, 1994). Phenomenology seeks to use specific analytic tools to get at the underlying nature and structure of meaning in common objects and processes.

Participant Observation

Participant observation is the basic strategy employed in such extensive field research methods as ethnographies and action research studies. The idea is simple—you go and you pitch in when and where you need to understand what is going on. Spradley (1980) is a classic reference for those interested in this process.

What Are Some of the Basic and Most Common Methods Used to Conduct Qualitative Studies?

Unlike quantitative articles, qualitative articles do not share many common characteristics. While they all raise questions and present and discuss findings, qualitative articles take on different forms based on the methods they choose to follow. Here are some of the common methods we find in the qualitative literature:

Ethnography

One of the keys to most forms of qualitative research is the idea of doing work in the field. The earliest field researchers in the social sciences were the cultural anthropologists. Cultural anthropological fieldwork was born at the turn of the 20th century when anthropologists like Franz Boas (1965) and Bronislav Malinowski (1961) traveled to faraway and exotic places and "went native." These field researchers lived with the people, learned their languages and customs, and sought to see the world through the eyes of these people. They actively avoided the very notion of predetermined methods. It was thought that if too much was done beforehand, and too much effort was spent on deciding how to study and record culture, then the fieldworkers ran the risk of looking for what they had been trained to see, rather than what was really before their eyes. Instead, novice field researchers were simply dumped on site and instructed to fend for themselves. Usually this fieldwork went on for at least a year. These anthropologists would take copious notes, and then go home and spend another year or so organizing their notes and writing their final reports. These techniques were known as *ethnographic* in nature, and research reports based on these efforts were called *ethnographies*.

The most prominent educational anthropologists were George and Louise Spindler (Spindler, 1982), who took the basic ideas of ethnographic field research and cultural anthropology and applied them to educational research. A number of important qualitative researchers in education, such as Harry Wolcott (1995) and Shirley Brice Heath (1983), came out of this tradition. The best introduction to traditional models of ethnography in education is LeCompte and Preissle (1993).

In recent years, there has been a tendency to conduct less extensive and time-consuming ethnographic studies. The main reason for this shift of emphasis is the fact that educational ethnographers are usually not going to faraway and exotic locales, but for the most part are sticking close to home. Therefore, the methods need to reflect the fact that there is not a big need to acclimate to the settings, as we might find in a more traditional ethnographic location.

Familiar settings, therefore, generally lead to less ambitious methods. For instance, the notion of *microethnography* suggests that field research can be done over a shorter period of time and with a more restricted target of interest. In a similar vein, *autoethnography* has also played a more important role in recent educational research. This technique, pioneered by Carolyn Ellis (1995), combines field research and autobiography in interesting ways.

Grounded Theory

Grounded theory is an important type of qualitative method that was born within sociology. Its founders, Barney Glaser and Anselm Strauss (1967), were medical sociologists. They were interested in using precise and focused field methods in order to build theory. In this way, sociologists would not have to be solely dependent on experimental methods and prior theories for their theories. It did not take long for this process to expand beyond medical sociology and sociology as a whole, and now it plays an important role in many qualitative studies in educational research.

Over the years, Glaser and Strauss diverged in their use of grounded theory. Glaser (1978) was more interested in the discovery nature of the method. Strauss was more interested in systemizing the process, particularly in the areas of data collection and coding. Strauss's mature understanding of grounded theory is reflected in Strauss and Corbin (1998). This work is the most influential and popular guide to grounded theory in use. Grounded theory has come to be the most analytic and "scientific-looking" type of qualitative research, and so it is often used by those who are more comfortable with traditional approaches to research.

Case Studies

A case study is nothing more than a rich and insightful look at an individual or a group. The key to a case study is the fact that it is an in-depth look. Researchers take their time to observe and probe, and often gather information from a variety of sources. Stake (1995) and Merriam (1998) offer differing but useful guides to creating case studies. Lawrence-Lightfoot and Davis (1997) is the definitive guide to a specialized form of case study known as *portraiture*. In portraiture, analytical and artistic modes and methods are deliberately combined to give readers a unique look at the research targets.

Narrative and Oral Historical Analysis

Narratives and oral histories have always played an important role in the dissemination of culture. For untold centuries, children have been instructed in the basics of their culture by such things as family histories, regional or national legends, and even fairy tales. Therefore, it makes sense for qualitative researchers to turn toward these rich and powerful sources of meaning in their work.

Narrative analysis can be as simple as recording stories and accounts, and as complex as analyzing word patterns, gestures, and intonations and pauses. Oral histories can be as focused as the accounts in a particular school on a particular day, to such broad areas as school culture or even urban legends. Polkinghorne (1988) is an excellent conceptual introduction to narrative thinking in the social sciences, and Richardson (1995) addresses basic issues in the study of narrative in research.

Critical Theoretical Analysis

Critical theory was born in the philosophical turmoil of the 20th century. The great philosophical question of the 20th century was this: How do we understand language and meaning? Critical theory, especially as it was practiced by the Frankfurt School, is one of the ways that this question was addressed.

The chief proponent of this version of critical theory was Habermas (1971). Habermas saw language and meaning related in terms of *ideology*. An ideology was some complex and coherent body of things that we believed, most often on an unconscious level. There was a problem, however—more often than not people held ideological positions that were actually against their own best interests. But since these ideologies were not part of conscious awareness, people clung to them without understanding how they were harming their chances for happiness and freedom and power.

Critical theory involves the use of an explicit interpretive frame to help people raise their conscious awareness in terms of these sorts of ideologies. The idea is this—once people see how they are deluding themselves by holding these sorts of unconscious ideologies, then they will be empowered to set aside these destructive ideologies and move in a better, and healthier, direction.

Within education, there is an exciting variety of practicing critical theorists. Lather (1991), for instance, uses a feminist framework to conduct critical theoretical analysis. McLaren (1998), in concert with many critical theorists in history, has adopted a Marxist perspective.

Other key critical theorists in education draw their insights from important postmodern thinkers. For example, Giroux (1988) has based much of his critical work on Foucault. Some critical thinkers, such as Kincheloe (2002), work within an overall postmodern critique of culture, where the goal is to improve "practice" as understood on multiple levels.

Action Research

We have mentioned action research before. Here, we simply wish to take note of some of the varieties of action research that are most common in educational research. At one end of the spectrum is an international movement directed toward the empowerment of teachers and learners. Very often, these efforts are fueled by a perspective known as *critical pedagogy* (see Wink, 2000). McTaggart (1991) has provided an excellent history and summary of these efforts.

On the other end of the spectrum, we find the "teacher as researcher" movement. These efforts emphasize that everyday conduct by teachers is in itself a form of research, since teachers are constantly working and experimenting with ways to improve their practices. While these efforts might seem more modest when compared to the efforts to empower students and teachers as a whole, the "teacher as researcher" movement has played a steady and important role in qualitative research. It is especially important in the area of research as practice. Hopkins (2002) provides a practical overview, and Hubbard and Power (2003) and Stringer (2004) detail specific methods that teachers and other educational action researchers can use.

Qualitative Educational Evaluation

Historically, much of the early work in qualitative research in education was done by educational evaluators. Back in the 1960s and 1970s in particular, many educational evaluators were growing more and more frustrated. It was commonplace to go into an educational setting and find many good things happening. Students and teachers were happy and productive, serious learning seemed to be going on, and there was excitement in the air. When these innovations were tested using traditional means, however, gains tended to be minimal or nonexistent.

These findings created a quandary for researchers—it was as if they could not trust their eyes and ears. A number of evaluators, led primarily by Egon Guba and Yvonna Lincoln (see Lincoln & Guba, 1982), decided that a paradigm shift was in order. As a result, qualitative educational evaluation came into being. This mode of evaluation still respected the need to find the truth, but it acknowledged that new paths and methods were needed to try to get at the whole truth. To this day, qualitative educational evaluation continues to play an important role in educational evaluation in general. Patton (2001) has written the most comprehensive guide to contemporary educational evaluation.

We Need to Look at Qualitative Articles in Order to Understand Them

In Chapter 3 we looked at training articles, and corresponding real articles paired with them, that were quantitative in nature. Using the same basic strategy, we will look at four qualitative training articles and their paired real articles. The qualitative training articles are as follows:

Ivan Asimov—"Exploring a Community Based Calculus Program in an Inner City Housing Project"
Albert Charles Clarke—"Use of Current Slang by Recent Southeastern Asian Immigrants in an Urban School System"
Rhonda Bradbury—"Analyzing the Web Journals of Three School-Age Shooters: Similarities and Differences"
Agnes Davidson—"Working With Parents on a Supplemental Character Education Program for Elementary School Children"

The corresponding paired real articles are:

Ailish O'Boyle—"The Changing Identities of History Teachers in an Irish School"
Karen James, Eve Bearne, & Elise Alexander—"'Doggy's Dead': Reflecting on a Teacher Research Study About Young Children's Sociodramatic Play"

Shannon E. Wyss—"'This Was My Hell': The Violence Experienced by Gender Non-conforming Youth in US High Schools"

Melanie Nind—"Enhancing the Communication Learning Environment of an Early Years Unit Through Action Research"

Each of these article pairs serves to illustrate one of four basic categories of qualitative articles. We will examine some of these categories next.

What Are Some of the Basic Categories or Types of Qualitative Articles?

Since qualitative research is so diverse and so divergent, it is hard to come up with basic categories to characterize this form of research. We can, however, look at the goals and aims of researchers as they conduct qualitative research. Are they interested in taking a deeper look at something? Are they trying to make sense out of a complex or puzzling situation? Are they seeking needed enlightenment or insight? Or are they just trying to make things better?

When we look at these sorts of outcomes, then four categories come to mind.

Investigative

The first general type of qualitative article is the *investigative* article. The primary goal of an investigative article is depth. When we find ourselves in situations that just do not quite seem to make sense, then it is time to investigate. More often than not, we are trying to bring in our own frameworks without paying attention to what is there before us in the situation. As we dig into the setting and circumstances, then things begin to fall together. Pieces and parts that at first seem to be insignificant may come to play important roles. It is as if we are detectives, hot on the trail of understanding.

The Asimov article was written to illustrate a simple investigative article. On the surface, Asimov found a puzzling phenomenon. How was it that young and very poor children, some of whom had very limited English skills, could be so proficient in advanced mathematics? To get the answers, Asimov needed to investigate. He went on the scene, and talked with students and teachers. He looked for the rules that held this learning community together. Rather than come in with a set of possible rules, he took his time and dug deeper and deeper. As he did so, a pattern began to take shape. He came away with some important in-depth findings.

O'Boyle, in her paired real article, sets out to investigate the history and dynamics of the History Department in a private Irish secondary school. She attempts to forge a new and deeper understanding of past and current roles of History in the school she investigates by talking in depth with, and observing, the teachers who currently comprise the History faculty.

Interpretive

The next general type of qualitative article is the *interpretive* article. The primary goal of an interpretive article is clarity of focus. When we have a situation that seems to be built of parts and pieces with no coherent frame to pull those parts together, then it makes sense to take an interpretive approach. Here, we are like puzzle masters, looking for the best ways to put the pieces together to come up with the clearest and most informative picture. As we settle upon our interpretive themes, we come to see things in clearer focus.

The Clarke article was written to illustrate a simple interpretive article. Clarke found that Southeast Asian immigrant children were adopting East End London slang. But were they adopting all the terms, or just some of them? And did these terms have the same meaning for these immigrants as they did for the other children? Clarke saw that it was not enough to identify and record types and patterns of use. These usage patterns and types had to be interpreted from the perspective of the Southeast Asian immigrant children themselves. To do this, Clarke had to go to the streets and find out what was happening and what it meant to those involved.

In the paired real article, James and her coauthors are employing a number of interpretive approaches in their research project. First of all, she attempts to interpret the findings of her study regarding sociodramatic play among young children. Secondly, she reflects upon the collaborative nature of her research, looking at the interactions between her and her research assistant and academic mentor. Finally, she reflects upon the process of research itself, and what this process has taught her.

Illuminative

The third general type of qualitative article is the *illuminative* article. The primary goal of an illuminative article is insight. Illuminative research often occurs when we are looking at an elusive phenomenon. It is as if we cannot get our arms around it. When that happens, part of the problem is usually conceptual. We may not know enough about the phenomenon, or we may need to look at it in a new way or from a new angle. An illuminative approach allows us to "get out of the box" and take a fresh look at things. Suppose everyone has been looking to the left. What happens when we look to the right? Are we able to see something that has been overlooked, or make links to things that may not have been considered earlier? In illuminative research, researchers are often examining and challenging their assumptions and presuppositions, to make sure they have not settled into a counterproductive way of looking at things.

The Bradbury article was written to illustrate a simple illuminative article. This article describes a situation that most of us find puzzling—why do seemingly normal children in seemingly normal schools and communities perform horrific acts of violence? All of us have our assumptions and presuppositions in areas like these, but the illuminative researcher must set these aside and try to get insights that have previously eluded us. Bradbury, by studying the blogs of three shooters, is able to weave together a common thread that might indeed shed light on these, and possibly other, shootings.

In the associated real article, Wyss explores issues of violence and harassment suffered by seven gender-nonconforming high school students. She paints a rich, complex, and vivid set of portraits of several gender-nonconforming high school students, allowing us access into their worlds and their perspectives.

Participatory

The final general type of qualitative article we will examine is the *participatory* article. Remember, the hallmark of a participatory research project is the desire to make things better. Very often, in participatory research, the boundaries between research and practice come to be blurred. Of all the forms of educational research, qualitative or quantitative, it is the one that is the hardest to pin down. More often than not, the research proceeds in the direction needed to make things better. Therefore, participatory research can shift and alter almost before our eyes. So long as the researchers are clear on their ultimate goals, however, these momentary twists and turns are of minimal importance.

The Davidson article was written to illustrate a simple participatory article. Davidson was convinced that character education could play an important role in bringing together different groups within an educational setting. She was an important practitioner in this setting, but she was also wise enough to hold back and allow the communities themselves to shape the solutions as much as possible. This sort of "bottom up" decision-making and empowerment strategy is quite common in good participatory research.

Nind examines a participatory action research project in the related real article. In this article, she documents and discusses a collaborative effort to enhance communication learning skills with very young children.

One last point needs to be made about this set of paired training and real articles. When we look at many qualitative research articles, we rarely find studies falling exclusively within one category or another. It is not in the least unusual to find investigative, interpretive, illuminative and even participatory dimensions in any given article. These dimensions are simplified in the training articles merely as a learning tool. Therefore, we should not be surprised to find these dimensions interwoven within in our primary articles. After all, the goal of research is to get at understanding and truth, not to conform to some a priori model of conduct.

Our Emerging Literacy Orientation

The qualitative perspective is an entirely different way of looking at empirical research. Qualitative researchers examine the role of meaning, and how people craft their understandings of the world. Qualitative research is best suited for those settings where our understanding is not rich or nuanced enough. Good qualitative research sheds light into dark corners, and changes the ways that we look at things. Qualitative researchers immerse themselves in their projects and their settings, and bring us back new and insightful things as a result.

Because qualitative research is so different in nature and intent from its quantitative ken, we should expect to read qualitative articles differently. Qualitative research questions need not make sense from a quantitative perspective, and qualitative methods should not be examined in the same light as quantitative tools. Is it possible to mix qualitative and quantitative methods in a single study? At this point in time, we will sidestep that issue. It is better for us to understand each of these methods on their own terms, without rushing to figure out how to bring them together just yet. It is surely the best way to learn to read each type of article.

Practice Makes Perfect

It is now time to practice some of the insights and skills you have explored in this chapter:

- *Meaning.* Can you compare and contrast assumptions about meaning in qualitative and quantitative research? What assumptions do they have in common? How do they differ?
- *Key aspects.* The treatment of meaning is one of the key aspects of qualitative research in general. We discussed three other differences. Can you name them? How would you rank them in importance?
- *Qualitative procedures.* We discussed seven tools and procedures that are often used in qualitative research. Can you identify them? Which are of most interest to you?
- *Methods.* In addition to tools and procedures, we also looked at seven common methodological areas. Can you give examples of each? How do they differ from tools and procedures? Which are of most interest to you, and why? Which seem less interesting, and why?
- *Investigative studies.* Which training article is based on investigation? Discuss the key points of this approach briefly, using the training article as your example.
- *Interpretive studies.* Which training article is centered on interpretation? Discuss the key points of this approach briefly, using the training article as your example.
- *Illuminative studies.* Which training article focuses on illumination? Discuss the key points of this approach briefly, using the training article as your example.
- *Participatory studies.* Which training article is based on participation? Discuss the key points of this approach briefly, using the training article as your example.

Titles and Opening Points

When we read articles, we need to start at the beginning. That beginning is usually the title. Too often, we merely glance at the title for its main content and then press on to the main contents. Sometimes, it pays to linger a bit and really read the title. What can the title tell you, beyond the basic contents of the article? Can the title help you understand how the researchers have approached their topic?

After the title, usually a research article then has an abstract. For now, we will set aside the abstract. Since it is so important, we will give the abstract its own chapter (which, coincidentally, is the very next chapter). Instead, we will spend some time here considering the opening of the article. As a very rough guideline, the opening of an article can usually be found in the first three sentences (or the opening paragraph). We will look at these openings to see what they tell us about the purpose of an article. Why is this research important to the researchers? Why should it be important to us? In what manner should we approach this research? These are all questions, on top of the basic matter of content, that openings often address.

In this chapter we will consider literacy issues related to titles and openings:

Title Literacy

Title literacy is a matter of learning how to read titles, both for their content and for their form. This is an important part of educational research literacy, but it is neither very hard nor all that time-consuming. When we read titles, we want to be able to extract some very basic information from them. We will save our hard work for the articles themselves. But there are a few "tricks" we can use to read titles that will help us orient ourselves better to those things that articles are trying to tell us.

A Title Can Tell Us a Variety of Things About an Article

Every research article begins with a title. The job of the title is to tell you what to expect from the article. In a way, the title is like a picture frame. It creates boundaries for the reader. A title should tell you at least about the research topic. Beyond that, a title might tell you something about the circumstances of the research, which variables are critical, what sorts of situations are involved, and who the target groups for the research are. In fact, titles often fall into categories, depending on what they are trying to say.

Titles are written carefully. In fact, the title is often one of the last parts of an article that is written. Researchers are trying to summarize key aspects of their articles in their titles. As a result, titles can often be categorized in a formal way. Five of the most common examples are *descriptive*, *equation*, *situation*, *process*, and *theoretical* titles.

The Descriptive Title

The simplest and most basic type of title is the *descriptive* title. Here, the reader is simply pointed toward an area that will be examined by the article. The title makes no claim other than the fact that some content area will be targeted.

Two of the training articles have descriptive titles—"Gender and Early Career Characteristics of High School Valedictorians From Different High Schools" and "Use of Current Slang by Recent Southeastern Asian Immigrants in an Urban School System."

The first title is descriptive because it merely promises a list of characteristics of valedictorians from different types of high schools. It does not suggest where these characteristics come from, what sorts of things might influence them, or even how these high schools are different. Readers are promised information, and nothing more.

The second title has a similar structure. The focus of the title is on the use of slang. Readers are promised a description of how certain types of slang are being used by a certain group in a certain setting, and nothing more. There is no guarantee, in the title, that slang use will be compared to other groups or other settings.

One of the paired real articles also has a descriptive title—"Effectiveness of School Staff Meetings: Implications for Teacher-Training and Conduct of Meetings." This title simply tells us that the concept of effectiveness will be examined, and that any findings in this investigation will be applied in some way to general strategies for conducting meetings and teacher training. Actual details of this effort are left to the article itself.

Descriptive titles can be useful as guides for readers. More often than not, however, researchers want to say something right away about the nature of the phenomena that are being examined. One way to help insure this result is to map out key relations among various phenomena in the title itself. This leads to the notion of the equation title.

The Equation Title

In an *equation* title, the title identifies a relation that will be explored in the article. Rather than merely describe the presence of relevant phenomena, as the descriptive title does, the equation title goes a step further to link those phenomena together.

What is an equation? That answer can be surprisingly complex. When examining equation titles, you are best served by keeping the idea of an equation simple.

Here is a simple made-up equation title—"The Impact of Noise on Sleep." This title has three parts. The first part is the first variable, which in this case is "noise." The second part is the second variable, which in this case is "sleep." The third part is the relationship, which is "noise impacts sleep."

Most relationships in equation titles are asymmetric. That is, they only go in one direction. In this example, "noise impacts sleep" but "sleep does not impact noise." Therefore, the order of the variables matters. Some common relationship terms and phrases are "the impact of," "the role of," "the effect of," and so on.

More often than not, titles will not be as explicitly "equational" as the simple example above. Instead, they will use a more implicit or perhaps less formal statement of the equation in question. This is the case for the two practice articles that use equation titles.

The first equation title example is from the training article—"Comparing Rates of Practice to Midterm Grades in Four Eighth Grade Magnet School Science Classrooms." In this example, the first variable is "rates of practice" and the second variable is "midterm grades." The relationship is "comparing." If this title were merely a descriptive title, then it would read "Rates of Practice and Midterm Grades in Four Eighth Grade Magnet School Science Classrooms." The relationship of comparing, which may be implicit in a descriptive title, is made explicit in the equation title.

The second equation title example is from the training article—"Testing the Relative Effects of High Protein Snacks on Quiz Grades in Afternoon High School

Math Classes." The first variable is "high protein snacks" and the second variable is "quiz grades." The relationship is "testing the relative effects." Again, a descriptive version of the title would simply read "High Protein Snacks and Quiz Grades in Afternoon High School Math Classes."

There is something else involved in the relationship in this title as well. The title promises the article will not only test "the effects" but "the relative effects." That is, the title suggests that there might be multiple comparisons. In this case, the effects of high protein snacks might be tested not against the absence of snacks, but perhaps against other types of snacks instead. In one neat little move, the title opens up the possibility for several testing conditions in the same study.

The third equation title is from the linked real article—"College Students' Ratings of Student Effort, Student Ability and Teacher Input as Correlates of Student Performance on Multiple-Choice Exams." In this title, we are being told that student performance on multiple-choice exams is going to be examined in light of three major variables—student effort, student ability, and teacher input. Furthermore, those three major variables themselves will be measured using student ratings. In a sense, the title is almost a first draft, or sketch, of the research design to follow.

The key assumption of the equation title (and usually, the descriptive title as well) is that variables and their relationships are the real key to the article. Sometimes, however, there are other aspects of a study that are more central. The next three title types reflect some of these other domains of importance.

The Situation Title

With the *situation* title, the article promises to lay out critical details and circumstances and explanations needed to understand a particular situation.

Our first situation title example is from the training article—"Analyzing the Web Logs of Three School Shooters: Similarities and Differences." The situation being described in the title is the fact that three school shooters all left web logs. A web log, or blog as they are known, is a sort of Internet diary that some young people (and some folks who are not so young) keep as an ongoing and updated public record on their web sites. The title is not talking about variables that are being extracted from the web logs. The research activity is described using a fairly global and generic term; the logs are simply being "analyzed" as such. The real importance is the fact that these logs exist, that researchers have access to them, and that at least some researchers have found out things about these logs by comparing and contrasting them to each other.

Three of the linked real articles have situation titles—"Situational Influences on Children's Beliefs About Global Warming and Energy," "The Changing Identities of History Teachers in an Irish School," and "'This Was My Hell': The Violence Experienced by Gender Non-conforming Youth in US High Schools." Each of these titles focuses on a different key situation that serves as the focus of the article. In the first case, beliefs about global warming are central. The second title informs us that history teachers in Ireland and their changing states of affairs will be our focus. Finally, the third title uses what is presumably a student quote to describe the focal situation of that particular study—the fact that being a gender-nonconforming student can be hell.

Situations are often important in educational research, but so are processes. This is reflected in the fact that many educational research articles have process titles.

The Process Title

In many ways, the *process* title is a special case of the equation title. There are usually variables and relationships present. The difference is the fact that there is also usually some goal or target present as well. This goal or target is the point of the research, and the variables and their relationships are part of the process of reaching that goal or target.

Our first training article process title is "Exploring a Community Based Calculus Program in an Inner City Housing Project." Here we have a situation that is clearly important—this research was conducted in an inner city housing project. But more importantly, it also describes the workings of a community based calculus program.

Part of the interest of this title is the fact that one aspect of it—the community-based calculus program—suggests a grassroots effort that almost certainly has specific goals and aims. Generally, the target audiences of such a program are those sorts of students who will go on soon to college careers, perhaps in such areas as mathematics, science, and engineering. Such training, and such programs, often requires resources and personnel that, frankly, are usually out of the reach of most inner city housing project dwellers. Therefore, the title not only promises a description and analysis of a process, but perhaps some intrigue as well.

The second training article process title example is "Working With Parents on a Supplemental Character Education Program for Elementary School Children." In this title, there is not only a program that presumably has clear goals and aims. There is a second process in place, as well. The researcher is also describing her process of working with parents to implement this program. This process of working with parents has its own goals and aims as well.

Two of the linked real articles also have process titles—"'Doggy's Dead': Reflecting on a Teacher Research Study About Young Children's Sociodramatic Play" and "Enhancing the Communication Learning Environment of an Early Years Unit Through Action Research."

In the first real article, the key process that is signaled is one of reflection. We are led to believe that this particular study will not just simply report findings regarding young children and sociodramatic play, but that the researchers will take the process one further step to reflect on the study itself.

In the second real article, the process appears to be a bit more straightforward. In this case, the researchers have committed to enhancing communication in an educational setting for young children. Furthermore, they will attempt to further this enhancement process by using a specific research process—namely, action research.

Situations and processes often contextualize and focus on conditions and factors beyond the relationships of variables. There is a third sort of activity that also goes beyond simple descriptions and relations. This activity involves the creation of abstract models or theories of understanding that can be used to capture events and circumstances in a broad, overarching fashion. This involves the creation of theory, which is often signaled by the use of theoretical titles.

The Theoretical Title

In the *theoretical* title, there is the promise that some theory or model will be put to the test in some fashion. A theoretical title goes beyond the simple relation described in an equation title, and is often more global in its claims than either a situation or process title.

Our first theoretical title example comes from the training article—"Critical Factors for Understanding Male Juvenile Offenders: Developing an Empirically Based Model." You know that this is a theoretical title since the title states that the article will be concerned with building a model. Most of the time, the notions of "model" and "theory" will be interchangeable. The title acknowledges that there are critical factors that play a role, but it does not identify them. In this case, it is because the article is trying to find at least some of those critical factors.

Our second theoretical title example comes from the linked real article—"Some Strategies to Improve Performance in School Chemistry, Based on Two Cognitive Factors." While the title suggests that they are going to employ a fairly straightforward educational process, namely to improve chemistry learning, they indicate that they will do so by employing a theoretical strategy. In this case, the researchers are focusing on two cognitive factors, which we presume to be more abstract than learning skills applied directly to the teaching of chemistry. As we read on, we find that we are correct—the researchers are using factors straight from the cognitive science literature.

Do these five title categories exhaust the list of possible ways to categorize titles? Of course not. They do cover quite a bit of territory, however, and they can help you anticipate themes and directions within articles.

Title Categories Often Point Out the Nature and Content of Articles

Determining a title category can sometimes help you decide what sort of article you might be reading. These informal guidelines can help you orient yourself toward the sorts of research strategies you might expect to find in the article. For example, situation and process titles often tend to signal articles that take a more qualitative approach. Equation titles are more likely to be quantitative. Descriptive and theoretical titles can go in either direction.

You can also use title categories to begin to understand how content is addressed. Are the researchers looking to isolate and test key variables? Are they looking at their topic as a complex situation? Or are they seeing it as a process? Or should you expect a more theoretical treatment? A title category can help you anticipate the sorts of information you might be getting from the article in question.

Is it absolutely critical to get the exact correct category for a title? Not really. Interestingly enough, the real value of using these categories comes into play when we are able to rule out which categories do not really apply. For instance, if we are sure that the title is not theoretical, then this tells us that we will probably not be finding some sort of complex model or extended theoretical discussion in the article itself. This, of course, is only a working assumption, and if we do find such models or discussions, then we need not be all that concerned. After all, we are evaluating the titles in order to orient ourselves, not to lock into place some sort of absolute way to read or understand the article.

What if a title can legitimately be assigned to more than one category? Should we be concerned about this? The answer again is no. The whole point of categorizing titles is to save us work, not to make more work for ourselves. If we have a good sense of what a title is trying to tell us, by using one or more categories, then this helps us anticipate what the article itself will be trying to tell us as we read it.

Article Opening Literacy

Article opening literacy is a matter of learning how to read the first few sentences of an article, to see what it is trying to accomplish and why. Why did the researchers do this research in the first place? Why do they think it is important? Are their concerns addressing the concerns that directed you to this piece of research in the first place? In these first few sentences or paragraphs, the researchers must connect with you, the reader, to convince you to read on and to take their research seriously. Were they able to do that? Why, or why not? These are the sorts of literacy issues that comprise our examination of the openings of research articles.

The First Few Sentences Should Tell You the Basic Point of the Article

It is fun and informative to play around with titles to see what they will tell you, but this process takes you only so far. Now you need to begin to address the actual body of the articles themselves.

When you begin reading an article, the first question you might ask yourself is this—what is the goal or aim of the author or authors of this particular piece?

One good question leads to many others. Why did they do this research, and why did they choose to write it up this way? What are they trying to show us? Are they trying to alert us to some condition or situation that needs correction or repair? Are they trying to address a gap in our knowledge or understanding? How do they feel about the people and the circumstances they are studying? The list goes on and on. However, none of these questions will engage you fully until the authors have shown you, at the outset, some point in doing the research in the first place.

At the very beginning of every research article, the researchers need to set up at least one reason for doing the research. As a good rule of thumb, these reasons or points should usually surface within the first three sentences of the article. If you are not clear on the point by the first three sentences, then read on a bit. Before long, the point of the article should be evident.

In other words, articles usually start out with *points* they are trying to make. These *opening points* can direct you toward the goals and purposes of the researchers. There are at least six different categories of opening points used in research articles.

An *opening point* is the initial set of issues that a research article brings to the table. While these issues may or may not serve as the basis for the rest of the article, they do serve the role of alerting the reader as to the potential importance of both the research and the article itself. To repeat a rule of thumb—you can expect the opening point of any given educational research article to usually show itself within the first three sentences. Surely it should reveal itself by the end of the first paragraph, in most cases. If, however, you have to read a bit more, then so be it. You should expect, however, that the article will strive to make some opening point fairly soon in the going.

In a similar fashion to titles, opening points can also be categorized. These categories can be useful in orienting us to the goals and purposes of the article. Six of the most common opening points include the *crisis point*, the *importance point*, the *lacuna point*, the *depth point*, the *commitment point*, and the *synopsis point*.

The Crisis Opening Point

Crisis point articles are not uncommon in educational research. There are many difficult and troubling conditions in education that need to be ameliorated. There are crises galore in education. Whether it is overcrowding or underfunding, falling test scores or increasing violence, formal education is beset with problems that can rightfully be labeled as crisis areas. It is no wonder that researchers become concerned with these sorts of issues, and strive to conduct research to help make things better.

Consider the first three sentences of the training article by Bradbury, talking about her research looking into web journals left by school shooters. She starts off by emphasizing some of the reasons that Iowa is considered such a great place to live and raise families:

> Iowa is the very model of an ordinary, All-American state. In addition, it takes particular pride in its school systems. Iowa has one of the highest literacy rates in the country.

So far, there is no crisis. This reads like it might be straight out of a Chamber of Commerce pamphlet. The paragraph continues:

> Iowans are also proud, community-minded citizens. Towns and whole areas rally around their local schools, supporting high school athletics and conducting car washes and bake sales to raise money for school libraries. Truancy and delinquency rates are also near the bottom of the scale, nationwide. In short, Iowa is a great place to live, and a really great place for children to get an education.

And yet, you know from the title of the article that something very bad is being examined in this research. Moving along, you come to the second paragraph, which lays out a stark contrast to the points discussed earlier:

> Imagine the shock, then, that fateful first week in May of 2004. Within four days of each other, across the state and in different sorts of schools, three shooting sprees broke out in Iowa schools.

In this article, Bradbury took two paragraphs to lay out the crisis point of her research. The first paragraph used short sentences to make points of fact and perception concerning the safety and normalcy of education in Iowa. The second paragraph created the crisis by simply describing incidents that were seemingly incomprehensible in a place like Iowa. By doing so, she pointed out that there are really two crises—a crisis of safety, and a crisis of understanding. Implied in her simple prose is the notion that the crisis of safety cannot be resolved without first resolving the crisis of understanding. Therefore, tackling the crisis of understanding is the opening point of this article.

More often than not, opening points are laid out more explicitly. Such is the case of the opening crisis point of the following article. Here are the first three sentences from the training article by Chagall, on creating a model of critical factors for youthful offenders:

> Male juvenile offenders who receive effective intervention are 40% less likely to enter the adult correctional system (Santayana, 2002). Given the growth of delinquency among young males, and given the serious consequences of delinquency on both the young males and society proper, it is past time to try to put a halt to this epidemic. Understanding the dynamics of proper intervention is a critical priority for all parties.

Delinquency is described as an "epidemic," which conjures up notions of both disease and maladies that spread rapidly and are often out of control. The increasing delinquency rate is described as a crisis both for society and the young males who fall into delinquency themselves. Therefore, both young males and society itself stand to benefit from effective interventions.

Two of the real articles begin with a crisis point opening. First of all, Devine-Wright et al. start off with a warning about global warming:

> Global warming is widely recognized as a serious threat to natural ecosystems and human existence (Intergovernmental Panel on Climate Change, 2001), caused mainly by the combustion of fossil fuels (for example, coal, oil and natural gas) for the human requirements of mobility, power, heat and light.

To compound the crisis, they go on to point out that responding to this threat is also fraught with difficulties of its own:

> From a psychological perspective, response to this complex, large-scale environmental problem presents formidable difficulties. Greenhouse gases, which are the main causal agents of global warming, are not perceptible using human sensory mechanisms and conventional human learning mechanisms that link cause and effect are likely to be inadequate. (Pawlik, 1991, pp. 493–494)

In this opening, Devine-Wright et al. point to two serious crises that must be addressed in contemporary life. By doing so, they set into motion their arguments, which will eventually lead to their research questions.

Wyss also confronts a crisis issue in her real article. She begins by pointing out that high school is a difficult period for most adolescents:

> High schools are institutions that provide a location for dynamics among various groups to play themselves out, and adolescence in the USA is a period of life when many teens become increasingly aware of the differences between them (Eckert, 1989). Consequently, this time is a difficult one for many teenagers,

who find themselves confronting social challenges that were unknown in elementary school.

Within this general aura of difficulty, Wyss goes on to single out a particular subgroup of adolescents who are in particular danger. In this case, it is hard to argue against fear for physical safety as a crisis situation:

> While most young people face some difficulty, youth who belong to one or more minority populations often face additional risks. Because images of homosexuality since the 1980s have become so much more prevalent in the USA than in previous decades, teenagers are now able to associate themselves with 'alternative' sexual and gender categories at younger and younger ages (Burgess, 1999; Human Rights Watch, 2001; Wilchins, 2002). As a result, some youth are beginning their high school years already having claimed a lesbian, gay male, bisexual, transgender, or queer (LGBTQ) identity (Human Rights Watch, 2001).
>
> Unfortunately, because of their peers' hatred—a hatred that mirrors the prejudices present in adult culture (Eckert, 1989)—out-of-the-closet teens often confront situations in which they are not safe (Mallon, 1999a).

A key aspect for most articles that begin by making a crisis point is the fact that you can expect them eventually to offer some sort of research-based set of insights or alternatives to the conditions that are engendering the crisis in the first place. Therefore, you should be alert to the presence of such instances or alternatives, and you need to pay particular attention to them when they finally arise in the article itself.

The Importance Opening Point

Similar to the crisis point, but without the warnings or the urgency, is the importance point. Consider the opening from the following training article by Miro:

> Research has shown that afternoon high school math classes consistently lag behind morning classes in overall performance (e.g., Fudd, 1999; Bunny, 2002). Given that not all students can schedule math in the morning, it is important to try to identify some of the causes of these general disparities, and to help remedy the effects. Otherwise, half of our students will suffer to some degree in their high school math preparation.

Miro makes it clear that there are important practical consequences to understanding how snacks can help students in afternoon classes. She does not present her case as a life or death proposition, but that does not mean that it is not an issue of critical importance.

Among the real articles, Klein is a good example of an importance point opening. In fact, he makes quite a case for meetings and cooperative efforts and planning. The scope of such efforts is quite sweeping:

> Each day, throughout the world, groups of people gather to make laws, achieve peace, stimulate economic or cultural progress, or just to have fun. There are parliamentary and business conferences, meetings to promote religious or social consciousness, lectures, political rallies, clandestine assemblies in

secluded rooms and celebrations which may or may not be appreciated by the neighbours.

Not only are meetings important, states Klein, but it is also important that we know how to do them well. Klein finishes his point by showing how society and culture as we know them depends on knowing how to meet well. How much more important can you get!

> While individual motivation and initiative underlie many aspects of human progress, the development and perpetuation of society are dependent to a large extent on the pooling of human resources and talents and the cooperative formulation and implementation of decisions.

What are some of the general criteria for identifying and evaluating an importance point? First, a point may be important because it brings in other sources of information or perspectives that might not have previously been linked to the topic of the study. Second, it might refine your understanding of how and when the results of the research might play a role in educational theory or practice. Finally, it might seek to clarify unclear areas of understanding within the broad framework of the topic area. It may take the entire article for such an effort to be achieved, but you should see some resolution of the importance point in the discussion section of the article in question.

The Lacuna Opening Point

"Lacuna" is a technical term for a gap or hole in something. It is often used when describing old records or manuscripts. Therefore, it is perfect for describing holes in theories or research records or programs.

The first example of a lacuna point comes from the training article by Picasso. In her first paragraph she makes some general statements about valedictorians:

> School communities hold valedictorians in high regard. Valedictorians are also more likely than the average student to get into a good college or university (Shakespeare, 1999), earn a high salary in their first job (Milton, 2002), and to assume leadership positions in their communities (Blake, 2000). For these and other reasons, it seems like being a valedictorian is a valuable accomplishment for a high school student.

Sometimes, when making a case for a lacuna, researchers must first make a case for why the topic matters in the first place. That is what Picasso was doing in the first paragraph. In the second paragraph, she goes on to point out the lacuna in the research record:

> Being a valedictorian is often a ticket for a bright future. This study will examine existing archival data about valedictorians to address two questions. First of all, are there any gender differences in the likelihood of being a valedictorian? That is, are males more likely to be valedictorians than females, or vice versa? Second, are there early career differences between valedictorians from wealthier suburban schools and poorer inner city schools? Are suburban

valedictorians more likely to go to college or vocational schools over their inner city counterparts, or vice versa? Research is needed to fill this knowledge gap about valedictorians.

Not only does Picasso argue that there are a number of lacunae in the systematic and research-based understanding of valedictorians, she goes on to raise a number of important questions whose answers might help fill those lacunae.

There are many sorts of lacunae that can serve as the basis of a lacuna point. There might be research where there are puzzling gaps in the knowledge base that need to be filled. In other cases, a theory might predict certain behaviors or consequences that have never been observed. There may be gaps in theoretical understanding that prevent the prediction what might happen under certain circumstances. The authors might be talking about people or places that have never been studied by researchers before. All of these things, in their own ways, are lacunae.

You can expect an article that begins by making a lacuna point to move toward filling some gap in the current knowledge or the current level of understanding. Articles that begin by making lacuna points are sometimes more abstract and more theoretically driven than, for instance, articles that begin by making crisis points. This is because the act of trying to fill a lacuna in a knowledge base or theory can be more dispassionate and more cerebral. Just because it does not have some immediate social or cultural "payoff," however, does not mean that it is not as important as more socially driven forms of research. If researchers fill in gaps in knowledge and understanding, who knows what payoffs might be down the road?

The Depth Opening Point

When researchers open an article with a depth point, they are usually signaling that they are going to be looking at something that needs to be examined thoroughly in order to be understood properly. Consider this training article example by Asimov:

> Magda is twelve years old. Her parents left Hungary to immigrate to Baltimore when she was five. She started school knowing no English. Her father soon died, and the family had no money or resources of any kind. Magda, her mother, and her younger brother moved into Camden Acres, the toughest housing project in inner city Baltimore. As one of only a handful of nonminority families in the project, and speaking broken English at that, they were soon targets for harassment and even threats. Magda's mother feared that her talented daughter would fall behind in her new, poverty-ridden school.

Asimov starts us with the sad facts of Magda's life. It would not be unusual for you to assume that Magda has fallen onto hard times, and is struggling in school and life. But Asimov surprises us when he goes on to say:

> On the day I first met Magda, she was huddled in a grimy hallway of the Community Center at Camden Acres with an adult and five other children. They were studying the Chain Rule for taking derivatives.

This is not the sort of thing you might expect to hear about Magda's current life. Asimov acknowledges this fact as he goes on to set up his depth point:

> How did Magda, and five other children, go from the hopelessness and dead
> end educational surroundings of her neighborhood to differential calculus?
> This study intends to explore that question in some depth.

In this study, Asimov says that we need to explore these surprising circumstances
in some depth in order to understand them. He brings that point home to his readers
by setting them up for the surprise of Magda's success in highly unlikely circumstances. By feeling this surprise themselves, his readers are more likely to be able
to follow the in-depth exploration of the dynamics of Magda's case.

Two of the real articles use depth openings. First of all, the Williams and Clark
articles suggest to us that we need to look closer at some of the common objections
that both teachers and students raise against the use of multiple-choice test items:

> College courses with high-enrollment often use multiple-choice exams as an
> efficient means of assessing student performance and providing timely feed-
> back to students regarding their performance. Yet many faculty and students
> object to the use of multiple-choice exams for a variety of reasons, some of
> which are not well grounded in empirical research.

Williams and Clark go on to lay out a few of these major objections, thereby giving
us the sense that the article as a whole will explore, in some depth, whether or not
such objections are empirically valid:

> A common objection is that multiple-choice tests assess only surface knowl-
> edge, rather than deep levels of thinking about subject-matter. Some students
> believe that the very structure of multiple-choice tests restrict students' ability
> to demonstrate their knowledge and reasoning. Students are not permitted to
> explain their reasoning for chosen options or to construct other options that
> might better answer a particular question.

James et al. also opens with an examination of depth, but from a much different direction:

> My view of young children and their ability to take ownership of their own
> learning was transformed during my M.Ed. research. As I observed children
> and listened to their views, expressed so articulately, I made discoveries that
> offer a fresh perspective on young children's sociodramatic play.

James, who is clearly the author of this introduction, then goes on to summarize
some of her major findings. The nature of the study then returns to the reflective
tone of the opening few sentences, by making that reflection the key to the very article itself. In addition, James explicitly draws in her co-authors as part of the reflective process. The article itself, then, is an invitation to dig deeper into the research
process to see how it unfolds as a collaborative process:

> Having completed my study I reflected on the key moments in the research
> process, and the main influences, which provide the framework of this arti-
> cle. Undoubtedly, the input of both Elise, my research assistant, and Eve, my

academic mentor, was influential at these points and therefore I asked them to contribute their comments.

As we have seen, depth points can go in a variety of directions. Sometimes, depth is based on a need to explain surprising circumstances. Sometimes depth is sought by trying to get a richer and more research-based definition of a key concept. Other times, researchers might pursue a depth of presence, or a sense of feeling what it is like to be there and involved in the activities being discussed and presented.

When an article begins by making a depth point you should expect it to enhance your understanding of the issues or circumstances it lays out at the outset. Therefore, you must also evaluate the potential importance of those concepts or issues. They are obviously important to the researchers, but are they as important to you, the reader?

The Commitment Opening Point

When an article opens with a commitment point, the researchers are being honest about their personal investment in the topic and the study.

The opening of the Davidson article shows her commitment to her topic:

> In this action research study, I was invited by a coalition of parents and administrators to help design an after-school program in character education for 1st and 2nd grade students at a local elementary school. As is the case with many action research studies, this one was precipitated by a series of problems. It was my job to come in and help make things better, and I welcomed the challenge.

Davidson is conducting this research as an action researcher. Action research is quite different from many other typical forms of research (McTaggart, 1991; Wink, 2000). Action research calls for commitment by the researchers. Minimally, researchers are committed to leaving a research setting in better shape than it was when they started their research. More often than not, researchers are furthered committed toward empowering the people they are working with and studying (Freire, 1983).

Most often, studies that open with a commitment point are qualitative in nature. There is often reluctance on the part of quantitative researchers to be so open an advocate for any position. These researchers prefer to advance theoretical positions and then test those positions to see if they are upheld in the data. While they are often committed to a theoretical position, quantitative researchers, more often than not, prefer to operate through a more objective stance.

The Synopsis Opening Point

When an article begins with a synopsis, there is a sense that things are already up and running. The point the researchers wish to make is this—let us get you up to speed right away so we can get on with this study. Researchers often begin with a synopsis when they feel that the research seems to need very little contextualizing. Furthermore, there is little need, as the researchers see it, to spend time justifying the purposes for conducting the research. Any reasonable person, they might conclude, can infer the value of this study just by reading how it has been set up and run.

Cassatt begins his training article in just this fashion:

Students in math and science magnet middle schools tend to be highly moti- vated (Ra, 2001) and they also tend to put in many hours of homework (Mul- ligan & Baker, 2002). With grades being competitive and the stakes being high (i.e., entrance into selective special high schools and colleges), it is no wonder that middle school math and science magnet students work so hard. But does all that hard work pay off? The purpose of this study is to compare large-scale practice rates of middle school math and science magnet students to their eventual midterm grades. Earlier studies have shown that moderate practice rates for average math students are positively related to their grades (Coltrane, 1997). But these same trends have never been explored in magnet middle school classrooms, where average student performance is much higher and the pursuit of grades is much more competitive. To get at these effects with higher performing students, much greater practice effects are needed. These higher rates are the target of this study.

Cassatt talks briefly about the competitive nature of middle school magnet programs in math and science, but mainly as a way to introduce the main point of the study. Cas- satt delves into the details of the study right away. Do the more competitive nature of magnet schools and the overall higher performance rate of these students alter the dynamics of practice as they are currently understood? These central issues are pre- sented as if they needed little or no justification—of course it makes sense to study how the best and brightest students learn, at least from Cassatt's perspective.

In the second example, the training article by Clarke, the researcher begins right away with examples of his data:

"Mind the wookie, mate" or "Strabble me backwards." Any teacher in the East London school system expects to hear these sorts of expressions while walking down the halls of school. Most often, these kinds of slang terms and phrases come from working class children in and around the East End of Lon- don. However, these terms and phrases are being picked up with surprising speed and fluency by very recent Southeastern Asian immigrants. What sorts of terms and phrases do they pick up? Where do they learn them? How do they become fluent so quickly? Are they using them in the same ways that their more native East End counterparts are?

Clarke is jumping right into the research because he is curious about these matters. It surprised him that recent Southeastern Asian immigrants would be using this slang so readily and so fluently, and he simply assumes that his readers will be just as sur- prised as he is. Since this topic has engaged his curiosity, he seems to feel that there is no need for any other justification for doing this research. While one could make a case for learning how to foster greater social acceptance for these recent immigrants by learning how they are adopting all sorts of language usages, Clarke does not even bother. Curiosity, as far as he is concerned, is reason enough to do this work.

It is not unusual for authors of real articles to use synopsis strategies to open their articles, given the need to communicate basic contextual details to their read- ers. In fact, three of the real articles did adopt such an approach.

In the first case, Danili and Reid summarize the state of affairs of chemistry instruction in Greece. Such an opening allows them to demonstrate the need for instructional reform in the teaching of chemistry, which is the main point of their article:

> In Greece, chemistry is taught for the first time as part of an integrated science course in the fifth and sixth year of primary school (ages 11 to 12) and, as a separate subject, in the second and third year of lower secondary school (12 to 15) and in all the years of upper secondary school (15 to 18). The majority of the schools are not equipped with laboratories and it is only in recent years that, in many schools, teachers have started experimental work. In research related to chemical notation, atomic and molecular structure, chemical equations and simple stoichiometric calculations, Tsaparlis (1991, 1994) has already established that the chemistry understanding of the majority of pupils in secondary education is poor.

Description of the setting is often an important part of framing a research study, as well. In the Nind study, she takes great care in laying out the details of the school that is the target of her action research study. She starts by describing the locale of the school:

> Honilands School is a large, vibrant primary school in the London Borough of Enfield. The Enfield statistical directory describes the population in the school's ward as being high in the multiple deprivation rankings as well as child poverty indicators. There is high unemployment, poor health, poor housing and little access to higher or further education. A considerable portion of the school's children are on the special needs roster.

Having established the dynamics of the neighborhood, Nind then gives us a picture of the school itself:

> The Early Years Unit (EYU) of the school comprises a nursery and two reception classes with three teachers, two nursery nurses and two classroom assistants and 120 children (not all of them full-time). The environment is an open plan, with base-room areas, a small quiet room, and a well-used outdoor play area.

The final example of a synopsis opening is found in the real article by O'Boyle. In this case, a complex mix of history and social issues is being summarized, in order for us to be able to understand the role of history instruction in Ireland, and how that role has changed. This context is necessary in order to understand and interpret the findings of the study:

> When the Irish State was established in 1922, History was assigned a central role in the school curriculum as a means of promoting fervent nationalism and asserting Irish independence from British rule. Teachers experienced a socialisation process, orienting them towards a form of military and political history that emphasised a republican tradition of anti-Britishness, violence and revolution. The History curriculum gave primacy to content and the learning

of facts about the great events and the valiant rebels of Ireland's heroic past. However, the outbreak of 'trouble' in Northern Ireland in the 1970s brought about a reassessment of the role of History and how it was taught. The Republic's membership of the European Union also spawned a social and economic transformation that made the 'Old History' seem redundant and irrelevant in modern Ireland.

In most cases where researchers dive right in, the justifications for going immediately into the study are straightforward. Sometimes, however, researchers assume that their research and its goals are more straightforward than they actually are. Just because the researchers do not feel the need to make a case for their research does not mean that a case might not need to be made. Is the assumption that the inherent value of a study is self-evident a case of being in touch with the basic values of research, or an example of the theoretical or cultural naïveté of the researchers? Is it possible for a reasonable researcher operating in good faith to take an alternative or even opposing position regarding the inherent importance of the study under discussion? You need to be aware of these sorts of issues as you read articles that begin by diving right into the research.

The opening direction of a research article can also be a map for accessing information in an efficient and straightforward way.

An opening point can do more than just lay out the reasons and rationale for a piece of research. It can also lead us to anticipate certain directions that the research might follow in addressing those reasons. For example, if an article begins by discussing a crisis, then you will most likely find research-based practical knowledge sometime before the article is done. Articles that start off by claiming their topics are important also tend to produce practical knowledge as well, but they are often oriented toward theoretical issues as well. Personal beliefs and insights are usually highlighted in articles that start off with commitment statements. Depth openings often lead you in exploratory or investigatory directions. When articles start by diving right into synopses, they often end up dealing with issues that are familiar to, or of interest to, a wide spectrum of educators. Finally, articles that point toward closing lacunae will most often focus on producing theoretical knowledge.

More Often Than Not, Articles Will Proceed to Make More Than One Point

Crisis point articles might also develop lacuna points later on, or commitment point articles might also emphasize crisis points. Usually, however, researchers will lead with the perspective that they feel is most relevant to their research efforts, so it is within those perspectives that you tend to find the most important information being generated.

The most common exception to this last point is often found in synopsis point articles. More often than not, a synopsis point article will make another point fairly soon. That is, they often lead right into importance or lacuna or depth issues. The nature of that other point will depend on the content of the article and the purposes of the researchers. More often than not, that follow-up point will not be a crisis point, however. This is because crisis points are best and most effectively made right at the outset.

Our Emerging Literacy Orientation

Educational research writing is like other forms of writing in many respects. Here is one of them—a good research article must grab your attention right away. In addition, a good research article will let you know what it is all about as soon as it can.

Good titles and good opening paragraphs and statements address both of these goals. A good title will capture your interest, or at least let you know if the article is aimed at a reader like you or not. Furthermore, a good title will tell you quite a bit about its article. It will not only reveal content—more often than not, it will tell you something about the manner in which the research was conducted. The opening points are even more directed toward your potential desire to read the article. In the very beginning, researchers often make their case for why you should read their research in the first point. All researchers feel their research is important. The best researchers make their work as clear as they can, while convincing you that this research ought to be important to you, as well.

Practice Makes Perfect

It is now time to practice some of the insights and skills you have explored in this chapter. First of all, you need to turn to the literature. It should be easy to find journals with primary articles that are interesting to you. Gather together about three to four articles that you can understand to some degree, based on your knowledge of the field. Now do the following:

- Identify the title type for each article. Do not worry about covering all types. Just see if you can handle the act of labeling real titles.
- Each of these articles also has an opening. Can you identify their openings? Again, do not worry about covering all types of openings.
- If possible, share your results with your classmates. What sorts of titles and openings did you find? Were some types of titles and openings more common than others? Did these various types seem to depend on the content and form of the articles, or the topics covered?

The Abstract

Once you have used the title and the opening sentences to get your bearings, then you are ready to tackle the article as a whole. Sometimes, however, an article may appear (at first) to be right up your alley, only to end up being something totally different from what you had expected after you have started reading it. This can be both a frustrating and a time-wasting experience. Fortunately, there is a way to sample the article in a quick fashion, so that you can decide whether or not to read the whole piece. There is a tiny version of the article, right at the beginning, which you can read and then decide whether to read on. This little "article in miniature" is called the *abstract*.

The Abstract Is the Front Door to a Research Article

The abstract is the front door to a research article. Researchers use abstracts to show readers what they can expect from the article as a whole. Abstracts typically use one paragraph to present a brief synopsis of the nature and contents of the article. Abstracts also invite readers to take a quick look, to see if they want or need to investigate the article further.

There Are Specific Guidelines for Creating an Abstract

Abstracts for research articles are written using specific guidelines. Curtis (2001) points out that, first and foremost, an abstract is short. It summarizes the major points of the article and most of the time it does not include bibliographic citations. December and Katz (2003) suggest that writing an abstract involves "boiling down the essence of a whole paper into a single paragraph that conveys as much new information as possible." Kies (2003) describes six pieces of information that every well-constructed abstract addresses. These include the purpose of the article, its scope, the methods used, the results of the study, critical recommendations, and conclusions.

The definitive format guide for most research articles in education is the *American Psychological Association Publication Manual*. The manual defines an abstract as follows:

An abstract:

- must be an *accurate* reflection of the contents of the article. All information, findings, and conclusion must be represented properly. Nothing can be in the abstract that is not also in the paper itself.
- must be *self-contained*. That is, the reader should not be required to turn to the article to identify terms or concepts. Abbreviations should be avoided, citations must be complete, tests must be specified, and unique terms must also be defined. In short, the abstract must be able to stand by itself as a summary of the research article.
- must be *concise*. In general, it should not exceed 120 words. It should also start with the most important points or information, and move from there into more detail or clarification.
- must be *non-evaluative*. The job of the abstract is to report, and not to make judgements. Do not include comments about the data or topic that are not present in the main article.

- must be *coherent*. One of the best ways to be coherent is to be readable. Simple writing tips apply here: using simple sentences, using the active voice, and so on. Procedures should be described in the past tense, while results are described in the present tense (pp. 14–15).

There Are a Number of Different Types of Abstracts

There are a number of different types of research articles in educational research. Therefore, it makes sense that there are a number of different types of abstracts.

The APA Manual describes four different types of abstracts, and specifies differing content for each of them (see pp. 14–15 for more details):

- For the standard *empirical* article, the abstract should define the research problem, participants, methods, findings, and conclusions.
- For a *review* or *theoretical* article, the abstract should define the topic, the purpose or thesis, sources used, and conclusions.
- For a *methodological* article, the abstract should define the general class of methods, essential characteristics of the proposed method, range of application, and operating characteristics of the method in practice.
- For a *case study* article, the abstract should define the subject and that subject's relevant characteristics, the nature of the issue illustrated by the case study, and questions raised for further work.

The APA Manual concludes its discussion of abstracts by stating that: "An abstract that is accurate, succinct, quickly comprehensible, and informative will increase the audience and the future retrievability of your article" (p. 15).

Abstracts Foreground Important Content

Regardless of the type of abstract, each and every abstract has one basic job to do. Since it is not long enough to address every aspect of an article, an abstract functions as a foregrounding tool. A foregrounding tool brings some elements forward and pushes other elements back. By bringing some elements forward, it highlights those elements so that readers will be sure to pay attention to them.

Since abstracts are limited to a few words, they can only foreground a few things. And to save even more words, they often talk about those foregrounded elements in highly stylized language. When researchers use such stylized language, in a very real sense they are writing in code. Since coded language is often more concise than regular ordinary prose, researchers can then save precious words that they can use to foreground an aspect of the article.

Abstracts Can Be Coded and Decoded

Abstracts seem straightforward enough but, as is often the case, looks can be deceiving. While abstracts are short, they are usually information dense. This information richness and density can make abstracts quite difficult to read and understand.

Since abstracts are so formal and dense in nature, it makes sense to look for coding patterns within abstracts. The basic coding pattern is actually quite simple. Think of an abstract as a device with seven switches. Each of those switches can be set to either the "on" position or the "off" position. If the switch is on, then the content area is present in the abstract. If the switch is off, then the content area is not explicitly mentioned in the abstract. The content areas and the usual order of those seven switches are as follows:

PURPOSE—PROBLEM—PARTICIPANTS—DESIGN—
ANALYSIS—RESULTS—CONCLUSIONS

This code, of course, is nothing more than a miniature model of the article itself. The full article usually has all of these seven content areas. But some of these content areas may be more important than other content areas within a given article. It is the job of the abstract to cue readers on which aspects of the article are most important. If a particular content area is present, then its switch is on and that aspect of the article is reported in the abstract. If that content area is missing from a given abstract, then the switch will be said to be off and that aspect is not reported in the abstract.

The other aspect to the code, in addition to which content areas are covered, is the order of presentation. The order outlined above is, more or less, the standard pattern of presentation in most educational research articles. But there is no requirement that an abstract conform to this order. Instead, abstracts tend to order those aspects that the researchers feel are most important for readers to know in order to do a quick analysis of the potential usefulness of the article. Sometimes, this involves pointing out the most important findings right away. Other times, it makes sense to direct readers to the uniqueness of the sample or participants. Each study has its own unique pattern of important elements. While the article itself might unfold in a typically standard fashion, sometimes the abstract will foreground those unique elements in a much less standard order.

The best way to understand how abstracts can be coded and decoded is to dive right into the process of reading and coding them. Consider the following abstract from the training article by Picasso:

This study looked at gender and early career characteristics of valedictorians from high schools with differing sociocultural dimensions. Archival data from 30 schools from suburban areas and 30 schools from inner city areas were examined. Overall gender differences across high school groups were not significant. Immediate career plans were also examined, with suburban valedictorians more likely to go to college and inner city valedictorians more likely to go to vocational school. There were no differences between employment data. A combined analysis of these data suggested that suburban males were more likely to go to college over inner city males, and that inner city females were more likely to go to vocational schools than suburban females.

First of all, the abstract is 115 words long. This places it within the 120-word limit recommended by the APA Manual. As you will see, this limit is not hard and fast, but researchers often try to at least stay close to this limit. Furthermore, some journals are very strict about adhering to a word length limit for abstracts, while others are more lax. Therefore, the 120-word limit should be considered as a basic rule of thumb.

Next, you should determine which of the switches are "on" and in what order. Here is one way to lay out that array for this abstract:

PURPOSE—PARTICIPANTS—DESIGN—
ANALYSIS—RESULTS

In this abstract, the order of the content areas followed the standard pattern quite closely. Its only key deviation was that it eliminated the PROBLEM and the CONCLUSIONS components. The following is a more detailed look at each content area as it was present in the abstract itself:

> [PURPOSE] This study looked at gender and early career characteristics of [PARTICIPANTS] valedictorians from [DESIGN] high schools with differing sociocultural dimensions. [ANALYSIS] Archival data from 30 schools from suburban areas and 30 schools from inner city areas were examined. [RESULTS] Overall gender differences across high school groups were not significant. Immediate career plans were also examined, with suburban valedictorians more likely to go to college and inner city valedictorians more likely to go to vocational school. There were no differences between employment data. A combined analysis of these data suggested that suburban males were more likely to go to college over inner city males, and that inner city females were more likely to go to vocational schools than suburban females.

When the abstract is coded, then the reader can see that most of the abstract (80 of 116 words) focused on reporting the results of the study. This is not an uncommon balance for abstracts to take. Very often, it is the findings themselves that are of most interest.

The second example is drawn from the Chagall article. This article is more complex than the Picasso article, and this fact is reflected in the abstract:

> Male juvenile offenders are 40% less likely to enter the adult correctional system if they receive proper intervention (Santayana, 2002). This study began the process of developing an empirically based model of critical factors related to proper assessment and intervention. Key variables selected to measure for this study included peer support, missed homework, victim awareness, part time employment, and positive drug testing, and success in school. Factor analysis identified two factors among these variables: one factor dealing with "adopting a responsible role", and a second factor dealing with "social awareness." Implications of these findings for developing a model to support assessment and intervention of male youthful offenders were discussed.

This abstract is 109 words long, which is almost exactly the same length as the first abstract. Unlike the first abstract, however, this abstract violates the rule of thumb of not including bibliographic references, but it does so for a good reason that will be addressed below. The coding structure of this abstract, also, is a bit unusual:

PARTICIPANTS—RESULTS—PURPOSE—DESIGN—
ANALYSIS—RESULTS—CONCLUSIONS

This abstract begins by identifying the general class of participants—youthful offenders. Then, it violates the bibliographic rule in order to present the crucial result from previous research that offenders are 40% less likely to enter the adult correctional system if they receive proper intervention. Such an important claim requires immediate support, and so Chagall cites her source even in the abstract. It is important to note that these are results, even though they are results of research that is not part of this study. Next, the purpose of the research is clearly stated, followed by the design and analysis strategy of the study. Results and conclusions dealing with the implications of the study then follow.

Here is the coded version of the abstract:

[PARTICIPANTS] Male juvenile offenders [RESULTS] are 40% less likely to enter the adult correctional system if they receive proper intervention (Santayana, 2002). [PURPOSE] This study began the process of developing an empirically based model of critical factors related to proper assessment and intervention. [DESIGN] Key variables selected to measure for this study included peer support, missed homework, victim awareness, part time employment, and positive drug testing, and success in school. [ANALYSIS] Factor analysis [RESULTS] identified two factors among these variables: one factor dealing with "adopting a responsible role", and a second factor dealing with "social awareness." [CONCLUSIONS] Implications of these findings for developing a model to support assessment and intervention of male youthful offenders were discussed.

The third example is from one of the qualitative training articles. This article is by Bradbury:

This article investigates the use of web journals (called "blogs") to investigate possible causes for a series of seemingly unpredictable and incomprehensible attacks by three young males in different sections of Iowa. Contents of blogs kept by all three 15-year-olds were combined and analyzed using a computer tool. A common theme of "bigness" and "littleness" regarding physical stature seems to be at the heart of each attack, although manifested in different ways by each of the young shooters.

First of all, this abstract is 78 words long. Because it is so short, there is a sense of compression to it. It also conforms nearly perfectly to the basic coding design:

PURPOSE—PROBLEM—PARTICIPANTS—
DESIGN—ANALYSIS—RESULTS

The only aspect of the coding structure missing is the CONCLUSIONS section. Here is the coded version of the abstract:

[PURPOSE] This article investigates the use of web journals (called "blogs") to investigate possible causes for [PROBLEM] a series of seemingly unpredictable and incomprehensible attacks by [PARTICIPANTS] three young males in different sections of Iowa. [DESIGN] Contents of blogs kept by all three 15-year-olds were combined and [ANALYSIS] analyzed using a computer tool.

[RESULTS] A common theme of "bigness" and "littleness" regarding physical stature seems to be at the heart of each attack, although manifested in different ways by each of the young shooters.

As is often the case with qualitative articles, there is no testing per se going on, and so results are presented as being more plausible than probable. This is reflected in the language of this abstract, where the RESULTS of bigness and littleness "seem" to play a central role. Often, you will see authors of quantitative research being equally cautious in their language when they cannot pin down results more precisely.

The final training article example also comes from one of the qualitative articles. This article by Davidson is an action research article:

> This action research study was conducted with eight sets of parent-led groups of first and second grade children from a diverse sociocultural setting. This particular setting was in socioeconomic decline, and the three key groups that comprised the setting all distrusted each other. It was decided by the community that the best long term remedy for this distrust was character education taught by parents and monitored by the whole community. After a six-month program of character education for diverse cultural groups based on the work and curriculum of Shaftoe (2001), children were interacting much more with each other on an informal basis. Follow up data will be collected to see if these results persist over time.

This abstract is 116 words long, so it is essentially the same length as the Picasso abstract. The structure, however, is much different. Its coding pattern is as follows:

DESIGN— PARTICIPANTS—PROBLEM—
PURPOSE—RESULTS—CONCLUSIONS

In this study, it was important to state at the outset that it was an action research study. Action research studies follow different rules and have different goals than more standard types of research. It is not surprising, for example, that the ANALYSIS component was not foregrounded in this abstract, since analysis in action research is often ongoing and interactive, and is often confounded with the RESULTS. Again, there was no actual discussion of CONCLUSIONS per se in the abstract, but the call for future research does in fact point in that direction. Again, here is the coding pattern on the abstract itself:

> [DESIGN] This action research study was conducted with [PARTICIPANTS] eight sets of parent-led groups of first and second grade children from a diverse sociocultural setting. [PROBLEM] This particular setting was in socioeconomic decline, and the three key groups that comprised the setting all distrusted each other. [PURPOSE] It was decided by the community that the best long term remedy for this distrust was character education taught by parents and monitored by the whole community. [RESULTS] After a six-month program of character education for diverse cultural groups based on the work and curriculum of Shaftoe (2001), children were interacting much more with each other on an informal basis. [CONCLUSIONS] Follow up data will be collected to see if these results persist over time.

The most interesting aspect of this abstract is the fact that its PURPOSE comes after its PROBLEM, and not before, as is usually the case. This is not uncommon in action research, however. Very often, the PARTICIPANTS must work together to see what their common understanding of the problem is, and it is from that common understanding that the purpose evolves.

The next four examples come from the real articles. The first abstract is from the Devine-Wright et al. article:

> This paper explores children's beliefs about global warming and energy sources from a psychological perspective, focusing on situational influences upon subjective beliefs, including perceived self-efficacy. The context of the research is one of growing concern at the potential impacts of global warming, yet demonstrably low levels of self-efficacy amongst both adults and children to effectively respond to this large-scale environmental problem. Empirical research was conducted on a sample of 198 UK children and adults to explore the influence of a cooperative learning environment upon children's beliefs about global warming and energy. A comparative design was adopted, contrasting 9-12 year old members of the Woodcraft Folk educational organisation with non-members of similar age and with adult members of the same organisation. Results indicate that cooperative learning environments can have a significant and positive effect upon children's beliefs about large-scale environmental problems. In particular, Woodcraft Folk children reported significantly higher levels of personal awareness and perceived self-efficacy in relation to global warming in comparison to their peers. Secondly, unexpected differences were identified between levels of perceived self-efficacy in children and adult Woodcraft Folk. The implications of these differences for the design of educational programmes seeking to empower children to respond to global warming are discussed.

First of all, we see that this is a very long abstract. At 203 words, it is well beyond the limit recommended by the APA Manual. At the same time, it is very easy to decode. Its coding pattern is:

PURPOSE—PROBLEM—PARTICIPANTS—
DESIGN—RESULTS—CONCLUSIONS

Applying the coding pattern to the abstract, we get the following:

> [PURPOSE] This paper explores children's beliefs about global warming and energy sources from a psychological perspective, focusing on situational influences upon subjective beliefs, including perceived self-efficacy. [PROBLEM] The context of the research is one of growing concern at the potential impacts of global warming, yet demonstrably low levels of self-efficacy amongst both adults and children to effectively respond to this large-scale environmental problem. [PARTICIPANTS] Empirical research was conducted on a sample of 198 UK children and adults to explore the influence of a cooperative learning environment upon children's beliefs about global warming and energy. [DESIGN] A comparative design was adopted, contrasting 9-12 year old members of the Woodcraft Folk educational organisation with non-members of similar age and

with adult members of the same organisation. [RESULTS] Results indicate that cooperative learning environments can have a significant and positive effect upon children's beliefs about large-scale environmental problems. In particular, Woodcraft folk children reported significantly higher levels of personal awareness and perceived self-efficacy in relation to global warming in comparison to their peers. Secondly, unexpected differences were identified between levels of perceived self-efficacy in children and adult Woodcraft folk. [CONCLUSIONS] The implications of these differences for the design of educational programmes seeking to empower children to respond to global warming are discussed.

The second real article example is from the Klein study. His abstract is as follows:

On the basis of reports of the limitations of staff meetings in various professions, the contribution of such gatherings to pedagogic activities and faculty cooperation was investigated. Organizational characteristics that differentiate between effective and ineffective conferences were also examined. Two hundred and ninety-four teachers from 64 public schools provided information on meetings in which they had participated and noted the factors that contributed to their success. The findings verify the limited contribution of general meetings, and point to the advisability of consultations of smaller groups of specialized staff. The results indicate a need to imbue school principals and others who conduct teachers' meetings with skills in communication and constructive collaboration. The implications of the findings on management of staff meetings via Internet are discussed.

This abstract is 124 words, which is more in line with recommended lengths. It can be broken down as follows:

PROBLEM—PURPOSE—DESIGN—PARTICIPANTS—
DESIGN—RESULTS—CONCLUSIONS

Applying the coding pattern to the abstract, we get the following:

[PROBLEM] On the basis of reports of the limitations of staff meetings in various professions, [PURPOSE] the contribution of such gatherings to pedagogic activities and faculty cooperation was investigated. [DESIGN] Organizational characteristics that differentiate between effective and ineffective conferences were also examined. [PARTICIPANTS] Two hundred and ninety-four teachers from 64 public schools [DESIGN] provided information on meetings in which they had participated and noted the factors that contributed to their success. [RESULTS] The findings verify the limited contribution of general meetings, and point to the advisability of consultations of smaller groups of specialized staff. [CONCLUSIONS] The results indicate a need to imbue school principals and others who conduct teachers' meetings with skills in communication and constructive collaboration. The implications of the findings on management of staff meetings via Internet are discussed.

The third example is from one of the real qualitative articles—the Wyss study. Her abstract is as follows:

This paper explores the experiences of harassment and violence endured by seven gender non-conforming youth in US high schools. Based on a larger research project, it opens an inquiry into the school-based lives of gender-variant teens, a group heretofore ignored by most academics and educators. Breaking violence down into two main types (physical and sexual), this work uses informants' voices, along with 'doing gender' theory, to analyze the experience of butch lesbian girls, trans teenagers, and genderqueer youth. The author also examines the impact of this violence on their self-esteem, academic achievement, substance abuse and sexual lives. This paper points out the similarities and differences between gender identity groups and suggests specific areas for school-based and cultural reform that would protect such teens.

At 122 words, this abstract also conforms to normal length criteria. Also, while its topic is innovative, the actual structure of the abstract is quite traditional:

PURPOSE—PARTICIPANTS—DESIGN—
ANALYSIS—RESULTS—CONCLUSIONS

Applying the coding pattern to the abstract, we get:

[PURPOSE] This paper explores the experiences of harassment and violence endured by [PARTICIPANTS] seven gender non-conforming youth in US high schools. [DESIGN] Based on a larger research project, it opens an inquiry into the school-based lives of gender-variant teens, a group heretofore ignored by most academics and educators. [ANALYSIS] Breaking violence down into two main types (physical and sexual), this work uses informants' voices, along with 'doing gender' theory, to analyze the experience of butch lesbian girls, trans teenagers, and genderqueer youth. [RESULTS] The author also examines the impact of this violence on their self-esteem, academic achievement, substance abuse and sexual lives. [CONCLUSIONS] This paper points out the similarities and differences between gender identity groups and suggests specific areas for school-based and cultural reform that would protect such teens.

Our final abstract to decode comes from the Nind study. It reads as follows:

This article reports on an action research project in which an external consultant, special education needs coordinator and staff of the early years unit of a mainstream school worked together to understand and enhance the communication learning environment provided for 3-5 year-old pupils. A transactional rather than deficit model was adopted, such that bi-directional influences in communication difficulties and communication learning were fully recognised. The focus for deliberation and action was the role, style, talk and interaction behaviour of the adults. Concepts of optimal interactive styles from studies of caregiver-infant interaction were applied. Activity included a mixture of observation, discussion and reflection on current and changing practice and related research. Developments evolved that were judged to have enhanced the communication learning environment, including increased use of small group time and greater use of child-led 'show and tell' and sharing time. The article is written from the perspective of the external consultant and includes discussion of the action research process.

This abstract, at 159 words, is another fairly long abstract. The actual form of the abstract is a bit complex and unusual:

PURPOSE—PARTICIPANTS—PROBLEM—PARTICIPANTS—
DESIGN—ANALYSIS—RESULTS—CONCLUSIONS

Applying the coding pattern to the abstract, we get:

[PURPOSE] This article reports on an action research project in which [PARTICIPANTS] an external consultant, special education needs coordinator and staff of the early years unit of a mainstream school [PROBLEM] worked together to understand and enhance the communication learning environment provided for [PARTICIPANTS] 3-5 year-old pupils. [DESIGN] A transactional rather than deficit model was adopted, such that bi-directional influences in communication difficulties and communication learning were fully recognised. [ANALYSIS] The focus for deliberation and action was the role, style, talk and interaction behaviour of the adults. Concepts of optimal interactive styles from studies of caregiver-infant interaction were applied. Activity included a mixture of observation, discussion and reflection on current and changing practice and related research. [RESULTS] Developments evolved that were judged to have enhanced the communication learning environment, including increased use of small group time and greater use of child-led 'show and tell' and sharing time. [CONCLUSIONS] The article is written from the perspective of the external consultant and includes discussion of the action research process.

In summary, abstracts can vary quite a bit. They can be simple or complex, very short or somewhat longer, linear or recursive. The actual form and shape of a given abstract depends upon the study, what the researchers wish to communicate and foreground, and the nature and policies of the journals. In the final analysis, however, each and every abstract must act as a short guide for an article.

Our Emerging Literacy Orientation

Conventional wisdom says that we should start the task of learning how to read and understand research articles by first looking at abstracts. We have gone against that conventional wisdom here for two reasons. First of all, we did not want to overlook the importance of titles and opening paragraphs. Secondly, abstracts are often dense and complicated pieces of text. If we start with abstracts, we run the risk of scaring away readers, or at the least making our readers think the process of reading articles is harder than it might really be.

Having begun to master the art of reading abstracts, we now understand how valuable they really are, and why we should take some time in reading them carefully. As we become skilled, we tend to adopt the following procedure for evaluating an article:

- We start by reading the title. As we know, the title can tell us quite a bit.
- Now we read the abstract. This gives us a short, information dense picture of the article as a whole. We now have a sense of the general aims and directions of the article.

- Finally, we read the first paragraph or so. Here, we are looking for the researchers to make their case for the importance of the research. If we cannot find a case after reading a few sentences or paragraphs, then we have reason to be concerned about the value and clarity of the article.

After we have looked at these three pieces, we should have a good idea about the article. Do we want to read it? Could it be important for our own work? If we decide the article is worth reading, then we need to learn how to address its meat—its main points and findings. As we move through the next five chapters, we will be looking at each major part of the article as we find it.

Practice Makes Perfect

It is now time to practice some of the insights and skills you have explored in this chapter:

- First of all, there are four training articles and four real articles whose abstracts have not been coded. Try your hand at coding these abstracts. Compare your results with those of your classmates.
- Take a look at the three to four articles you had gathered previously. Now that you have looked at their titles and openings, take some time and code their abstracts as well. Given that you understand their content areas, does this help you code their abstracts as well? Share your results with your classmates.
- Finally, try your hand at writing an abstract yourself. Try to use all of the coding categories as you create your abstract, and try to keep it under 125 words. You can make up any kind of study you like. When you are done, share your results with your classmates.

Introductions

At this point, you have explored those aspects of articles that serve to introduce basic ideas and prepare you to follow the main points. Following in the footsteps of many good literacy strategists, you have built up sets of expectations and anticipations. You now have a general feel for what an article might tackle and how it might tackle it. You also have a sense of why the researchers think this research was worth doing. Using the abstract, you have a concise little map of the key points that the researchers want you to take away from their work.

Now you are ready to wade into the article proper. Most articles consist of four basic sections: Introduction, Methods, Results, and Discussion. Sometimes those parts are clearly labeled. Sometimes, one or more parts are left unlabeled (if there is only one unlabeled part, it is almost always the Introduction). Sometimes, particularly in qualitative articles, they have different labels. Sometimes, because of the specific needs or aims of particular studies, they may contain additional sections. Usually, though, this four-part organization scheme is at the heart of most educational research articles.

This chapter will address literacy issues relevant to Introductions. These issues include the identification of research goals, stating and developing research questions, and the use of literature reviews to support and ground research questions.

Researchers Pursue One or More Goals When They Do Research

The key to the Introduction section of an article is the research question, and so we need to start by moving in the direction of the research question. The first step toward getting a picture of the research question is to understand the goals of the researchers. Understanding research goals is different from understanding opening points. When we were looking at opening points, we were looking at how researchers were trying to describe to their readers the importance of doing their research. Now, we are looking at the actual goals of the researchers themselves. What, in broad terms, are they trying to accomplish in their research studies? How are they first presenting and then approaching those goals?

The following is a list of various broad goals that researchers might have. This is not an exhaustive list by any means. Also, researchers may be pursuing more than one goal in any given study. This list functions as a sampling of the sorts of goals we might expect to find in various research studies:

- to explore an area that is not well understood
- to predict some result by manipulating and controlling important factors
- to explain some previously unexplained setting or situation
- to organize and interpret facts and information that currently have not been brought together
- to compare two or more important processes or factors to see how they might relate to each other in a given setting or situation
- to replace a current understanding or theory or model with a better one
- to understand change within a complex setting or situation
- to reflect upon the impact of research on self or others

These broad goals obviously influence the methods and analyses that researchers use, but they also influence the type and nature of questions and arguments that researchers use as well.

Sometimes researchers do not explicitly state their goals. Instead, the goals are reflected in the research questions that researchers ask, the arguments they use to support these questions, and the prior knowledge that researchers consider important for understanding their research. In our examples, though, the researchers have actually made goal statements.

Here are some examples of research goals from some of our articles.

To Explore Relationships That Are Not Well Understood

Sometimes, researchers are most interested in exploring. For example, in the Picasso article, we find a clear example of exploration. This goal is summarized in the first set of questions that Picasso raises:

> What are the students who win this competition like? What kind of person is the average high school valedictorian? We already know that valedictorians have the top grade averages in their graduating classes. Are there other characteristics that we might expect from them?

From these broad and general questions we can see the basic exploratory goal of the research. In a bit, we will consider the actual research questions that Picasso crafts from these more general goal-setting questions.

To Predict Results by Manipulating and Controlling Important Factors

Predicting how differences among clearly identified processes or factors will affect some outcome is often a goal of research. A clear example of this can be found in the Miro study:

> The purpose of this study is to provide a direct comparison among all three snack categories . . .

Miro moves immediately from this goal statement into a discussion of the research question, as we will see shortly.

To Explain Some Previously Unexplained Setting or Situation

In the Asimov study, we have a situation that appears to be like the Picasso study, in that something is identified as the target of exploration. Asimov's exploration is more pointed, however:

> How did Magda, and five other children, go from the hopelessness and dead end educational surroundings of her neighborhood to differential calculus? This study intends to explore that question in some depth.

Asimov wants to explore this area not only because it is poorly understood, but because it is also hard to explain. Many times, researchers are trying to explain how bad situations and results persist in the face of efforts to change them for the better. Here, we have a more positive problem—how do we explain good results in conditions where we would expect the opposite?

To Organize and Interpret Facts and Information That Currently Have Not Been Brought Together

Clarke is a good example of bringing together two areas to help us understand how they interact. In short, Clarke is studying slang and immigrant enculturation at the same time:

> "Mind the wookie, mate" or "Strabble me backwards." Any teacher in the East London school system expects to hear these sorts of expressions while walking down the halls of school. Most often, these kinds of slang terms and phrases come from working class children in and around the East End of London. However, these terms and phrases are being picked up with surprising speed and fluency by very recent Southeastern Asian immigrants. What sorts of terms and phrases do they pick up? Where do they learn them? How do they become fluent so quickly? Are they using them in the same ways that their more native East End counterparts are? As a consulting practical linguist for the London school system, I have made it my practice to gather and study these sorts of linguistic intrigues.

Clarke is using his linguistic skills and his ethnographic and qualitative skills to bring together two areas of study, so as to understand both areas a little better.

To Compare Two or More Important Processes or Factors to See How They Might Relate to Each Other in a Given Setting or Situation

Devine-Wright et al. start out with the assumption that education is a critical link in dealing with global warming but point out that conventional environmental education often ignores such situational factors as economic, political, cultural, and other issues. The goal of their research was to help remedy this lack of understanding within the environmental education community:

> The research sought to further understanding of situational influences upon children's beliefs about global warming and renewable energy.

To Replace a Current Understanding or Theory or Model With a Better One

Current educational strategies in chemistry in Greece, according to Danili and Reid, require students to wrestle with complex and abstract material. This approach seems to be based on the notion that the goal of chemistry education is to present the basic facts of chemistry to students without regard for the students' characteristics as learners. Danili and Reid offer a different approach, based on understanding the potential roles of memory store and field dependency in science learning in general, and chemistry education in particular:

> This study seeks to explore two psychological factors which may influence performance in chemistry and to develop teaching strategies which minimize the effects of these limiting factors in allowing pupils to become more successful.

To Understand Change Within a Complex Setting or Situation

O'Boyle developed a rich and complex case study of eight History teachers in an Irish school. The actual article is broken down into biographical, historical, and craft dimensions. The goal of the article is much broader however; it is to weave these various threads together to create a complex and situated picture of change:

> This article explores how the nature of history as a subject has shaped the subcultural identities of the eight teachers in the History Department of an Irish post-primary school. . . . It questions whether changing attitudes to the subject have altered the professional craft knowledge they apply in the classroom and concludes as these teachers grow older and the subject loses its significance within the curriculum, a crisis of identity becomes perceptible.

To Reflect Upon the Impact of Research on Self or Others

James et al. is in fact a study within a study. The presumed main goal of this complex article was to discover and explicate crucial issues of sociodramatic play in young children. At the same time, James sought to illustrate the complex dynamics of collaborative research:

> Having completed my study I reflected on the key moments in the research process and the main influences, which provide the framework for this article. Undoubtedly, the input of both Elise, my research assistant, and Eve, my academic mentor, was influential at these points and I therefore asked them to contribute their comments. . . . Elise's and Eve's perspectives help to give a fuller picture of the difficulties and surprises that may be associated with teacher research.

Research Questions Build Upon Research Goals in Specific Ways

Developing and answering a research question, however, is not just about addressing some set of goals. It is about looking for specific things in specific ways. Before we get to the art of finding these specific questions, however, it is useful to look at certain broad domains that often frame more specific research questions.

The first broad domain of research questions is nothing more than basic curiosity. Many research questions are modifications of one simple question: I wonder what is going on here?

Another broad research question domain can be identified as, Am I on the right track? Researchers might wish to test current models of understanding, to see where these models seem to be correct and where the models might be wrong. Even if the researchers might feel that their work is on the right track, they may wish to conduct research to help nail things down somewhat more precisely.

Finally, a research question can be paraphrased within the following broad domain: What am I missing? You might wish to see if you have overlooked something important that might change your understanding of some process or phenomenon.

What is going on? Am I on the right track? What am I missing? These broad domains give us a sense and flavor of actual research questions. These domains can help us anticipate the directions that researchers might pursue, and allow us to work within a bigger, less specific, and more global overall picture. In short, broad domains can be useful tools in helping us see the forest and not just the trees.

Some Research Questions Are Basic and Some Are Applied

Regardless of the question, most researchers are still driven to some degree by basic curiosity. This basic curiosity is one of the most useful tools for both individual researchers and for the field of research as a whole. For researchers, curiosity helps keep them fresh and intrigued. For the field of research, seemingly idle curiosity has been the route for most, if not all, critically practical discoveries. Usually, research that is primarily motivated by curiosity is called *basic research*.

Often, research studies focus on issues of effectiveness, accountability, exploration, and the like. There are many different reasons to turn to the world of experience to look for answers. Researchers might want to see if some practice is actually effective. They might want to see if further practical efforts might be useful. All of these efforts are motivated by questions: Is this working well? Are these things working the way they were expected to work? Is there a need to get involved further? All of the preceding reasons for looking to the world of experience are important and involve research in important ways. Very often, these efforts are called *applied research*.

Closely related to the idea of applied research is the process of *evaluation*, where research tools and principles are used to help determine if something is operating in optimum or expected ways. In other words, evaluators might want to see if someone or some organization has actually done what he or she or they have promised to do at the outset. In general, evaluation questions are much more focused and practical than research questions, even applied research questions.

Most of the studies used in this book are more basic than applied, but many of them have important practical goals or applications. In particular, action research often blurs the boundaries between basic and applied research.

Finding Research Questions Is an Important Research Literacy Skill

It is almost impossible to understand a research article without finding the research question. Fortunately, most researchers make it fairly easy to find research questions. To see this, let us jump right into the process and track down the research questions for some of our articles.

Research Question: Picasso Article

Here are the research questions for the training article by Picasso:

> First of all, are there any gender differences in the likelihood of being a vale-dictorian? That is, are males more likely to be valedictorians than females, or vice versa? Second, are there early career differences between valedictorians from wealthier suburban schools and poorer inner city schools? Are subur-ban valedictorians more likely to go to college or vocational schools over their inner city counterpoints, or vice versa?

This researcher is asking two broad questions, which she then clarifies in more spe-cific terms. Since her data are strictly archival data, Picasso can do nothing with these data except to gather them and compare them in a descriptive way. She is most interested in these comparisons, but they are all comparisons of naturally occurring incidents.

Research Question: Miro Article

Miro, in another training article, asks a simple question:

> Given that students seem to need a nutritional "boost" in the afternoon in order to perform well in math, what sort of nutritional boost is most beneficial?

Miro starts her question by making a claim—students need a nutritional boost in the afternoon in order to perform well in math. This claim is actually a summary of her argument. Arguments will be covered in a bit, but it is important to note that claims of fact, like these, must be supported by evidence. That is where a review of literature often comes into play. Here is a good illustration of how the question, the argument, and the literature review all work together.

Once Miro has made the claim that a nutritional boost is beneficial, the pri-mary research question is then presented—what sort of boost is most beneficial? This sort of question suggests that the researcher will be making controlled com-parisons in order to see which type of boost works best.

Unlike the study by Picasso, Miro will not depend on naturally occurring con-ditions. Controlled comparisons are usually much stronger than comparisons of naturally occurring things, since controls allow researchers to either eliminate or control possible contaminating factors whenever possible.

Research Question: Asimov Article

Qualitative studies also ask research questions, but they often are quite different in nature. Consider this apparently simple question by Asimov in his training article:

> How did Magda, and five other children, go from the hopelessness and dead end educational surroundings of her neighborhood to differential calculus? This study intends to explore that question in some depth.

Asimov's question is framed by diametrical opposites. Dead end hopeless educational settings do not foster children who are learning differential calculus. At least, that is the unexamined assumption that many readers would be prepared to make, going into this study. Asimov shows us that sometimes assumptions are off base, and that when they are, researchers need to explore and document these unexpected and surprising cases.

Whenever researchers can account for these sorts of unexpected findings, they are also expanding our base of understanding. Qualitative researchers often target these sorts of unexamined assumptions in order to move research into a more in-depth examination of things often taken for granted. These sort of unexamined assumptions are often best challenged in unusual circumstances, where the "rules" are sometimes less clear-cut.

Research Question: Clarke Article

Unusual circumstances also play a role in Clarke's question, from his training article:

> "Mind the wookie, mate" or "Strabble me backwards." Any teacher in the East London school system expects to hear these sorts of expressions while walking down the halls of school. Most often, these kinds of slang terms and phrases come from working class children in and around the East End of London. However, these terms and phrases are being picked up with surprising speed and fluency by very recent Southeastern Asian immigrants. What sorts of terms and phrases do they pick up? Where do they learn them? How do they become fluent so quickly? Are they using them in the same ways that their more native East End counterparts are?

In a way, these research questions resemble Picasso's questions. Both are looking at descriptive aspects of naturally occurring phenomena. In Clarke's case, however, there is a key difference. The circumstances are much more puzzling. There is no reason to suppose that Southeastern Asian immigrants would be picking up East End street slang, much less so quickly and thoroughly. Like many qualitative studies, this question almost seems like a riddle. How can Clarke sort out what is really going on here? This is a much different situation than that found in Picasso's study, where two settings are being compared along fairly well understood and clear dimensions.

Just like the training articles, the real articles also have clearly delineated research questions. We will look at the following four examples:

Research Question: Devine-Wright et al. Article

These researchers are concerned about the effectiveness of global warming education, as reflected in their research questions. These questions were posed in the form of two hypotheses:

> With an emphasis upon cooperation, empowerment and an opposition to individualistic and competitive values, the researchers hypothesized that children who had experienced cooperative learning as members of the Woodcraft Folk would be more self-efficacious and ready to act on global warming, in addition to indicating stronger levels of environmental concern and feelings of personal responsibility to do something about it, in comparison to a control sample of children the same age who had not been exposed to such a learning situation. . . . Secondly, it was hypothesized that adult Woodcraft Folk would report even higher levels of awareness, concern, responsibility and self-efficacy than the children . . . .

This is a good example of a general set of research questions that have been turned into testable statements. Essentially, the researchers are saying that Woodcraft Folk children are more likely to be willing to do something about global warming than their non Woodcraft Folk peers, and that their adult teachers are even more committed to working against global warming than the children are. By turning it into a comparative set of statements focused on specific measurable variables, the researchers are making an explicit link between their research questions and the methods they will use to answer them.

Research Question: Danili and Reed Article

Danili and Reed are concerned about the poor performance of secondary students in Greece when they study chemistry. It was their belief that two important psychological processes, namely working memory storage and field dependency, need to be minimized in order to allow all students to learn. To this end, they conducted two studies.

In the first study, they sought to compare the two psychological factors to test performance:

> The two cognitive factors outlined above were examined in relation to pupils' performance in chemistry tests. For that purpose, the following measurements were made:
>
> - The working memory capacity of the pupils;
> - The field dependency of the pupils; and
> - Pupils' performance on chemistry tests.

The second study's research question was built directly on the findings from the first study:

> The first stage demonstrated that pupil performance is related to their working memory space and extent of field dependency. The purpose of the second

stage was to develop an instructional approach to improve students' conceptual understanding of two difficult areas of the syllabus: atomic and bonding theory. The aim in designing this new instructional approach was to minimize learning situations where a high working memory was demanded, thus making the chemistry more accessible for all pupils, irrespective of their working memory space.

The use of sequential development of a series of research questions that build upon prior findings within the same article is not unusual. It is particularly common in prestigious empirical journals, which encourage researchers to report upon an entire program of research, and not just one or two related questions.

Research Question: O'Boyle Article

O'Boyle sought to examine critical issues in the teaching of History in an Irish school by taking a historical perspective. As such, the focus of this research turned toward an examination of biography and how this sort of narrative history relates to identity as teachers:

> Studying History teachers' biographies and locating their careers within a life-cycle framework conveys how the changing contexts of the workplace and the process of ageing shape the adoption of situated identities in the formal context of St. Colman's.

Research Question: James et al. Article

James et al. is a good example of a study that is grounded in specific field-based observations. James starts with her assumption about the demands that are placed upon young children in Early Years learning settings:

> When the study commenced I was concerned that, even in the early years, children were asked to do 'too much, too young'.

This opinion based on casual experience did not become a research question until it was combined with specific issues within a field setting:

> It was only when I began teaching in the nursery that I noticed the fragmented nature of children's sociodramatic play. This intrigued me because I was unsure how children were making meaning from the role-play scenarios. However, I believed these would provide rich opportunities for me to learn from children.

Researchers Use Arguments to Support Their Research Questions

It is not enough for an article to have a research question. The research question must also make sense. It must be relevant to the basic areas of interest of the researcher.

It must be defensible logically. All of these aspects, and others, require that when we find a research question, there must also be an argument present. Therefore, once we find the research question, it is important to find and understand the argument that supports it.

A good argument supports and enhances its research questions, pulls together what is already known, lays the foundation for the design and analysis of the study, and helps make the results clear and easy to interpret.

A flawed argument, on the other hand, undermines the entire study. If a research study is not put together in a clear and logical fashion, then we cannot be confident that the question is well supported, or the results follow from the design and analysis. We cannot be sure that the research question, as stated, is the best way to approach the topic or if the researchers' conclusions are warranted.

It is usually fairly easy to find a research question. Most researchers want us to find it, and so they point it out. Research arguments, on the other hand, are often less easy to find in their entirety and to evaluate. However, it is critically important to find and understand the research argument of a study.

The training articles were deliberately designed to have simple and concise arguments. Going through these articles carefully will help us develop our basic skills for finding and laying out a research argument.

We need a few tools to help us find arguments. For these simple training articles, we can use the following simple tools. Arguments are always related to research questions. Sometimes, the argument comes before the question to help *set up* the question. Other times, the argument comes after the question in order to *support* the question. In more complex cases, the research question is both set up and supported.

To see these principles in action, consider the following examples of research arguments.

Setup Arguments

In the first example, a very simple argument is used to set up the questions. The following is the beginning of the Picasso article:

> School communities hold valedictorians in high regard. Valedictorians are also more likely than the average student to get into a good college or university (Shakespeare, 1999), earn a high salary in their first job (Milton, 2002), and to assume leadership positions in their communities (Blake, 2000). For these and other reasons, it seems like being a valedictorian is a valuable accomplishment for a high school student.

Next, Picasso makes an important but obvious point:

> Being a valedictorian is often a ticket for a bright future.

At this point, there is an implied argument that everyone should have a fair chance to this sort of fair ticket to a bright future. Picasso does not make this argument explicitly because it is such an integral part of the belief system of this culture. She does let us know that she is looking at target areas for fair treatment—gender and sociocultural levels. The focus of that target is early career choices. Picasso does not state, but seems to assume, that college is the most likely road to success, followed by vocational school and then by working right out of high school. All these factors inform her research questions, which immediately follow:

> This study will examine existing archival data about valedictorians to address two questions. First of all, are there any gender differences in the likelihood of being a valedictorian? That is, are males more likely to be valedictorians than females, or vice versa? Second, are there early career differences between valedictorians from wealthier suburban schools and poorer inner city schools? Are suburban valedictorians more likely to go to college or vocational schools over their inner city counterpoints, or vice versa? Research is needed to fill this knowledge gap about valedictorians.

Although it does not say so directly, this research argument seems to be concerned with the fairness of existing conditions. Later on, when the data suggest that there are indeed some differences that might be related to fairness, Picasso makes her concerns known. Note that she waited until she actually had data, and analyzed it, before raising these concerns explicitly:

> If valedictorians from poor areas and impoverished schools are not getting an equal chance for continued education at the highest levels, then eventually all society must suffer from this case. Therefore, it is important to continue research along these lines, to make sure we are not wasting one of our most precious resources.

In summary, this is an example of using points to build toward stating the research question. By the time we read the actual question, we also have a sense that it is well supported conceptually.

Support Arguments

Sometimes, the argument is used primarily to support the question. In this situation, there is little or no setup involved. Asimov, in his training article, starts with the question and uses the argument to build support. First, the question is stated:

> How did Magda, and five other children, go from the hopelessness and dead end educational surroundings of her neighborhood to differential calculus? This study intends to explore that question in some depth.

After the question, Asimov starts developing his argument by looking at previous examples of after school programs to see if they can address his question:

> Over the years, researchers have looked at successful programs to try to see how they succeeded, as well as looking at where unsuccessful programs might have gone wrong. The results have been divergent. Blackwood's (2000) look at math whizzes in the South Bronx suggests that the first impressions of the children toward community educators are critical. On the other hand, Machen

(2001) seemed to find that his amateur astronomers from East Los Angeles required extensive trust-building sessions in order for the learning to take effect. Are these indicators of regional or cultural differences, or are there other critical dynamics at play?

Asimov has shown that the literature alone cannot answer his research question. Therefore he turns in a theoretical direction:

> I draw my main theoretical inspiration from the work of James (1999). In this landmark work, James asserted that the urban poor are kept poor by their lack of power. This power, according to James, is rooted in their inability to filter out the hustle and bustle of most poor urban neighborhoods and settings. She advocated the establishment of semi-permanent "enclaves" of peace and quiet within such urban settings as housing projects, where community educators and children can come together and pursue intellectual efforts in relative peace and tranquility.

As is often the case, arguments can lead toward a refinement or clarification of the question itself. In this case, Asimov uses enclave theory to adjust his research focus:

> Did such enclaves work in real life? How could they be founded? How could they be sustained?

Finally, Asimov puts the argument into perspective by addressing how his look at theory will be realized in his field efforts:

> I sought the answers to these and other questions not by trying to build such an enclave, but by seeing if one (or more) already existed. If I could find such an enclave that had arisen naturally, then it would be strong evidence that such enclaves were successful. Also, such an enclave would provide a naturalistic "road map" for creating and designing other enclaves.

By starting with the question, Asimov was able to move forward through a process of practical and theoretical support to arrive at a particular focus for the study. This sort of focusing activity is often important in qualitative studies, where there are no preexisting sets of hypotheses to test. The researcher builds support for a focus, and then hopes it will be a fruitful source of insight and new knowledge.

Setup and Support Arguments

The next example provides a simple version of a common argument approach, especially for quantitative articles. Miro uses a fairly standard model for her argument. It has both a setup and a support component to it, with the question sandwiched in between. The setup component is used to establish a context for the research question:

> Research has shown that afternoon high school math classes consistently lag behind morning classes in overall performance (e.g., Fudd, 1999; Bunny, 2002). Given that not all students can schedule math in the morning, it is important to try to identify some of the causes of these general disparities, and to help

remedy the effects. Otherwise, half of our students will suffer to some degree in their high school math preparation.

The question is now presented as following logically from the context:

Given that students seem to need a nutritional "boost" in the afternoon in order to perform well in math, what sort of nutritional boost is most beneficial?

Finally, the question is supported by an explicit statement of the purpose of the research:

The purpose of this study is to provide a direct comparison among all three snack categories, to see which type of snack has the most beneficial impact on student performance in an afternoon math class.

In this type of argument, the researchers have used their argument first to set up the question and then to support it. This is a common design in cases where the research is part of an ongoing process of exploration of a topic. The reader is first grounded in the existing work and thought on the topic, and then as the question emerges it is supported by past work as well.

Grounding the Argument in Experience

There are times when the argument is not that clearly stated in the article. This often happens in the case of qualitative articles that are based on field experiences.

Clarke's study is typical of much field-oriented research. Much like the Asimov study, Clarke begins with an anomaly. It is this anomaly itself that argues for the need of the study. As Clarke points out:

"Mind the wookie, mate" or "Strabble me backwards." Any teacher in the East London school system expects to hear these sorts of expressions while walking down the halls of school. Most often, these kinds of slang terms and phrases come from working class children in and around the East End of London. However, these terms and phrases are being picked up with surprising speed and fluency by very recent Southeastern Asian immigrants.

This simple but puzzling state of affairs is all the support that Clarke feels his research questions need. Therefore, he simply follows by stating his questions of interest:

What sorts of terms and phrases do they pick up? Where do they learn them? How do they become fluent so quickly? Are they using them in the same ways that their more native East End counterparts are?

This example seems particularly terse, even for one of the training articles. But that is one of the goals of the training articles. While these training articles have artificially short and concise arguments, they do mirror many of the strategies and concerns used in the development of actual research arguments.

Literature Reviews Are Used to Tell Us What Is Already Known

Up to now, we have seen references to the literature in some of the research arguments. This is one of the most common uses of the research literature. The other primary use of the research literature is to build a picture of prior knowledge that informs both the research and the reader.

More often than not, researchers will address a great number of topics when they cover areas of prior knowledge. A good and simple guideline is to find the three most important topics of prior knowledge in a given research article. These three topics, taken together, can give you a quick picture of the key areas being addressed in that study.

Here are those key topic areas for four of the training articles covered in this chapter.

The Picasso Article

The three most important areas of prior knowledge for this study dealt with characteristics of valedictorians:

1) Gender differences have been the topic of some research. Voltaire (1998) documented that most valedictorians in his sample have taken Advanced Placement courses, regardless of whether they were male or female. This is not surprising, since many selective colleges expect to see Advanced Placement courses on the transcripts of applicants. Rousseau (2003) has argued that selective colleges also expect extracurricular activities from their applicants, and so she expected valedictorians to be well represented in school and club leadership positions. She also found no gender differences in terms of extracurricular activities. There were no studies that examined whether or not there were gender differences in the total number of valedictorians, however.

2) There are very little data on sociocultural differences among valedictorians. Preliminary data from the National Consortium of Secondary School Varsity Leadership Initiatives (2002) seems to indicate that valedictorians who play varsity sports do not differ in terms of academic courses taken across suburban and inner city schools. No data on career plans or aspirations were gathered, however.

The third source addressed the reasons for not looking at a characteristic that might be reasonably included in this study:

3) One other potential area of comparison is race. Rockwell (2001), for instance, pointed out that minority students who do well in school often have different career plans and goals from their white counterparts. Race was not included in this study for two reasons. First of all, the topic has been explored in some depth recently. Secondly, the racial differences between the suburban schools and the inner city schools are already substantial, and these pre-existing

differences might affect any valedictorian data. In contrast, gender should be nearly equal across schools, and career plans are more subject to variation and change than, say, a demographic factor like race.

The Miro Article

Prior knowledge in this study first showed that there is a performance gap, and then that this gap might be metabolic. Finally, types of snacks were also shown to be at least somewhat effective:

> 1) Research has shown that afternoon high school math classes consistently lag behind morning classes in overall performance (e.g., Fudd, 1999; Bunny, 2002).

> 2) Coyote, in his work on this topic (Coyote 1998, 2001; Coyote & Sam, 1999, 2003) has explored the possibility that the increased metabolic rate of high schoolers creates a "nutrition gap" for them during afternoon hours. Coyote & Sam, in their latest findings (2003), have shown that this gap does appear to exist and does seem to affect performance as predicted.

> 3) Bird (2000) has argued that fruit sugars provide the quickest boost and therefore should be used. Sylvester (2002), drawing upon decades of athletic nutritional research, suggests that a high carbohydrate snack is most beneficial. Both of these studies appear to clash somewhat with the Coyote & Sam (2003) study, which used high protein snacks exclusively and came up with dramatic effects.

The Asimov Article

This is the first qualitative study in this particular list. First of all, Asimov looks at supplemental educational programs that have been tried in the past. He then looks at literature that tries to explain these sorts of programs and why they either succeed or fail. Finally, Asimov documents a particular theoretical concept that has been previously shown to be important in situations like the one he is studying:

> 1) Studies of supplemental educational activities with bright, disadvantaged children have been conducted for decades (cf. Lovecraft, 2003, for a recent review of some of this literature). Poe (1975) is considered the landmark study. Working in his native Baltimore, Poe sought to bring poor and culturally isolated children to the state aviary on a regular basis, where they were able to join in efforts to track and identify rare birds throughout the region. The results were dramatic; the majority of these children were able to continue their education through the college level, and several of them earned doctorates.

> 2) Over the years, researchers have looked at successful programs to try to see how they succeeded, as well as looking at where unsuccessful programs might have gone wrong. The results have been divergent. Blackwood's (2000) look at math whizzes in the South Bronx suggests that the first impressions

of the children toward community educators are critical. On the other hand, Machen (2001) seemed to find that his amateur astronomers from East Los Angeles required extensive trust-building sessions in order for the learning to take effect.

3) I draw my main theoretical inspiration from the work of James (1999). In this landmark work, James asserted that the urban poor are kept poor by their lack of power. This power, according to James, is rooted in their inability to filter out the hustle and bustle of most poor urban neighborhoods and settings. She advocated the establishment of semi-permanent "enclaves" of peace and quiet within such urban settings as housing projects, where community educators and children can come together and pursue intellectual efforts in relative peace and tranquility.

The Clarke Article

Clarke is interested in establishing proper groundwork for identifying and understanding the uses of slang that he found. He starts by looking at a working categorization system for slang. He then establishes that slang is important for socializing immigrants, but that this socialization process often occurs on their own terms and with clear areas of importance for immigrant populations:

1) According to Oakley (2002), there are four main classes of slang terms and phrases in the East London region.

2) Earp (1999) contends that slang is an important socialization tool for new immigrants. This is especially true when these immigrants differ racially and ethnically from the prevailing residents.

3) Bonney (2002) has noted that immigrant groups in general try to fit in when moving into a new culture, but they tend to do so on their own terms whenever possible. Hickock (2003) has suggested that personal protection from stigmatization is the key area where immigrant populations modify their existing cultural approaches.

For each of the studies listed above, there were obviously more than three topics of prior knowledge, and in fact there were more than three very important topics of prior knowledge. The task of finding the three most important topics is artificial and even misleading, but it should help you evaluate and rate various pieces of prior knowledge, and to not fall into the trap of treating them equally. Finding critical sources of prior knowledge is an important part of research literacy, and this exercise was designed to help move you along in that direction.

Reference Sections Can Also Be Mapped

The reference sections of the training articles were deliberately created to be very simple and short. Therefore, it was easier to get a grasp on the nature of their literature reviews by targeting three important content areas from the text of the article itself.

Real articles, on the other hand, most often cite a large number of references. While we can still find three important topics in the text, it is often equally useful to "map" those reference sections. When we map a reference section, we are organizing the information in two ways, to help us understand what resources were brought to bear to build the review of the literature for the article.

The first level of organization is by author, or team of authors. When we identify authors whose work is cited more than once, it is likely that the work of these authors had an important impact on the thinking of the researchers doing this particular piece of work. In fact, the more articles cited, the more impact we can expect. This is an important piece of information, and can provide us with a way of approaching and understanding the content of the article.

The second level of organization is by broad content area. Here, we need to be careful not to cast too fine a net; if we do, we find that we end up with an unwieldy number of content areas to juggle. Instead, we should strive to identify no more than five or six major content areas. We do not have to fit every article into one of the content areas, and each article need not fit perfectly into one of the areas. In addition, we might find articles that overlap two or more categories. We need not be concerned about building too precise a system of mapping. The goal of the mapping is to create content areas and bodies of work by authors that can serve as organizers for helping us read and understand the review of the literature in the articles themselves.

The best way to understand these mapping systems is by doing one. For this purpose, we have selected the following real quantitative article:

The Danili and Reid Article

Danili and Reid cite 53 articles in their reference section. First of all, we will look at the multiple citations by author or team of authors:

1. *The Johnstone team.* The work of A. H. Johnstone is cited extensively. First of all there are seven sources where Johnstone is either the only author, or the first author. These articles and books range from 1966 to 2001. There is also another article where Johnstone is second author, published in 1991. Johnstone is writing about science education in general, and chemistry education in particular. Therefore, it makes sense to assume that he is probably the major source cited in this research on the topic of chemistry education in general.

2. *The Goodenough team.* Goodenough and his coworkers supply four references related to issues in field dependency. This leads us to suspect that these researchers are important experts on this topic.

3. *The Tsaparlis team.* Tsaparlis contributes three references on issues of teaching chemistry in Greek schools.

4. *The Niaz team.* Two references from Niaz, one from 1988 and another from 1989, offer research support on problem solving and memory demand in chemistry learning.

5. *The Reid team.* It is not surprising to find two references to the work of Reid on problem solving and chemistry, since Reid is one of the authors of this article, and at least some of his earlier work ought to be related in some way to this effort.

The remaining 34 articles are all by single researchers or researcher teams. Their contents will be covered in the following topics analysis:

1. *Cognitive processes.* Eighteen references are on various topics related to cognitive processes from memory to problem solving.
2. *Chemistry education.* Twelve references are either on the explicit topic of teaching chemistry, or are drawn from chemistry education journals.
3. *General science education.* Four references are drawn from the general science education area, including mathematics education topics.

The map above gives us a clear indication of some of the important researchers, theorists, and topics that will be covered in the article. We will map one more reference section. This time, we will look at a real qualitative article:

The Wyss Article

The Wyss article cites 34 references. There are only three small teams of researchers, and the other 28 references are from single sources. The most interesting aspect of this reference section, however, is that four of the remaining references are from institutional sources.

The three teams are as follows:

1. *The Goffman team.* Two of the references are from landmark books by the famed sociologist Erving Goffman.
2. *The Mallon team.* Mallon's 1999 book on social services with transgendered youth is cited, along with an article by Mallon in the same book.
3. *The Wilchins team.* A book on genderqueer voices that is coedited by Wilchins is cited, along with an article by Wilchins in the same book.

Three of the institutional citations deal with reports on school violence: one from Human Rights Watch in 2001, and two from Safe Schools Coalition of Washington (1995, 1996). The fourth institutional citation is the American Psychiatric Association's 1994 diagnostic manual.

The remaining 24 references were divided among the following topics:

1. *Transgendered youth and identity.* Nine of the references looked at issues of transgendered youth and adolescence.
2. *Transgender issues.* Six references were on the larger topic of transgendered persons in society, including legal and social issues.
3. *Gender theory.* Five references were concerned with general and specific issues of gender theory.
4. *High school and issues of identity.* Two references tackled the general topic of high schools and adolescent identity.
5. *General reference works.* There were two general reference works. The first work covered issues of women's studies, and the second was a classic text by Garfinkel on ethnomethodology.

This work was quite a bit different from the first reference map. In this article, the researcher drew from a broader set of sources, including magazine articles, manuals, and reports. This is not unusual, given the topical nature of her area of investigation.

When you map a reference section, you now have another version of the argument that supports the research question. This is true because the vast majority of citations in research articles are made in order to support the article's research question. This map also allows you to access important background information quickly and efficiently. It also gives you a picture of the ideas that the researchers themselves considered to be important to their topics. All in all, it is an excellent way to supplement and summarize key aspects of an article's introduction.

Our Emerging Literacy Orientation

Questions and supporting arguments are at the very heart of every educational research article. No method, no matter how well planned or executed, can bring clarity and focus to a fuzzy question. No analysis, no matter how precise or detailed, will answer a poorly asked question. That is why it is important to find the research question, and why it is important that the question or questions be explicit and clear.

While it is important for a question to be clear, it must also be well supported. A good argument draws out the nature and importance of the question—it makes the question seem to be a logical part of the process of looking at the topic under investigation. A good argument can also guide our understanding and interpretation of research findings. Finally, a good argument can help us understand the methods and procedures used to attack the research question—in a real sense, the argument is the first line of attack upon the research question itself.

The final lesson we have pondered in this chapter is this—no research really stands alone. It is part of a larger ongoing process of research and understanding. This is why prior knowledge, most often captured in a literature review, makes so much sense for nearly every article. A good review of prior knowledge helps researchers and readers come to a common point of understanding, while serving to help us put the research questions and findings into a proper perspective.

Questions, arguments, and prior knowledge do not just serve to set up and contextualize the research methods and findings. On the contrary, they are often an important and necessary part of the overall research process. If these matters are not introduced and framed properly, then the rest of the study inevitably suffers.

Practice Makes Perfect

It is now time to practice some of the insights and skills you have explored in this chapter:

- First of all, there are four training article introductions and four real articles that have not been evaluated. You can also incorporate the three to four articles you have selected earlier.
- Can you find the research question for each of these articles? Compare your efforts with those of your classmates.
- Once you have found the research question for each article, see if you can identify the nature and style of the argument used to support that question. Compare your efforts with those of your classmates.
- Finally, see if you can identify three key topics of prior knowledge for each article. Compare your efforts with those of your classmates.

Methods and Procedures

Once the research questions have been established and the literature has been used to build support for both the question and the research itself, it is time to do the actual research. The four aspects that address the conduct of research are sampling, designs, methods, and procedures. Sampling deals with the selection of participants. Designs deal with the process of turning a research question into a test or other data-gathering process. Methods and procedures describe the ways that these tests or processes are actually conducted.

Sampling Techniques Should Match Research Goals

There are a variety of ways that participants can be selected for research studies. The process and strategy of participant selection, or sampling, should be based on what the research is trying to accomplish.

The first type of sample is usually the least desirable type from a research perspective. It consists of using those persons who are closest at hand, or who are most readily available. This sort of a sample is called a *convenience sample*. Sometimes, researchers have no choice but to use everyone, or nearly everyone, who is available.

A Convenience Sample From a General Population

Williams and Clark were interested in seeing how students rate the impact of certain factors on performance on multiple-choice exams. As university-based researchers, they turned to available students for their participants:

> Students in five sections of a large undergraduate human development course participated in various phases of the study ($N = 306$). . . . The sample consisted of 79% females and 21% males, with 76% of the students being second- or third-year students. Students earned a small amount of credit towards their grade for participating, but equivalent credit was available for non-research activities.

A Convenience Sample From a Specialized Population

Sometimes, the researchers need to choose participants who might not be commonly available in the general population. The Chagall study illustrates the use of a convenience sample from a specialized population. In this case, due to the small number of people who were readily available, Chagall was required to use all participants who were available:

> Thirty male juvenile offenders enrolled in an assistance program were used for this study. These offenders ranged in age from 16-18, and all were currently in the second semester of their junior year in high school. All of these students came from households whose income levels qualified them for free school lunch programs. Twenty-five of these students lived in one-parent households; most of the time these students were living with their mothers. Before enrolling in the assistance program, none of the students had held a part time job.

Even though Chagall is using a convenience sample, she nonetheless describes their relevant characteristics in some detail. In this case, she details their income levels, household situations, and employment records. These details help justify her use of this particular group of students.

Convenience sampling always casts the generalizability of a study into some doubt. That is why researchers would much prefer to use a more systematic and more defensible strategy for putting together their samples.

Random Sampling Is One of the Most Common Forms of Sampling

One of the most common strategies for selecting participants, especially in quantitative studies, is to use a *random sample*. In a random sample, every member of a population has an equal chance to end up being a participant.

Why are random samples so often used? There are a number of reasons.

First of all, random samples are relatively easy to gather. As a contrast, consider some of the sophisticated sampling procedures used by pollsters and large-scale marketers. These firms often create complex formulae that allow them to look for a certain number of each of the types of participants they feel they need. To create these formulae, the firms collect and refine and constantly update vast quantities of demographic and other data. As a consequence, their results are often quite impressive. They are able to make sweeping predictions after collecting very little actual data. But these formulae are closely guarded company secrets, so ordinary researchers could not use them even if they wanted to do so.

Compare this to the process of collecting a random sample. Each member of the target population is identified. Then, using a table of random numbers or a computer program that generates random numbers, certain members of the target population are selected one at a time until the necessary quota of participants is reached.

In quantitative research, this quota is usually based upon the number of participants that are needed to give stable statistical results. Obviously, if the sample is too small, then one or two atypical results could throw off the entire study. Researchers, however, are not interested in collecting more data than they need, and so they want to be able to get manageable but stable samples. The size of each sample will depend on the type of statistical test used—as a general rule of thumb the more complicated the test the larger sample pool you need. Sample size also depends on how powerful the effect is—in general, the weaker the effect the larger the sample needs to be to find it.

Second, random sampling allows researchers to avoid any systematic selection bias. Sometimes this bias is conscious, but most often it is unconscious. Imagine, for example, a research study measuring learning outcomes where all the treatment kids are in the gifted program and all the control group kids are in regular classrooms. Or a fitness program where all of the treatment students are varsity athletes, as compared to a control group of average students. These are extreme examples of selection bias, but more subtle versions show up if you are not careful. Randomly drawing from all available participants is your best strategy for avoiding bias. Random chance is rarely systematic.

Finally, random sampling usually "averages out" extreme cases within a given sample. Most often, the mean of a random sample is pretty close to the population mean itself. The sample might contain a few people who are really smart or really physically gifted, but then at the same time there are usually also those who are barely average or who have two left feet. If the sample is big enough, everything tends to even out due to the laws of chance, and the sample ends up being pretty representative.

Randomly Dividing Samples Into Equivalent Groups

The Miro study illustrates a fairly standard use of random sampling. From her total base of 90 students in three classrooms, she randomly assigned 30 of them to each treatment group. This assignment is done at the classroom level, randomly assigning 10 students to each treatment within each 30-person classroom, to make sure there are no accidental classroom effects:

> Ninety high school students were used in this study. These students were enrolled in three afternoon high school classes in a large Southeastern high school. There were 30 students in each class, and each class was a different section of Introductory Geometry. All three classes used the same textbook and curriculum, and Iowa Basic Test math scores were comparable for each class. Each class was also held during the last class period of the day. Students were randomly assigned into one of three groups. The first group received a dried fruit snack, the second group received a high carbohydrate snack, and the third group received a high protein snack. All snacks were precisely the same weight, and all snacks were packaged in identical foil pouches. Ten students in each class were assigned to each of the snack groups, so there were 30 students in each group across all three classes.

Sampling Often Needs to Match the Purposes of the Study

As powerful, useful, and simple as random sampling is, sometimes it is not appropriate for a given research study. This is where the use of other sampling procedures comes in. These sampling techniques fall under the generic heading of *purposive sampling*.

The first sort of purposive sampling strategy has already been discussed briefly. These are the techniques that try to create a sample that contains the same elements, in the same proportions, that are found in the population at large. This version of representative sampling is called *stratified sampling*. Stratified samples can be very useful and powerful, but researchers rarely have the resources or the sampling know-how to create a truly effective stratified sample.

There is one sort of stratified sample that is fairly common in educational research, however. This sampling process occurs at the classroom level. Specific types of classrooms with specific types of characteristics are selected, often in order to try to make sure that diverse and representative groups of students have been included. For instance, researchers might pick classrooms from both rich and poor districts, or classrooms with both racially homogeneous and racially diverse make-ups. Furthermore, researchers might weight the various numbers of classrooms they select in order to mimic proportions from their target population as a whole. Then, the researchers either randomize treatments or conditions within each classroom, or give everyone the same conditions or treatments. This is done so that potential research effects are not confined in any particular classroom, but are spread across the larger sample as a whole.

A Simple Stratified Sample at the Classroom Level

Here is a simple example of the use of stratified sampling from the Cassatt study. Note that he gives every student the same treatment condition, regardless of classroom:

> Four Advanced Algebra classes were selected from four math and science magnet middle schools. Two of these magnet schools are in the upper Midwest, one school is on the West Coast, and the other school is in the Southwest. There are 20 students in each class. Each class is using the Magnet School Standard Advanced Algebra Textbook and Curriculum series. The standardized Midterm Exam, created and normed for this particular school year, was also used in each classroom.

In qualitative research, purposive samples are quite common and are often the desired mode of sampling. These types of samples are often *target samples*. That is, specific participants are chosen because of their expertise, their insights, or their access to information.

A Purposive Sample of Unique Individuals

In some cases, researchers target unique participants. These participants are chosen because they are the only ones who can give the researchers the answers or insights these researchers are seeking. This was the case in the Bradbury study. Since she was looking into the backgrounds and motives of actual school shooters, then these shooters *were* her participants. She needed to go beyond demographics, however, and draw portraits of these young men as unique individuals. These portraits contained demographic information, to be sure, but they went beyond the mere collecting and detailing of facts:

> The first shooting was in Davenport. The shooter, whom we will call Abel (not his real name), walked into the cafeteria at noon, armed with an assault rifle. He began to spray the crowd with bullets, killing seven people. He then reached into his coat pocket and pulled out a grenade. He pulled the pin and ran after a teacher who was monitoring the cafeteria. The ensuing blast killed both Abel and the teacher. In all, there were nine dead and 23 who were seriously wounded. The second shooting occurred the very next day, in rural Paulina. A young man, whom we will call Baker (not his real name), fired upon a group of children waiting for a school bus to take them home. From his sniper's position he killed three children and one adult supervisor. By the time authorities reached his position, hidden on a slight bluff among a grove of trees, Baker had

shot and killed himself. The final incident occurred in Cedar Falls, two days after the second shooting. A junior high school student named Cain (not his real name) walked into the student union at the University of Northern Iowa. He walked deliberately toward a particular table, and shot the young couple sitting there with a pistol he had concealed in his jacket. Before he could be overtaken, Cain turned the pistol to his own temple and shot himself once. After a week in a coma, he died as well.

Portrait of a Shooter

Another thing that jumps out of this situation is the fact that all three shooters had many things in common. All three were 15-year-old white males. They were all honor students, and they all came from homes that were at least economically comfortable (Cain's family was quite affluent). Each boy had a desktop computer, a CD player, a radio, a television, and a DVD player in his bedroom. Two of the boys had their own personal phone lines, and Baker had a phone extension in his room. All three boys had high speed Internet access to their computers, and each maintained a "blog." Blog is the slang term for a "web log", or an ongoing personal journal kept on a web page. Blogs are a growing phenomenon across the Internet, and especially with young adolescent males. (Montini, 2003)

Sampling Sometimes Takes Place Over Time

Informants make up another important class of target participants in qualitative research. Informants are people in a given field setting who have specialized or privileged information. Gathering informants is often a slow process, and finding good and dependable informants is often a matter of trial and error. Good informants, however, are critical for most field studies.

Sampling Informants in a Field Setting

In the Clarke study, four informants were identified and described. Clarke recruited all four informants from his target population, and assigned each a pseudonym to protect his or her identity:

Jin is a 12-year-old male whose family has lived in England for 3 years. Jin is a good student, and is popular with his classmates, both Asian and non-Asian.

Jen is a 17-year-old female who is an average student. She is quiet and has a small circle of friends, mostly Asian. She has lived in England since she was 10.

Jan is a 24-year-old male who works in the neighborhood as a clerk. Jan is quite outgoing and observant. Jan came to England when he was 20.

June is a 15-year-old girl who has many friends, mostly non-Asian. She has been living in the East End for 2 years.

Developing a Sample of Participants in an Action Research Context

In the case of action research, the very notion of sampling becomes problematic. Researchers and participants work hand-in-hand to solve problems and to make things better. In a sense, action researchers "sample" problem situations, and then help guide the people on the scene to eliminate the problems. These dynamics are clearly on display in the Davidson study:

Forming Community Groups

Upon inspection, there were three main demographic groups in this newly altered community. The first group we called the Old-timers. Old-timers were the remnants of the original occupants of the area. Many of them were retired and did not wish to move from their homes. Others were still employed in the mill, even though its production had been drastically cut over the years. That is, they were the survivors of the layoffs and downsizing efforts of the last ten years. They desperately wanted to maintain the old ways of the area, because of their roots to the recent past.

The second group consisted of mainly racial minorities who had come into the area from the nearby metropolis, seeking cheaper housing and a better way of life. They sustained themselves mainly on low-income service jobs and public assistance. We called this second group the Urbanites. They were committed to the effort of keeping the community safe and thriving, but as a group lacked the financial means to help sustain most of the sorts of efforts needed to help the community to prosper and grow. As property values in the region continued to decline, so did the property tax base. This led to less money for schools, public works, and local social services. The Urbanites were not only frustrated by their inability to help turn the community around, but also at the dislike and mistrust directed toward them by the other two groups.

The third and final group consisted of recent immigrants to this country, mainly from the Middle East. We called this group the Newcomers. The Newcomers were also committed to a better way of life, especially for their children. At the same time, however, they were reluctant to abandon all of their traditions and ways of life. These traditions, which looked strange to the other two groups, brought them under constant suspicious scrutiny. Coupled with recent tensions and actions in and from the Middle East, the Newcomers were concerned with the willingness of the others to give them a chance to become productive members of the community.

Finding Common Problems

Volunteers to serve on the initial planning board were identified for each community group. These volunteers were then placed on a ballot that was distributed to all members of that community group. Members of the community elected three representatives to sit on the board. Counting myself, there were a total of ten people on this board.

As we can readily see, often the distinction between participants, researchers, and even samples are blurred in action research. This is because action research is dedicated to the notion of positive change—niceties in design and performance must take a back seat to the need to make things better.

Research Designs Drive Both Quantitative and Qualitative Research

The research *design* is the *plan* for answering the research questions that drive a particular study. Quantitative research studies tend to focus on more strategic plans, while the research designs for qualitative studies tend to be more tactical. For both types of studies however, methods and procedures tend to flow out of the research design.

The following designs are some of the most common in educational research:

- Quantitative Descriptive Design
- Quantitative Comparative Design
- Quantitative Experimental Design
- Quantitative Predictive Design
- Qualitative Investigative Design
- Qualitative Interpretive Design
- Qualitative Illuminative Design
- Qualitative Participatory Design

Quantitative Designs Tend to Be More Strategic

The next four examples illustrate some of the most common types of quantitative designs. Note how these designs are focused on answering certain questions, and on arranging the nature and terms of data collection efforts so as to give the best and clearest possible answers to those questions. This is the essence of methods and procedures in a quantitative study—to allow for unambiguous control over data collection to ensure the cleanest possible answers:

A Simple Quantitative Descriptive Design

Devine-Wright et al. knew that they wanted to examine children's views on global warming, and how various social factors might influence those views. In cases such as these, surveys are often used. The researchers start off discussing issues of survey creation and distribution:

> Data were collected from children using a survey that addressed global warming and the specific issues of energy conservation and renewable energy. The survey form was piloted with adults and children and amended before a final version was produced. The survey was distributed in two ways: over the internet on the Woodcraft Folk website and using paper versions.

The researchers also broadly specified the types of questions asked:

> Respondents were asked specific questions that formed the dependent variables in the research concerning issues of awareness, concern, perceived responsibility and self-efficacy. These included questions about levels of

awareness, specifically awareness that changes to weather patterns were happening, exposure to specific sources of information (school, friends and family) and awareness of practical actions to deal with global warming; questions about perceived self-efficacy in reducing negative consequences of global warming; and finally, concern and perceived responsibility about specific energy issues.

Finally, the details of the survey and the sorts of response choices available were also described:

> Questions were in two formats. Yes/No/Don't know responses were used for probing sources of information, awareness of practical actions and feelings of responsibility. Likert-type scales (e.g., strongly disagree/strongly agree) were used for questions concerning self-efficacy, concern and general awareness of the environmental problem.

By discussing the nature and creation of their main data-gathering tool, Devine-Wright et al. give their readers a sense of what kind of data they collected, and how their participants responded to the questions they were asked.

A Simple Quantitative Comparative Design

Sometimes, researchers are interested in making comparisons among variables. In an experimental study, those variables are controlled and the changes are measured and possible causal links are inferred. Sometimes, however, we cannot control variables. We can only measure them and compare them. This is the basic design of the Williams and Clark article.

Williams and Clark were interested in comparing student ratings of perceived factors on actual performance when multiple-choice exams were used. First of all, they describe the course units that were used in their large class. The content of these units formed the basis of the multiple-choice exams:

> Issues related to human development provided the framework for five course units: physical, cognitive, psychological, social and character development. The five class sessions in each unit followed a standard sequence: session 1 involved viewing and discussing a video tape related to the unit; sessions 2 and 3 consisted of a teacher overview of pivotal issues in the unit; session 4 began with a brief essay quiz related to selected issues in the reading materials and then continued with the teacher overview; and session 5 included a multiple-choice exam over the unit and feedback to students regarding their essay quiz and multiple-choice exam performance. Students signed a class roster each day they attended class but received no credit for attendance. Virtually all students attended class on quiz and exam days.

Williams and Clark also describe how the exams themselves were created:

> At the end of each unit, students took a 40-item multiple-choice exam with four possible choices per item. The lead teacher initially developed all the exam

items, which graduate teaching assistants (GTAs) later took and edited for clarity of wording. A majority of the items, as determined by the lead teacher and the GTAs, required higher-order reasoning that involved synthesis of course information and evaluation of possible conclusions from that information.

Then, the researchers discuss how the rating scales were created:

> The 12-item rating scale targeted three areas: (a) student effort (e.g., amount of time I spent studying for the exam, my level of reading in this unit), (b) student ability (e.g. my ability to take this type of exam, my ability to master the type of subject-matter addressed in this unit) and (c) teacher input (e.g., level of clarity in teacher presentations in this unit, degree of match between teacher presentations and exam content, clarity of wording on the exam). Four of the items reflected student effort, two items related to student ability and six items targeted teacher input.

Finally, Williams and Clark discuss technical details, so that we understand how the students made their ratings and how the researchers evaluated those ratings. We should also point out that the measures of internal consistency were made in order to determine how reliable these scales were. For experimental data, these scales are reasonably reliable. In the end, all major design details have been clarified prior to the presentation and interpretation of the findings:

> Students rated the magnitude of potential contributors to exam performance of a 1 to 23 basis: 1 = low, 2 = medium and 3 = high. . . . Internal consistency measures across units were 0.72 for student effort, 0.61 for student ability and 0.64 for teacher input. In addition to rating the magnitude of student effort, student ability and teacher input, students also circled the five items on the exam-rating scale they considered the most important contributors to their performance on the exam taken the previous class session.

A Simple Quantitative Experimental Design

One of the oldest and most venerable designs in educational research is the simple experimental design. The simplest type of this design is the basic Treatment vs. Control design. In this design, an overall sample is taken. Members of that sample are randomly assigned to either a Treatment or a Control group. The Treatment is then delivered to the Treatment group, and then the dependent variable is measured for each group. If the Treatment has had an effect, then the scores for the Treatment group will differ from the scores of the Control group. Researchers usually predict in advance the impacts they expect the treatments to have, and then the results either confirm or deny those predictions.

The Miro study uses a version of this design. In this study, there are three Treatment groups but no actual Control group. In a sense, each Treatment group acts as a Control for the other groups. This way, each student is eating something, and it is the difference in what is eaten that is the target of the study. The dependent variable is each student's score on the quiz. Miro also predicted that the students in the Protein group would have the highest scores on these quizzes. Note how every effort was made by Miro to standardize these snacks, so that the Protein-Carbohydrate-Fruit difference was the only consistent difference among these groups:

> Students were randomly assigned into one of three groups. The first group received a dried fruit snack, the second group received a high carbohydrate snack, and the third group received a high protein snack. All snacks were precisely the same weight, and all snacks were packaged in identical foil pouches. Ten students in each class were assigned to each of the snack groups, so there were 30 students in each group across all three classes. Students then received a 30-minute lecture on new material, and at the end of the lecture, all students were given a pop quiz. Scores on the quiz could range from a zero to a ten. Scores were tabulated, and used in later classes for diagnostic purposes. Students were also told, immediately after handing in their papers, that the quizzes were part of a research study and would not be used to affect their class grades.

A Simple Quantitative Predictive Design

In quantitative studies that are more exploratory in nature, the basic design is to identify, measure, and then compare important variables. This is the case in the design of the Chagall study. The key aspect of this study is the careful definition of each variable that will be used in the exploratory process:

> Data were collected over the first semester of the junior year from a variety of sources:

> *Peer Support Rating.* Each juvenile offender was rated by his primary caseworker regarding that student's degree of positive peer support, following the protocol developed by Bacon & Pepper (1998). This rating ranged from a zero to a 9. A score of zero meant that this student had no peer-aged positive role models; that is, all of his contacts with peers were linked to his delinquent behaviors. At the other end of the spectrum, a score of 9 meant that the offender had found a crowd of positive peer role models, who were actively involved in trying to help him stay out of trouble. The ratings of the primary caseworkers were reviewed by the researcher and the director of the assistance program, to assure that the ratings were reasonable.

> *Missed Homework.* School officials supplied the assistance program with missed homework data. Each homework assignment that was not handed in during the first semester of the junior year, across all classes, was counted as a data point.

> *Victim Awareness Survey.* One of the keys for rehabilitation of youthful offenders is making them aware of the consequences of their actions on others. Victim awareness classes are also a major part of the assistance program. To help measure this awareness, each student completed a Victim Awareness Survey (Plato, 1999). Scores on the survey ranged from 0-9. The higher the score, the greater offenders' awareness of the harmful consequences of their crimes.

Part-Time Employment. Since most offenders live in poverty-level households, lack of money often plays a key role in their choices to commit crimes. To help alleviate this personal lack of money, as well as give these students something positive to do in their free time, the assistance program tries to place these offenders in part-time jobs. Students can spend as little as four hours per week working, up to a maximum of 20 hours per week.

Positive Drug Testing. Drugs play a major role in the lives of many youthful offenders, and all of the students in this sample have tested positively at some point for drugs. Helping students break drug habits is a priority for the assistance program. Students are tested daily for the presence of drugs, and each data point in this area is an indication that the student tested positive for some kind of drug on a given day.

Grade Point Average. A key indicator for school success is grade point average, or GPA. All of the students in this study were marginally passing high school after the first semester of junior year. Therefore, all they have to do for the next three semesters is to maintain a GPA over 2.00 in order to graduate. Data reported are their GPAs for the second semester junior year, which is the targeted time frame for this study.

Qualitative Designs Tend to Be More Tactical

Tactical efforts often play key roles in educational research. As has already been discussed briefly, many qualitative studies replace the notion of a formal or strategically based design with a tactical plan for looking at an important area. Examples of this sort of process are as follows:

A Qualitative Investigative Design

The essence of the Asimov study was an act of discovery by the researcher—the fact that an enclave of high-powered mathematical instruction existed in a highly unlikely setting. Therefore, the heart of the design was investigation of this phenomenon in its natural setting. When this is the case, researchers often turn to field study approaches:

> I used an ethnographic participant observation approach in this study. I had learned of the existence of the "calculus enclave" from casual conversations with teachers in the local elementary school and from residents in the neighborhood.

As Asimov conducted his initial investigations, he began to learn more about how this particular math enclave came into being. The first and most necessary piece was the presence of a competent and willing instructor. Asimov came to discover the story behind this particular teacher and mentor:

> I came to find that a retired math teacher from the local high school named Jerry (not his real name) had moved into Camden Acres after a series of

financial reversals regarding his retirement income sources. Jerry soon became a highly respected member of this community, especially among the parents, and was granted special consideration and protection within these sometimes harsh and demanding circumstances.

And so, out of this situation of mutual need and respect, the informal math learning sessions began to come into being. Asimov, by virtue of his investigation into this topic, had uncovered a plausible set of motives to explain why these courses were functioning:

> As a token of his appreciation and in order to keep busy and active, Jerry set up a number of informal math programs. Most of them were short-lived by intention, designed to help students grasp basic math points in order to do better in school. The calculus enclave, however, took root and is still going strong to this day. At the time of this study, there were six regular "students" in this program.

Now that he had established the necessary background for understanding the existence of this phenomenon, Asimov needed to investigate it in some depth. To do so, he needed to make some choices. The first choice had to do with the selection of his participants, and why:

> In this study, I decided to concentrate upon Magda. There are several reasons for this decision. First of all, Magda is very articulate and self-reflective. Secondly, her cultural experiences are the most far-removed of her peers. Because American culture is so new and strange to her, she sees things that the other students might ignore out of familiarity. Finally, Magda has been a member of the enclave for the longest time. She was one of the original three volunteers to work with Jerry, and is the only one to still be involved with the enclave.

Now that he had decided to focus on Magda as his learner, Asimov needed to establish some field rules for working with Jerry, the instructor. As is often the case, the research participant took the lead in defining the parameters of the field experience:

> Jerry was very cooperative in allowing me to observe and even participate to some degree, but he was adamant in his refusal to be interviewed or to discuss the nature and operation of the enclave. I never pressed him for his reasons for not talking about the enclave; I was content to be allowed to be involved. Parents were also reluctant to talk about the nature of their children's involvement, and so I respected their wishes as well.

After Asimov had negotiated such necessary entry issues as ground rules on whom and what to study, he engaged in classic participant observation activities. That is, Asimov spent his time in the field watching and learning and documenting:

> With the permission of Jerry and the parents, I became a regular fixture of the enclave for six months. It has no permanent meeting place; this is partly due to the lack of public meeting space in Camden Acres, and partly due to the need to keep the enclave free from harassment by local gang members, thugs, and toughs. Jerry has a sort of blanket immunity even from these groups, but

the kids (especially the newer and younger members) always risk teasing and even physical harm. The enclave meets for three times a week for two hours at a time, and the meeting spots for the next sessions are always settled at the end of the meeting. Hallways are a common meeting spot, followed by outdoor picnic tables when the weather is nice and the occasional meeting in a parent's apartment. By common agreement, none of the meetings are ever held in Jerry's apartment.

From these initial and evolving field-based and situation-based rules, the structure and texture and flow of the research project began to evolve. Once Asimov felt that he had a sufficient handle on his main questions, he then moved into the process of gathering his information, organizing it, and reporting his findings.

A Qualitative Interpretive Design

We are going to look at the James et al. article as our example of an interpretive design. This design was both emergent and complex. As James continued through her research process, she turned to her assistant and her mentor for guidance at every turn. While these collaborative sessions were important for the overall growth and development of the study, they make for complicated reading. To simplify our examination of her design, we will focus only on the design issues related directly to gathering data from the children themselves. James signals to us, at the outset, just how complicated this study will be:

> I tried to capitalize on the benefits of a qualitative approach by analysing the selected scenarios in detail, using a broadly ethnographic approach. During the study many unexpected issues emerged, which informed the next stage of data collection and analysis. Sometimes the surprises were challenging, particularly gender differences and the powerful way children can play without needing adult intervention.

James starts by describing her basic field-oriented data collection procedures:

> I needed to capture what children say and do in their play and what they say about their play, so I chose to collect data through observation, video recording and interviewing children after they had watched themselves on video. Ethical considerations were foremost in my mind: I gained permission from my head teacher, parents and tacit agreement from children, discontinuing data collection if they appeared uncomfortable.

She also collected her own thoughts, impressions, and interpretations as the research process proceeded:

> As I was interested in children's social behaviour, I used a running record to collect observations. This enabled me to write a rich narrative account, reflecting the complex nature of the children's interactions, showing children exploring issues such as life, death, hunger and love.

Videotaping in particular was new to James, and she was initially wary, but came to realize its key importance to her study:

> Videotaping provided a sophisticated method of data gathering despite my lack of technical expertise. My initial reservations about using videos were allayed as I found I was able to capture the children's interactions during sociodramatic play in a dynamic form. As a means of sharing data with both practitioners and children, videos were unsurpassed. Videos acted as a catalyst for children to reflect on the importance of their play, instilling them with confidence when they were interviewed in pairs or trios. The children expressed powerful ideas, which showed that they understood, and influenced, each other's meaning.

A major breakthrough came when James realized that it was very useful to look at the videotapes without listening to the sound:

> Eventually, I decided that owing to practical limitations (both the time constraint of the study and with class teacher responsibilities) I had collected enough data. So I began to analyse in more depth. . . . I tried watching the videos without sound. . . . My attention was focused on the corporeal dimension, which was a thought-provoking experience and provided a key moment in shaping my understanding. I realised that young children often express themselves through physical means with greater eloquence than through their verbal interactions.

Finally, as she began to accumulate mounds and mounds of data, it became clear to James that she needed a system to organize and refine her data. She describes that system in some detail:

> The amount of data I accumulated was excessive! Needing to extract key issues, I filed, sorted and indexed the data with piles strewn on the floor until, after much paper shuffling, I was left with four key scenarios. . . . I made grids of key moments from observations of each of the scenarios and drew charts tracking different children's movements. I identified patterns across the children's play and within the gesture and dialogue of particular individuals, comparing these with themes identified from analysis of the interviews. Coloured mind maps became an important way that I made sense of my data and kept it within a cohesive framework. . . . At the polishing stage, I redrafted, whilst paring unnecessary phrases to make the points more emphatically. . . . My 12-year-old son seemed to empathise with each scenario, able to recall from his own experiences how the children were interacting. Their play seemed more accessible to him than to me, so he offered me interpretations.

This study is an excellent example of the potentially fluid nature of a qualitative research design. As James learned more and more about her topic, her methods and style of gathering data and insights also began to change. While she was able to keep her initial focus on child sociodramatic play, her approach toward researching that topic continued to expand and evolve.

A Qualitative Illuminative Design

Strategic planning is critical for most quantitative designs. In a previous quantitative design example, Miro tried to either randomize or standardize every possible source of a systematic effect other than the one that she was explicitly testing. This sort of concentration and attention to detail is absolutely necessary, especially in an experimentally oriented study.

Qualitative research, on the other hand, is often much more tactical in nature. Researchers need to allow things to unfold in front of them, without trying to control these processes. However, there are times when strategic planning is just as critical for a qualitative study.

Strategic planning, for instance, was important in the Bradbury study. In this case, most of the data that could be used was already available. The young men who did the shootings were already dead, and so their input could only be garnered from their records. Bradbury conducted interviews to gain additional background knowledge on these young men, but her research focus was clearly directed toward their computer writings. She turned to the use of a computer software package to help her sort through these writings to look for common themes, threads, and facets:

Investigating the Blogs

At the time of my fieldwork, all three blogs had been shut down and access to them had been sealed by the police. After some persuasion, and working under police surveillance, I was able to download the contents of each blog for my research purposes. The fact that the blogs had been sealed and isolated was a good thing, from a research perspective, since it meant that the data that was there had not been tampered with. Abel had been running his blog the longest, and it contained the most data. Abel's blog ran for six months, and he faithfully wrote a new entry each day. Baker had been running his blog for only three months, and he rarely updated it more than once a week. Cain had kept his blog for five months, with an average of four entries per week. Most of Cain's entries were done on the weekends. Content on each of these blogs were diverse as well. Abel crowded his entries with lots of links to political web pages. There appeared to be no consistent political position advocated. Baker talked about going hunting with his father and other men, and how the experience made him feel like an adult. Cain talked often of Wendy, of what she was doing now, about her ex-boyfriends, and the like. Even though there appeared to be no common link among these blogs, I decided to transcribe them and analyze them as a single group. If there were common themes, they might be uncovered in this manner. I used the Reveal software pioneered by Pacelli & Roncalli (2001) as a tool for looking for commonalities in diverse prose sources.

A Qualitative Participatory Design

Participants, design issues, and procedures are all intertwined in an action research study. This is because the problem is central in action research, and all of these aspects play a role in addressing the problem. More often than not, action research requires a constantly shifting focus between the people involved, their concerns, and the best way to get things going and underway.

Consider how all these elements are involved in the Davidson study. First, the nature of the participants has to be examined again:

Forming Community Groups

Upon inspection, there were three main demographic groups in this nearly altered community. The first group we called the Old-timers. Old-timers were the remnants of the original occupants of the area. Many of them were retired and did not wish to move from their homes. Others were still employed in the mill, even though its production had been drastically cut over the years. That is, they were the survivors of the layoffs and downsizing efforts of the last ten years. They desperately wanted to maintain the old ways of the area, because of their roots to the recent past.

The second group consisted of mainly racial minorities who had come into the area from the nearby metropolis, seeking cheaper housing and a better way of life. They sustained themselves mainly on low-income service jobs and public assistance. We called this second group the Urbanites. They were committed to the effort of keeping the community safe and thriving, but as a group lacked the financial means to help sustain most of the sorts of efforts needed to help the community to prosper and grow. As property values in the region continued to decline, so did the property tax base. This led to less money for schools, public works, and local social services. The Urbanites were not only frustrated by their inability to help turn the community around, but also at the dislike and mistrust directed toward them by the other two groups.

The third and final group consisted of recent immigrants to this country, mainly from the Middle East. We called this group the Newcomers. The Newcomers were also committed to a better way of life, especially for their children. At the same time, however, they were reluctant to abandon all of their traditions and ways of life. These traditions, which looked strange to the other two groups, brought them under constant suspicious scrutiny. Coupled with recent tensions and actions in and from the Middle East, the Newcomers were concerned with the willingness of the others to give them a chance to become productive members of the community.

It is important to see that this is not just a list of all the relevant participant groups who are on the scene. Each of these groups brings their own natures, traditions, histories, and perspectives to bear. All of these differing characteristics help compound the problems confronting this community, but on the other hand, this complex and dynamic set of characteristics can also serve as a palette for fresh and creative approaches to those same problems.

Davidson continues by documenting her efforts to help bring these groups together at the outset. The first order of business was setting up an elected group of representatives. Then, her efforts centered on helping them discover common understandings concerning the problems that they were confronting:

Finding Common Problems

Volunteers to serve on the initial planning board were identified for each community group. These volunteers were then placed on a ballot that was distributed to all members of that community group. Members of the community elected three representatives to sit on the board. Counting myself, there were a total of ten people on this board. During our first meeting, we decided to explore the issue of common problems. Our first group decision was to limit the scope of common problems to those which had a direct impact on the younger children. After some lively debate and a bit of give and take, the group reached consensus on this principle. The board then adjourned for a week. The next week, each representative came with a set of possible common problems. At the same time, I went into first and second grade classrooms to ask the children directly about problems they might be having with each other. During our meeting, we put all of these problems together for discussion and consideration. Those problems that were closely associated with one community group over the others were discarded. Once this sorting process was complete, there were three potential common problems left. They were 1) lack of mutual respect, 2) lack of mutual trust, and 3) unwillingness to see the world from another's perspective. After an extended discussion, it was decided that all three of these matters were related to the central notion of character and character education. I volunteered to gather information on character education models, and the group adjourned again.

The hallmark of a good action research process is that the key ideas for change come from the people at the scene, themselves. This is indeed what happened in this case, as Davidson documents:

One of the Urbanite parents then hit upon a brilliant notion. Why not let parents teach children from the other groups? We had all simply assumed that the character education lessons would be taught in homogeneous groups, so this was a revelation to us all. After serious discussion, it was decided that Newcomer parents would teach a mixed group of Old-timer and Urbanite children, and so on with mixed groups handled by Old-timer and Urbanite parents.

Finally, all that remained was for the details of the plan to emerge and then get finalized:

Implementation and Change

Parent teachers were then recruited and trained. It was decided that each member of the planning board would be responsible for monitoring and supervising a certain number of parents. After much discussion, consensus was reached that planning board members would supervise parents from their own community. My job was to supervise the supervisors, to make sure things were even across the board. The character education curriculum we used was modified from Shaftoe (2001). Specific questions and problem areas were incorporated into the basic curriculum. The character education classes started in September and ran through February of the following year. Carpools brought groups of children to designated teaching areas within the neighborhoods of the parents who were teaching those particular groups. There were 12 children in each group; three 1st graders and three 2nd graders from each of the two groups that were different from the group of the parents doing the teaching. Overall, the process was quite successful. In all, there were eight groups; three run by Old-timer parents, three run by Urbanite parents, and two run by Newcomer parents. One Old-timer and one Newcomer parent each had to be replaced due to their inability to control their children, but all the other parents did well.

In action research, even areas that might be thought of as being results or findings often play a role in design. Since many action research efforts are fluid and changing, it is important to incorporate at least early results into the overall design of the process. Once adjustments start to wane and the process starts working smoothly, it is then appropriate to start looking for results proper:

> After six months, we started to see tangible community change. Children in the two target grades were playing more with children from other groups. Children across groups were inviting each other to birthday parties and sleepovers. Even two months later, well after the end of formal classes, these trends were still in place

Our Emerging Literacy Orientation

Methods and procedures are used to take research questions and put them into action. Therefore, they are both important and often complex. We have looked at four key issues in this chapter that help us understand how researchers turn their ideas and questions into actual research.

The first issue is sampling. Different types of research call for different sampling strategies. In general, quantitative studies strive for typical people in their samples, often chosen at random. In contrast, it is not unusual for qualitative researchers to look for specific people for very specific and focused reasons.

After the notion of sampling comes the issue of design. Designs allow researchers to do things to answer research questions. In most quantitative studies, the chief role of the research design is to control or counteract those things that might interfere with our efforts to isolate and test certain processes or effects. In many qualitative studies, the point of the design is to allow us to be in the right place at the right time.

Finally, we have the notion of methods and procedures per se. For many quantitative studies, methods and procedures are designed to operationalize the ideas being tested in the study. As such, they are usually created in advance, and only modified if necessary. For a large percentage of qualitative studies, however, methods and procedures are often an historical record of the tactical efforts needed in order to bring about the research so that the research questions could be addressed.

In either qualitative or quantitative research, however, it is important for us to understand that goods methods arise from clear and well-argued research questions. If the research questions are not well formed, then the entire study is in trouble. No amount of clever methodological or design tricks can compensate for a muddled or unclear set of research questions.

Practice Makes Perfect

It is now time to practice some of the insights and skills you have explored in this chapter:

- First of all, there are four training articles and four real articles that have not been evaluated. You should also look at the three or four articles you have chosen to examine.
- Can you find the sampling strategy for each of these articles? Compare your efforts with those of your classmates.
- Once you have found the sampling strategy for each article, see if you can identify the nature and style of the design used to support its research questions. Compare your efforts with those of your classmates.
- Finally, see if you can identify the basic methods and procedures used for each article. Compare your efforts with those of your classmates.

Chapter 9

Qualitative Findings and Results

The heart of any research study is its findings and results. More often than not, however, this part of the study is the most intimidating for readers who are trying to build their research literacy skills. There are several good reasons, however, for readers not to fear these findings and results.

First of all, in a well-done study the findings and results flow right from the questions, arguments, and methods. Most of the findings and results are answers to questions that have already been stated and are merely being put to the test.

Second, complex statistical procedures or sophisticated theoretical frameworks that often accompany findings and results are usually based on simple ideas that can be clearly related to the questions being tested or addressed. This will be demonstrated over and over again in this chapter from a qualitative perspective and in the next chapter when we consider quantitative results and findings.

Finally, the findings and results often add an element of surprise and intrigue to the research. It is not at all unusual for researchers to not get exactly what they expect in the way of findings and results. This merely means that the researchers did not anticipate every aspect or nuance of the situation beforehand. Good researchers are delighted with findings that require some thought, because more often than not these sorts of findings can lead to entirely new directions for research.

What is the difference between a "finding" and a "result"? In actuality, nothing. There are a few conventions that can make it easier to sort through various ways of handling and presenting data, however. In the next two chapters, "Findings" will be used to describe descriptive or qualitative data, while "Results" will be used to describe the answers to various forms of statistical tests.

Since we need to look carefully at results, we will divide this task across two chapters. This will keep our efforts from being too overwhelming. In this chapter, we will look at qualitative results and findings, and in the next chapter we will do the same for quantitative results and findings.

What Are Qualitative Results and Findings Like?

Sometimes, qualitative results are the results of highly structured processes like axial coding (Strauss & Corbin, 1998) and cross case comparisons (Miles & Huberman, 1994). Other times, they seem anecdotal and narrative in nature. Across this diversity of types, however, there is a common thread. Qualitative results and findings are grounded in the discovery of meaning. There are four common procedures that qualitative researchers often use when handling their findings. First, they *sort their findings and discoveries*, pulling together bits and pieces to make a case. Quite often, these researchers will take care to *organize their findings* according to themes or codes or any other sense-making system. The next approach is based on *reflection and synthesis*, where researchers attempt to formulate new ways of looking at the data. Finally, the researchers might *take stock* of what they have, creating an account or narrative or tale that encapsulates and organizes their major findings. We will look at examples of each strategy in turn:

Sorting Findings and Discoveries

In many qualitative studies, researchers go into a situation looking for something unusual or overlooked that might shed light on matters. In these situations, the researchers have literally "found" things, and so the label of "findings" is quite appropriate.

More often than not, these "found" pieces have been gathered piecemeal. At this point, researchers often act like detectives, gathering these bits of evidence and putting them into some sort of coherent organization. Items of lesser importance, or items that seem to have no bearing to the overall emergent picture, are discarded. Those items that are left are then organized in a coherent fashion. This organizational activity often involves careful, and sometimes innovative, interpretations from researchers. In the end, the researchers have built a case for a new way of looking at the situations or events.

The best way to understand this process is to watch it in operation. The following are the key findings from the training article by Bradbury. She starts by looking at certain unusual aspects in the lives of each of the three shooters:

> Abel had dropped an American history course in mid-semester in order to preserve his perfect 4.00 GPA. He and the teacher had engaged in arguments during class time over trivial points in American history, and Abel stormed out of class on more than one occasion. Abel also spent nearly all his time in the evenings in his bedroom, which was well stocked with communication and entertainment devices.
>
> Baker had often bragged about the fact that he was one of the youngest members of a local shooting club. His father, an avid hunter, encouraged his son's prowess with a hunting rifle.
>
> Cain had covered a bulletin board in his bedroom with pictures and sketches of Wendy (not her real name), his former babysitter. Wendy was now a junior at Stanford University, and she even wrote him occasionally. Cain's parents thought that his obsession with Wendy was cute and harmless, but they were starting to get worried that he seemed to show no interest in girls his own age.

Bradbury begins with a set of facts about the lives of each of these shooters. Given that these young men had each committed a terrible crime, it makes sense that she would look for "cracks" in their seemingly perfect exteriors. Having waded through much biographical detail, she focused on the three aspects above as possible trails to follow when investigating the blogs.

The blogs themselves proved to be complex sources of data, so Bradbury turned to technology for help in sorting through them:

> Even though there appeared to be no common link among these blogs, I decided to transcribe them and analyze them as a single group. If there were common themes, they might be uncovered in this manner. I used the Reveal software pioneered by Pacelli & Roncalli (2001) as a tool for looking for commonalities in diverse prose sources.

Computer software programs are playing an increasingly important role in many qualitative research efforts. They are most useful when they can help researchers sort through large amounts of data looking for recurring patterns and occurrences that might elude ordinary perception. Bradbury is using the imaginary computer software package in this fashion, and it helped her sort out the various occurrences of her key themes. Computer software can also "bury" less frequent or even unique observations, however, and so they must be used with some care.

Researchers should also avoid relying upon computer sorting and organization solely. The human eye is exceedingly good at spotting unusual things, and the human ears are attuned to unusual sounds and statements; these are often the best tools that qualitative researchers can use.

Bradbury also had to deal with another major restriction in her treatment of the data:

> Because of the sensitive nature of the research material and the fact that there are still some legal matters that are pending, actual quotes from the blogs could not be used. Instead, I have summarized and categorized key points.

Now Bradbury is ready to launch into her major findings. She does not use a traditional "Findings" or "Results" heading. Instead, she is demonstrating that her findings needed to be assembled like a jigsaw puzzle:

Pulling Together the Pieces

> Once the blogs had been transcribed and analyzed using a computer program, a powerful common theme began to take shape. Two of the most common words used in these blogs were "little" and "big." Pattern analysis showed that these terms were equally common in relative frequency in all three blogs. I began to search for context for "little" and "big" and I found, in all cases, that the usages were autobiographical. All three boys were smaller than average, and it appeared to be a source of concern and discontent for each of them. This theme manifested itself in blog content that at least hints towards the acts that they each would soon commit.

Bradbury has found a common pattern in the blogs of each of the three shooters. First of all, she finds that the terms "big" and "little" are used often in each blog. These terms are linked to each other, and concepts like "big" and "little" can have powerful meanings for people. These facts, though, are not enough. She needs to go further and see how they are actually used in context:

> Abel reproached his history teacher over and over again for thinking of himself as some kind of "big man." This teacher was indeed physically large, and served as an assistant football coach. Abel created as many links to as many different history sites as he could, to demonstrate how much "bigger" his knowledge was, over the teacher. These links became increasingly stranger and more marginal over time, indicating the possibility that Abel was growing more and more unstable on this topic. Given the dramatic nature of his attack, this sort of mental deterioration is quite plausible. As he became less and less "linked" to reality, his natural ability to suppress his strange and obsessive thoughts might have diminished. It is worth noting that he started each blog with a measure of his height and weight. Over the last four months, there was no change in height. Abel noted this fact explicitly over the last week, often pointing it out using multiple exclamation points.
>
> Baker seemed to deal with his shortness by longing to be one of the "big hunters." He kept elaborating on his most difficult hunting feats, and longed for even more difficult challenges. His father had killed a Rocky Mountain

sheep, one of the most elusive native big game animals. Baker talked of his father in glowing terms, wanting not only to emulate his feats but to exceed them as well. Over the last week, he mused about a film he had seen where a "big strong" hunter hired a "little" man to be his prey on a deadly game of hide and seek.

Cain was almost torn between his desire to be both "little" and "big" at the same time. He remembered with fondness the many sessions where Wendy had been his babysitter. He longed to be tucked in by her, bathed by her, and read to late into the night. At the same time, he wanted Wendy to see him for the man he was becoming, as a "big" man. The couple that he shot, upon investigation, had been high school classmates of Wendy toward whom she had been decidedly cool. Cain talked about making things "right" for Wendy, so that she could see how "big" he had become so that she might return and take care of him again.

At this point, you need to realize the nature of the data that was presented above. First of all, these data are not causal. Nowhere is Bradbury suggesting that this fascination with "big" and "little" caused any of the crimes. Instead, they are identified as common themes that run through each blog and as such, are worthy of investigation.

Second, these data are not exhaustive. Nowhere is it suggested that these issues that are discussed are sufficient to explain the actions of the shooters. Certainly, there are many other issues that are in play for each situation. They are offered, instead, as data that might be overlooked but which give us a richer and deeper picture of what has transpired.

Finally, these data are not reductive. In fact, they are the very opposite. Findings such as these are meant to illuminate a perplexing situation. They shed light on a situation where understanding is elusive. As such, they give us a more complex picture of the lives and motives of these shooters, and not a simpler one.

Organizing Results

Very often, the key to presenting qualitative findings effectively is organization. More often than not, that organization has to be discovered by the researcher. In this case, Clarke uses his actual questions as his organizational structure:

What sorts of terms and phrases do they pick up?

This is Clarke's first question, and it is an obvious place to start. Clarke uses Oakley's set of four common classes, and then reports the degree to which each class is found in his field data:

According to Oakley (2002), there are four main classes of slang terms and phrases in the East London region. First, and most common, are the putdown terms and phrases. These are used by East End children and young adults to mock and tease each other. Some of the more common terms are "Parker" (a nerdy individual) and "tiptoe" (a coward). Common putdown phrases include "cave to the hoop" (to back down from a fight or confrontation) and "mind the wookie" (where the person being put down is compared to a hairy beast).

While these are the most common slang terms and phrases in the East End streets, they are the least used by the new Southeastern Asian immigrants.

The second class of terms and phrases, from Oakley (2002), deal with common places. Terms such as "picklepit" refer to school buildings, and phrases such as "the clinker closet" refer to juvenile detention centers. These usages are quite common among the newer immigrants.

The third class of terms and phrases, from Oakley (2002), deal with common activities. For instance, to "paginate" means to read, and to "cheese the runaway" means to pass intestinal gas. These usages are less common among Southeastern Asian immigrants.

The final class of terms and phrases, from Oakley (2002), deal with mock commands and pronouncements. Some of the most common are "twick the stick" (get over here right now!) and "strabble me backwards" (I'll be darned). Southeastern Asian immigrants tend to use these among themselves, but rarely with members of the larger East London community.

Clarke progresses to the next question:

Where do the immigrants learn these terms and phrases?

Once Clarke has established the type and frequencies of slang use, he then explores the issue of how the immigrants came to learn these terms. Here, he makes use of actual data from his informants:

All four informants focused on school as an important source for learning slang terms and phrases. According to June: The teachers want you to learn to read and write English right away, but in order to survive and fit in, you need to learn the street language as soon as possible. The quicker you learn what to say, and when to say it, the faster you will fit in. I knew a little bit of English when I came over here, so it helped me pick up things quickly.

Even Jan, who never went to school in England, acknowledged the importance of school as a place to learn slang: These school kids teach each other the slang very quickly. You see a few non-Asian helping out, but its mostly Asians teaching other Asians during lunch hours and break times.

Local media is an important source as well. Radio is particularly useful, as noted by Jin:

You learn to listen to the cool radio stations right away, and they help you pick up what slang is in and what slang is out. That is important to know, so you can fit in, you know?

Finally, these immigrants learn to hang out and listen carefully to passersby and people going about their ordinary lives in the East End. As Jan said, "You learn to be like a chameleon with big ears!"

The third question is then addressed:

How do they become so fluent so quickly?

Clarke is also impressed with the fact that these immigrants pick up the slang so rapidly. Again, he turns to his informants to try to find out how this happens:

Earp (1999) contends that slang is an important socialization tool for new immigrants. This is especially true when these immigrants differ racially and ethnically from the prevailing residents. Jen, even though she is quiet by nature, knew that this sort of socialization was critical: If I don't make an effort to fit in, then I will be on the outside always. In my case, I made some close Asian friendships immediately. They have helped me so much, especially in learning the "real" language. I do not want to sound like a textbook out here in the streets. They will torment me and call me a Parker. I do not want that, and so I want to learn as fast as I can.

Clarke's final question examines the socialization process a bit more closely:

Are they using them in the same ways as their other East End counterparts are?

Are the immigrants becoming more and more like their native East End counterparts as reflected by the ways they use slang, or are the immigrants assimilating the slang into their own preexisting culture to some degree?

> This is the most surprising finding, for me, in this study. There is a great deal of reluctance to use East End slang in exactly the same ways that the "native speakers" use it. It seems as if the Southeastern Asian community wants to demonstrate that it knows and can use the slang, but at the same time they do not want to go against long standing traditions within their own cultures regarding the use of language in appropriate and non-appropriate ways. Jin illustrates: I know all the putdowns but I don't use them. My parents would be sorely upset with me if I did. That is not the way we talk in our culture. If someone calls me a Wookie I just nod and smile, but I would never call them back. I just let them know I am joking and that usually works.
>
> Jen agrees: You can say bad things about the school and things, but not about other people. I know they are just teasing when they do it, but I cannot bring myself to do the same. It is just not in me. This can be hard to do sometimes, and sometimes I think they think we Asians are stuck up or goody-goody or something. Oh well, that is just how it will have to be, I guess.

Reflecting and Synthesizing

There are a number of qualitative research methods that draw heavily on reflection and synthesis. For example, reflection is a critical part of any action research study. It is built into the very fabric of the method—identify actions, implement, reflect and evaluate, and then modify and apply.

We can see the importance of reflection and synthesis in the Nind study. Prior to the actual data collection and gathering of findings, Nind worked with the teachers and assistants. Through the use of observation and discussion, the team was able to come up with a vision of where they wanted to go:

> The combination of observation, reading and heightened awareness of the issues centred on two key discussion-points: What would an optimum communication/language learning environment be like and how did the EYU match up?

We dedicated one of our sessions to combining our knowledge about optimum communication learning environments in infancy and in early-years settings. This was a pleasurable shared task that helped us to create a picture of what we wanted to work towards.

Nind and her team then generated the following set of optimal conditions:

Our ideal model was characterised by the following,

- Play that is child-initiated, mutually pleasurable and has familiar routines based on joint attention and turn-taking. Play that involves props to aid understanding, and adults modeling, guiding, questioning, reminding.
- Opportunities for children to talk to adults, peers, small and large groups and to use different types of communication.
- Adult speech characterised by a conversation-eliciting style (Ogilvy et al. 1992): speech that is slower than adult-adult speech, with simple sentence construction and vocabulary. Frequent open questions, with rising intonation and expectant pause. Lots of repetition, melodic intonation, exaggerated pitch and rhythm, and dialogue about activities, feelings, surroundings, and most importantly, the child's or a joint focus of interest.
- An interactive style that is relaxed and child oriented, responsive rather than directive, sensitive to possible initiations and intentions and well matched with the child's developmental level, learning style and interests. Use of eye contact, physical positioning, body language, facial expression, touch, and children's names to gain and hold their attention. Providing thinking time and giving positive responses whether or not answers are 'correct'. Attempting to use children's first language and checking their understanding, tuning in to individuals' idiosyncratic communications.

After implementation of these approaches, Nind returned to see how things had changed:

After a term of action I returned to ask what had changed in the EYU, and the following was reported.

- More opportunities had been created for small group work, e.g., smaller circle times, smaller group outings, more use of the small quiet room.
- All classes were using child-led 'show and tell'/sharing time sessions.
- Practical things had been done to eliminate the need for lots of interruptions and basic communications of needs for equipment (they had ordered more sticky tape).
- They were more likely to engage in a conscious process of decision-making when there were competing demands; sometimes they prioritised the quality of the communication over other needs.
- They had carried out observations of adult-child dialogue.

While these findings were important, Nind built upon them with a series of reflections and actions that are highly appropriate in action research settings. Some of the major reflections and modifications were:

All staff enthused about the greater effectiveness of the smaller groups where the less communicative children were now talking. This had an accumulative effect in encouraging staff to seek more opportunities for this.

On a less positive note, staff were still frustrated by how much conversation was getting interrupted as they played multiple, simultaneous roles (conversation partner, rule negotiator, keeping children on track, supplying equipment needs).

The child-led 'show and tell'/sharing time sessions were also felt to have led to much more child language in the base-room sessions. Staff reported that children with English as a second language were taking turns in this and using all kinds of communication strategies to get their meaning across.

As the project came to an official close, Nind continued to emphasize the importance of process and continual reflection and synthesis, as shown in these final observations:

> Leading on from the observed session, in our final session together we discussed some complex issues, without necessarily finding the answers. Firstly, how does the set rule structure help and how does it hinder? Does it mean that staff can speak less as the children are managing the activity for themselves— or do teachers have to intervene to enforce the rules? Secondly, are toys from home the best stimulus? They lead to a good deal of animation and interest, but they lead into demonstrations, holding and doing more than talking and explaining. Would this be the case with all objects? Thirdly, what balance is needed between practice and challenge? Do the children need to ask the much used questions such as 'where did you get it from?' over and over before they gain the confidence to try new questions. And once again, what is the adult's role in the sessions?
>
> In some ways it is important that we did not have all the answers to all these questions. This helped to keep everyone involved—in some ways equally—all and none of us were experts. We had our original compass, or good practice model as our anchor and we had our observations and our dialogue as our tools.

Taking Stock

When we look at the O'Boyle study, on the surface it appears to be an evaluative look at the history and change of a History department in an Irish school. Upon more careful examination, however, it becomes a chronicle of a number of facets and factors and issues that have all come together to impact the formation, evolution, and nature of this department. Furthermore, we can learn things from such analyses that we can apply to our own situations and circumstances.

Here, we will only look at one part of the results of this study—an examination of how the members of this department see themselves, and the various factors that need to be pulled together to understand this sense of personal and collective identity. That is, in order to take stock of the various complex threads in this issue of identity, the researcher has to examine each issue one at a time.

The first thread of identity is essentially anthropological:

This researcher and four other history teachers, Martin, Nick, Breda and Jerry (pseudonyms are used throughout), belong to a group of Senior staff, who call themselves the Oldies. The Oldies perceive themselves as committed 'professionals' (Mac an Ghail, 1992) and as 'activists' (Baldridge, 1971). They are the 'political wing' of the staffroom. . . . Though middle managers, Oldies do not identify with the role of 'officials' (Baldridge, 1971), but engage in ongoing cynicism and analysis of school decision-making.

A married couple, Jack and Liza, occupy the 'Smokers' Corner', a group which shares many ideological interests with the Oldies, but differs from them in micropolitical orientation. Their dominant perspective is one of pragmatism and a public facade of detachment, apparent in their unwillingness to discuss management issues, or participate in open decision-making.

Elsa, as a member of the 'Music Group' is one of four teachers who meet occasionally in the staffroom. They are deeply involved in the school musical, are 'entrepreneurial' (Mac and Ghail, 1992) in their professional approach, contribute to staff meetings and support school policies. Unlike the Oldies, whose loyalties are to the institution, this group view the Principal as the visible embodiment of the institution and see school management as a collective responsibility.

It is as if there were three different tribes in the History department, with each tribe moving in its own direction and addressing its own needs. As the researcher continues to explore these dimensions of identity, various aspects emerge that need to be brought together and reconciled in order to tell the whole story. Early experiences appear to play a key role:

The development of their identities as History teachers began in early childhood, where the family, the community and by extension the school were powerful influences in their introduction to and affection for History.

The History teachers believe that background and family experiences were possibly more influential than school in their pursuit of History at tertiary level.

Male primary school teachers gave History an ideological and revolutionary perspective that reflected popular educational thinking at a time when the 'national question' dominated Irish politics, and an event such as the 1916 rising (which laid the foundations for Irish independence from the United Kingdom) was celebrated as a great national triumph.

There are a number of other dimensions that differentiate identities within this department. An important one is age:

The biographies of Martin and Jerry, two of the oldest teachers at St. Colman's, reveal initial career satisfaction, punctuated by critical incidents and career disappointments.

Martin believes that his leadership role at St. Colman's, his political activism and History teaching over thirty years embodied his personal identity and professional fulfillment as a teacher. . . . His perceived diminution in status has reaffirmed the importance of the classroom as a means of professional fulfillment and a relief from the frustrations of his role.

Jerry has much in common with Martin. He came to St. Colman's in 1971 as an experienced teacher who wished to return to his own community to live and work. In teaching English and History, he endeavored to make them into living subjects through drama, visits to historic sites, and participation in local history projects. . . . His role and identity have changed over time. Though he adjusted his pedagogical style to meet changing education priorities, junior colleagues in the English and History departments replaced him at senior level, and his qualifications as remedial teacher are not utilised.

The experiences of younger teachers are much different:

For younger History teachers, the establishment of identity has been a differ-ent process. By the 1970s, free education had dramatically increased intake into third-level colleges and created a competitive academic environment. In contrast to their older colleagues, the social development of younger teachers was subordinated to the need to achieve honours degrees and compete in a contracting economic and jobs market. . . . However, by the 1980s, financial cutbacks by the government reduced the numbers in teacher-training courses, and teaching became a competitive profession to get into.

While Nick and Breda came straight from college, Jack, Liza and Elsa started as temporary teachers in other schools. When appointed, they were among the last staff at St. Colman's to get permanent positions.

Another important dimension is teaching area. Some areas appear to be much more important than others:

While the demands of family life have constrained Liza's and Breda's careers, an analysis of their career paths suggests that they are in search of identities that will confer status and a realisation of self-image. As graduates from Reli-gious Education Training College, they are employed primarily as catechists (teachers of Religious Education in Roman Catholic schools). They are not happy with their contracted identities as catechists, as Religious Education is not providing the career fulfillment and status that these teachers need. . . . A compulsory subject, it is firmly embedded in the philosophy of the school, but lacks external legitimisation (Reid, 1984), in that it is not an examinable subject in the national curriculum.

The low status of Religious Education has led catechists to reassess their career options within the school and Liza and Breda have sought institutional recognition as Senior History teachers.

Jack, Liza's husband, teaches Senior Religion and Junior History. He would prefer more History classes, but is content with his present status. Jack differs from his male History colleagues in that History does not foster any political interest or involvement. His identity is tied up with soccer at school and at national level.

Unlike the catechists, Nick and Elsa have well-established identities within the school. Music permeates Elsa's personal life and perspective on her teach-ing subjects. Music is the smallest department in the school, yet it holds an elite status, appealing to predominately middle-class female pupils.

Political orientation is another key factor in this attempt to synthesize a picture of identity:

> As with Elsa, Nick's socialisation and ideological and subject orientation bring a particular micropolitical perspective to his workplace. . . . Like other Oldies, he believes 'activism' is a measure of a teacher's commitment. His trade union role gives him a strong staffroom profile but he resents being branded as negative by colleagues in other groups.
>
> This political approach contrasts with that of his wife, Breda, whose ideological views on traditional teaching and discipline led to confrontations with management and a sense of victimisation at the hands of 'coercive power' (Johnson & Short, 1998). In interviews and in staffroom conversations, she constantly emphasises the career advantages of playing the game and survival at work (Blase, 1988, 1989) through practicing avoidance techniques and self-reliance; an attitude Fullan & Hargreaves (1991) see as symptomatic of a culture of individualism. However, despite her attempts at maintaining a situated identity, Breda's essential self re-emerges periodically, sustaining a cycle of confrontation and retreat.

O'Boyle then summarizes the view of these History teachers on History itself:

> History teachers in this study do not see themselves as historians, but as subject teachers, who try to promote a love of history as well as delivering the curriculum. . . . However, for most of them, history is more than just a textbook experience, but involves related pursuits that utilise their historical skills and training.

Finally, after this long and complex introduction, O'Boyle finishes with actual quotes from some of the teachers that illustrate these points. He provides two quotes from Nick:

> History drew me into politics. It gives you a very different view of things. One wouldn't be biased, but History helps you to see the waffle of politics. You look at the twenties and the foundation of the state, the role of De Valera—it helps you see things more critically.
>
> We have so many different personalities; but we are willing to speak our minds on a lot of topics. In History you are looking at cause and effect; you are picking out reality from propaganda. You take nothing at face value; you are likely to discuss it and look at the alternative. A History teacher has to be questioning and that translates into your normal view of things.

Breda offers her perspective:

> I would say they are people who seek the truth. . . . History is asking questions. People outside interpret their quest for information and all that as maybe conspiratorial . . . Teachers here with a History background . . . I see similar characteristics in your thinking and approach, your lack of fear, taking risks.

Martin then contributes the following two reflections:

> A lot of people have scant knowledge of History. Once they find out you are a History teacher they expect you to fill in the gaps. It puts you in a very comfortable position, if you can explain to people the origin of a current problem.
>
> I think history teachers are more serious-minded, more thoughtful, more critical . . . solid . . . have a great deal of commitment outside of school in politics, Third World issues and social action.

By weaving together these diverse threads, O'Boyle has come up with a complex pattern that accounts for many of the differences and tensions that are found within this department. This allows the researcher to continue to explore issues of the craft of teaching and the impact of change over the years.

Our Emerging Literacy Orientation

Research questions are always empirical questions. An empirical question is a question that can only be answered in the world of experience. No matter how certain we may be of the answer beforehand, and no matter how plausible our explanations and expectations are before the fact, we still must wait for the world of experience to give us our answers. And, more often than not, those answers surprise us.

Qualitative research thrives on research questions that lead us out of unclear and puzzling situations into new and often unexpected directions. Qualitative researchers believe that the world is full of meanings that are waiting to be discerned, and that the world of experience is a generous place. More often than not, qualitative researchers get more answers and more meaning than they ever could have imagined.

Results in qualitative research should be fresh, new, and insightful. Bad quantitative research is often done incorrectly. Bad qualitative research, on the other hand, is usually not good. Bad qualitative research tends to be too timid, too pat, and too predictable. All the research results in this chapter are based on researchers looking out, taking a chance, and striving to go down rarely traveled paths.

Practice Makes Perfect

It is now time to practice some of the insights and skills you have explored in this chapter:

- First of all, there are two qualitative training articles and two qualitative real articles whose results have not been examined. Try your hand at laying out the results, using the examples in this chapter as your guide. Compare your efforts with those of your classmates.
- If none of your personally selected primary articles are qualitative, find at least one qualitative article in a field of your interest. Can you follow the results more clearly now? What are some of your remaining problems? How might you address them? Compare your efforts with those of your classmates.

Quantitative Findings and Results

The heart of any quantitative research study is its findings and results. More often than not, however, this part of the study is the most intimidating for readers who are trying to build their research literacy skills. There are several good reasons for readers not to fear the findings and results.

First of all, in a well-done quantitative study the findings and results flow right from the questions, arguments, and methods. Most of the findings and results are answers to questions that have already been stated and are merely being put to the test.

Second, the complex statistical procedures or sophisticated theoretical frameworks that often accompany findings and results are usually based on simple ideas that can be clearly related to the questions being tested or addressed. This will be demonstrated over and over again in the remainder of this chapter.

Finally, the findings and results often add an element of surprise and intrigue to the research. It is not at all unusual for researchers to not get exactly what they expect in the way of findings and results. This merely means that the researchers did not anticipate every aspect or nuance of the situation beforehand. Good researchers are delighted with findings that require some thought, because more often than not these sorts of findings can lead to entirely new directions for research.

What is the difference between a "finding" and a "result"? In actuality, nothing. There are a few conventions that can make it easier to sort through various ways of handling and presenting data, however. In this chapter "Results" will be used to describe the answers to various forms of statistical tests.

When we looked at basic statistical literacy, we saw that there were four basic directions for statistical decision making. As we look at the findings of our quantitative articles, we find that each of these basic directions has been employed. We will look at an example of each of these four in turn.

Understanding Descriptive Data

We depend upon descriptive data in those settings where we cannot control the ways and situations that determine how the data are created. A good example of this is the Devine-Wright et al. study.

In this piece of research, the researchers were interested in collecting information on the beliefs and attitudes of their participants. In this case, those beliefs and attitudes were not shaped or modified by the researchers. Instead of trying to change beliefs and attitudes, the researchers instead tried to see if different groups held different beliefs and attitudes. Comparing these differences across these groups served as the heart of this research effort.

The researchers displayed their findings by using two tables. We will look at each table in turn.

Table 10.1 summarizes difference between Woodcraft Folk children and the comparison group of children. Five questions were raised, and response totals and percentages were tabulated for each of the two groups of participants.

Table 10.1 Descriptive statistical data for Woodcraft Folk children and the comparative sample describing responses to questions concerning global warming and energy

'How convinced are you that the earth's weather patterns are changing?'

	Not at all convinced	Not very convinced	Fairly convinced	Very convinced	Don't know	Total
Woodcraft Folk children	2 (2.5%)	2 (2.5%)	32 (40%)	33 (41.3%)	11 (13.8%)	80 (2 missing cases)
Comparison sample	3 (5.1%)	7 (11.9%)	29 (49.2%)	7 (11.9%)	13 (22%)	59

'How much of a contribution can you make to reduce the effects of global warming?'

	Not at all	Very little	A little	A lot	Don't know	Total
Woodcraft Folk children	1 (1.5%)	12 (17.6%)	27 (39.7%)	26 (38.2%)	2 (2.9%)	68 (10 missing cases)
Comparison sample	5 (8.9%)	10 (17.9%)	24 (42.9%)	7 (12.5%)	10 (17.9%)	56

'Where did you hear about these issues—friends, family and school?'

	Friends		Family		School	
	Yes	No	Yes	No	Yes	No
Woodcraft Folk children	30 (38.5%)	48 (61.5%)	57 (73.1%)	21 (26.9%)	60 (76.9%)	18 (23.1%)
Comparison sample	11 (19.6%)	45 (80.4%)	33 (58.9%)	23 (41.1%)	52 (92.9%)	4 (7.1%)

'Do you yourself feel a sense of responsibility for conserving energy?'

	Yes	No	Don't know	Total
Woodcraft Folk children	52 (69.3%)	18 (24%)	5 (6.7%)	75 (mv = 3)
Comparison sample	24 (46.2%)	11 (21.2%)	17 (32.7%)	52 (mv = 4)

'Do you yourself feel a sense of responsibility for using renewable energy?'

	Yes	No	Don't know	Total
Woodcraft Folk children	41 (56.9%)	23 (31.9%)	8 (11.1%)	72 (mv = 6)
Comparison sample	19 (33.9%)	19 (33.9%)	18 (32.1%)	56

Table 1 in the article "Situational Influences upon Children's Beliefs about Global Warming and Energy" in Appendix A

The first thing we need to do is to examine this table visually. How do the responses of these two groups of children differ, from question to question? Where are the striking differences? For instance, on the last two questions about responsibility for conserving energy and using renewable energy, the comparison sample were much less sure of their answers, as a group, than the Woodcraft Folk children. This is because almost a third of them answered "Don't Know" to these questions.

The researchers went on to test whether or not these differences were significant. As they state:

> A range of statistical tests were conducted upon the data to examine differences between Woodcraft Folk children and the comparative sample. Descriptive statistics for questions in this section are given in Table (10.1). Cross-tabular statistical analysis, using the chi-squared method, revealed a significant difference between the two sample groups ($X^2 = 17.42$ on 4 df, $p = 0.002$) concerning beliefs that earth's climate is changing.

Let us take a look at the chi-squared test so that we can interpret it properly. Remember that the chi-squared test is designed to determine whether observed differences are significantly different from expected differences. That is, are there specific and major differences that "leap out" from our tables, and get our attention? And, if those differences are present, are they real or merely apparent?

Chi-squared (X^2) is a decision-making tool based on probability. The smaller the chi-squared value, the more likely there are no real differences in our data. In the case of this chi-squared, the question is this—are there any likely differences in the patterns of response in Table 10.1? How sure are we that any differences we find are true, and not just an unlikely case that our sampling has picked up some extreme cases that have skewed our data?

The answer to the significance question is based on two sub-questions. First of all, just how different are the scores from what we might expect? And second, what are the odds that these differences are merely based on sampling quirks, and there are no real differences after all?

To get an answer to the first sub-question, we compute our actual chi-squared value. The larger this value, the more likely it is that the differences are significant. The closer the value is to zero, the more likely it is that the table is giving us the results we would expect to get if there were no overall differences anywhere. In this case, the chi-squared value is 17.42. This is a large value, but is it large enough?

The first thing we need to take into account in our evaluation of the chi-squared value is the number of comparisons that it makes. In this case, we are making five comparisons (since there are five questions) across two groups of children. As you might expect, the more comparisons you make, the more chance you have for random variations to cancel each other out. This factor is represented by the number called df, which stands for "degrees of freedom." We will talk about degrees of freedom much more extensively when we get to hypothesis testing. For now, we will say that the degrees of freedom involved in a chi-squared test is the product of each comparison type minus one. So, since there are five questions, the degrees of freedom for questions is $(5 - 1)$, or 4. Likewise, since there are two groups of children, the degrees of freedom for children is $(2 - 1)$ or 1. When we multiply 4 by 1, we get 4, which is the total degrees of freedom for this particular set of data.

Once we get the actual chi-squared value and the total degrees of freedom, we can then determine the probability that any apparently significant differences are merely a matter of chance. While there are specific probability equations that can be computed, most of the time we rely on precomputed tables of results. These tables give us the minimum values for each degree of freedom for a significant result at a given probability level. These researchers probably did their chi-squared analysis on a computer, which also went ahead and calculated the exact probability that these differences are not significant. In this case, they found that $p = 0.002$. This means that the odds that these results are not significantly different from what we might expect are 2/1000, or 500 to 1. That is, there is a 99+% chance that this chi-squared value is significant.

Once they have an overall difference, Devine-Wright et al. go on to look at more specific comparisons. Looking closer at the data in Table 10.1, they find:

> Cross-tabular analysis, using a chi-squared test, indicated significant differences between the two sample groups for friends ($X^2 = 5.44$ on 1 df, $p = 0.02$) and school (chi-squared = 5.25 on 1 df, $p = 0.022$) as a source of information about global warming, with statistics for family ($X^2 = 2.96$ on 1 df, $p = 0.085$) approaching statistical significance.

From these results, we come to find out specific comparisons are significant. When we look at the actual numbers in Table 10.1, we can figure out that the Woodcraft Folk children get more information on global warming from friends and family than the comparison group. The researchers go on to conduct six more chi-squared analyses on the data in Table 10.1, but there is nothing new for us to learn from these, methods wise. Suffice to say, however, that we ought to be somewhat concerned that they keep going back to the same set of numbers to make probability tests. Are they running a risk of doing so many tests on the same data that they might accidentally find a result that is merely a probability quirk? We must link our use of statistical tests with good old-fashioned common sense.

The second part of the analysis is based on Table 10.2. Table 10.2 looks at comparisons of attitudes between Woodcraft Folk parents and children.

Table 10.2 Descriptive statistical data for Woodcraft Folk children and adults concerning conviction and self-efficacy beliefs about global warming

'How convinced are you that the earth's weather patterns are changing?'

	Not very convinced	Fairly convinced	Very convinced	Don't know	Total
Woodcraft Folk children	2 (2.5%)	32 (40%)1	33 (41.3%)	11 (13.8%)	78
Woodcraft Folk adults	1 (1.8%)	24 (42.1%)	32 (56.1%)	0	57

'How much of a contribution can you make to reduce the effects of global warming?'

	Not at all	Very little	A little	A lot	Don't know	Total
Woodcraft Folk children	1 (1.5%)	12 (17.6%)	27 (39.7%)	26 (38.2%)	2 (2.9%)	68 (mv=10)
Woodcraft Folk adults	2 (3.6%)	4 (7.3%)	46 (83.6%)	3 (5.5%)	0	55 (mv=2)

Table 2 in the article "Situational Influences upon Children's Beliefs about Global Warming and Energy" in Appendix A

The analysis of the data in Table 10.2 is quite similar to the earlier data analysis:

> Finally, analysis revealed significant differences in the levels of perceived self-efficacy held by Woodcraft folk adults and children (chi-squared = 28.46 on 4 *df*, *p* = 0.001) with the descriptive statistics summarised in Table (10.2). The adults, who displayed higher levels of awareness and concern than the Woodcraft Folk children, who in turn tended to be higher than the comparative sample, had significantly lower levels of perceived self-efficacy, in comparison with the Woodcraft Folk children, in responding to global warming. Against expectation, the Woodcraft Folk children were significantly more likely to estimate a greater personal contribution towards reducing the effects of global warming in comparison with the Woodcraft Folk adults.

There are some concerns in the actual reporting of data here. Some of the comparisons, particularly in regard to Table 10.2, appear to be made across both Tables 10.1 and 10.2. Also, the last claim of significance was not actually tested, or else the resultant chi-squared value was not reported.

Overall, this article is a good illustration of the use of descriptive data and their analyses. Note that the data were presented in categories, and so the question of category frequency became the measure for looking for significant differences. In the remaining examples in this chapter, the nature of the data allow for more powerful statistical tests and comparisons.

Examining Patterns of Relationships

Williams and Clark were interested in looking at how students rated the importance of various aspects of multiple-choice exam items, and how those ratings compared to their actual exam grades. Table 10.3 lays the three variables that are being compared. The first column tabulates the average rating of each ranking item, on a three-point scale. Each item is also ranked. The second column is impact status, which is defined as the number of times the rating item was mentioned as a major contributor. The ranking value of that impact status is given in parentheses. Finally, the third column is the correlation of the rating item with actual performance on the unit exams.

When we look at the average ratings, we see that they range from 1.97 to 2.84 on a three-point scale. Five of the 12 items are rated at 2.50 or above:

> On the 1-3 scale, students assigned relatively high composite ratings across the units for their level of class attendance (2.84), note taking (2.69) and reading (2.53). They assigned their lowest rating to clarity of wording on exams (1.97). All other items received intermediate-level ratings, ranging from 2.21 to 2.51.

Next, the authors combined all items on each subscale to create composite ratings for student effort, student ability, and teacher input. The researchers refer to Table 2, but all that this table does is to confirm consistency of ratings across exams, and so we will not need to look at it in any detail:

Table 10.3 Student responses to exam-rating items

Item type	Average rating[a]	Impact status[b]	Exam r[c]
Effort items (n = 170)			
Amount of time spent studying for the exam	2.21 (11)d	269 (1)	0.03
Level of reading	2.53 (3)	235 (3)	0.16*
Level of notetaking	2.69 (2)	211 (4)	0.13
Level of class attendance	2.84 (1)	256 (2)	−0.02
Ability items (n = 170)			
Ability to take unit exams	2.25 (10)	126 (8)	0.37**
Ability to master unit subject matter	2.48 (6)	73 (11)	0.29**
Teacher-input items (n = 170)			
Clarity of instructor presentations	2.50 (5)	130 (7)	0.18*
Match between instructor presentations and exam content	2.51 (4)	147 (6)	0.28**
Match between study questions and exam content	2.48 (6)	168 (5)	0.41**
Balance between reading and class content on exams	2.41 (9)	89 (10)	0.19*
Clarity of wording on the exam	1.97 (12)	111 (9)	0.30**
Exam emphasis on higher order thinking	2.45 (8)	54 (12)	0.06

[a] Average item ratings across all units could range from 1 to 3.
[b] Impact status = the number of times each item was selected as a major contributor to unit exam performance across all units.
[c] Exam r = correlation between item rating and composite performance on unit exams.
[d] Numbers in parentheses = rankings of exam ratings and impact status.
* $p < .05$. ** $p < .01$.

Table 1 in the article "College Students' Ratings of Student Effort, Student Ability and Teacher Input As Correlates of Student Performance on Multiple-Choice Exams" in Appendix B

The composite ratings across exams were 2.57 for student effort, 2.35 for student ability, and 2.38 for teacher input. Independent samples t-tests revealed that composite teacher input and student ability ratings did not differ significantly, although both were significantly ($p < 0.001$) lower than the student effort ratings.

The students seem to feel that effort is the most important, then ability, and then teacher input in determining how they will fare on the exams. A look at the data in Table 10.4 tells a different story, however. Only one of the four effort items correlates significantly with exam performance, while both of the ability items and five of the six teacher input items correlate significantly with their exam performance.

This same pattern is repeated when the items are ranked:

The student effort items were the most frequently identified contributors (rankings of 1-4), whereas the student ability (rankings of 8 and 11) and teacher

Table 10.4   Correlations between exam ratings and exam performance across units

Rating scales	Exam A (n = 273)	Exam B (n = 245)	Exam C (n = 248)	Exam D (n = 244)	Exam E (n = 250)	Composite (n = 170)[a]
Student effort	0.10	0.26***	0.29***	0.16**	0.13*	0.16*
Student ability	0.37***	0.39***	0.36***	0.31***	0.43***	0.41***
Teacher input	0.29***	0.43***	0.30***	0.34***	0.26***	0.34***

[a] The number of students who took the exam and did the exam ratings varied from unit to unit. The n for the Composite category represents only those students who took all five exams and did the ratings for all five exams.

* p < .05. **p < .01.***p < .001.

Table 3 in the article "College Students' Ratings of Student Effort, Student Ability and Teacher Input As Correlates of Student Performance on Multiple-Choice Exams" in Appendix B

input items (rankings of 5, 6, 7, 9, 10 and 12) were identified less frequently as major contributors. Students identified amount of time spent studying for the exam as the number one contributor to their exam performance, but rated the magnitude of their exam study 11th in comparison to the rating of other items.

In Table 10.4, in the final column, we find our key correlational data for this study. Here we have the correlations between exam performance and student effort, student ability, and teacher input.

Williams and Clark go on to spell out these major findings:

> The correlations between composite exam ratings and composite exam scores across all units were 0.16 for student effort ($p < 0.05$), 0.41 ($p < 0.01$) for student ability and 0.34 for teacher input ($p < 0.001$). As previously indicated in Table (10.4), student ratings on only one student effort item (level of reading) significantly correlated with composite exam performance, whereas both ability items and all but one of the teacher input items correlated significantly with exam performance.

It is ironic that students tend to rate their own efforts as being important in terms of exam performance, and yet those efforts do not correlate well with their actual performance. On the other hand, ability factors and teacher input efforts were not rated to be nearly as important, and both of them correlate much higher with actual exam performance. It is as if the students had gotten things exactly opposite.

Could these unusual results be attributed to a split between perceptions of high performing and low performing students? Table 10.5 showed a difference in ratings between high performers and low performers on ratings of student ability and teacher input factors, with the high performers rating those two areas both higher. Regarding student effort, however, there were no differences.

Table 10.5 Exam-rating means for high and low performers on unit exams

Performance level	Exam A	Exam B	Exam C	Exam D	Exam E	Composite
Means for student-effort ratings per exam						
High performers	2.65 (55)	2.58 (53)	2.67 (51)	2.58 (55)	2.60 (54)	2.62 (47)[a]
Sig. level[b]	ns	0.05	0.01	ns	0.01	ns
Low performers	2.51 (46)	2.38 (34)	2.38 (41)	2.55 (35)	2.33 (40)	2.50 (17)
Means for student-ability ratings per exam						
High performers	2.59 (56)	2.64 (53)	2.59 (52)	2.65 (55)	2.59 (54)	2.59 (47)
Sig. level	0.001	0.001	0.001	0.001	0.001	0.001
Low performers	2.26 (46)	2.06 (35)	2.10 (42)	2.06 (36)	1.93 (41)	2.15 (15)
Means for teacher-input ratings per exam						
High performers	2.57 (56)	2.56 (53)	2.51 (52)	2.49 (55)	2.39 (54)	2.51 (47)
Sig. level	0.001	0.001	0.01	0.001	0.001	0.01
Low performers	2.33 (46)	2.17 (35)	2.29 (42)	2.19 (36)	2.09 (40)	2.30 (15)

Notes: Numbers in parentheses following means represent ns for the various cells in the table. Slight discrepancies in the ns across the three rating categories are attributable to items omitted in the ratings of a few participants.

[a] The ns for the composite exams are lower than for the individual exams, because only those participants who took all five exams and did the ratings for all five exams were included in the composite analyses.

[b] Sig. level represents significance level for differences between the ratings of the high and low performers for each unit exam in each rating area. For example, the means for the high and low performers' ratings of student effort were not significantly (ns) different for the Exam A. Independent samples t tests were used in computing the significant differences.

Table 4 in the article "College Students' Ratings of Student Effort, Student Ability and Teacher Input As Correlates of Student Performance on Multiple-Choice Exams" in Appendix B

This study is a good example of why investigating relationships among variables is often not just enough. These are indeed puzzling findings, and it is important to discover and uncover these sorts of things. At the same time, it is equally important to try to get to why these things are the way they are. That is where hypothesis testing comes in.

Testing a Simple Hypothesis

Many research studies, particularly if they are quantitative, are not in the business of exploring and organizing data. Instead, they have been designed and conducted to answer certain questions. In these situations, the results must be grounded in those same questions.

Again, this is best illustrated by going right to the heart of the matter. Consider the training article by Miro. In her study, she was interested in whether high protein snacks were better (over either high carbohydrate or fruit snacks) for enhancing performance of high school students in afternoon math courses. She defines "better performance" in terms of higher quiz grades.

Sometimes, it is easier to see what is being tested and what is not being tested by putting the research claims into simple equation form. Here are Miro's claims:

Protein > Carbohydrate

Protein > Fruit

Notice that there is nothing explicitly said about comparing carbohydrate snacks and fruit snacks. This is because Miro does not really care about these comparisons. All she really wants to do is to show that protein snacks are superior to the other two types of snacks.

Miro begins the proof process by taking a look at the descriptive statistics for quiz grades under all three snack conditions. These results are found in Table 10.6.

Table 10.6 Means and Standard Deviations for Quiz Grades for Each Snack Condition

Variable	mean	sd
Fruit	3.27	0.94
Carbs	4.67	1.12
Protein	6.90	1.16

N = 30

Table 1 in the article "The Effects of High Protein Snacks on Quiz Grades in Afternoon High School Math Classes" in Appendix C

These data have been collected from a total of 30 students, with 10 students in each of the conditions. First of all, it looks like Miro's claim is holding up so far. By comparing the means, it looks as if the protein snack group was averaging a quiz score of somewhere around 7 out of 10, as compared to roughly 5 out of 10 for the carbohydrate group and 3 out of 10 for the fruit group. However, Miro is far from having a convincing case as yet.

If Miro had many more than 10 students per group, and the members of each group got exactly the same score on the quiz, then there would hardly be any need to press on with the analysis. The results would be obvious. But neither situation is the case here. Look at the range you can expect for the typical quiz scores for each group:

Protein: 5.74 to 8.06
Carbohydrates: 3.55 to 5.79
Fruit: 2.33 to 4.21

In this case, you can see that there is quite a bit of overlap in these ranges. Even if there were no overlap, the fact that the sample sizes are fairly small would require you to get a more precise picture of what is going on here.

To do that, Miro performed an analysis of variance, or ANOVA for short. This statistical test allowed her to compare all three conditions to each other at the same time. The results are laid out in Table 10.7.

Table 10.7 ANOVA Results

Group	SS	df	MS	F	Significance
Between Groups	201.49	2	100.74	86.58	$p < .01$
Within Groups	101.23	87	1.16		
Total	302.72	89			

Table 2 in the article "The Effects of High Protein Snacks on Quiz Grades in Afternoon High School Math Classes" in Appendix C

This table consists of six columns. Each column tells an important story about the analysis.

Group

This column lays out the sources of variance. Obviously, there is some "Total" amount of variation. This is the variance associated with all 30 participants as a single distribution, regardless of what group they belong to. But how is this variance parceled out? If you think about it, there are really only two other sources of variation.

First of all, there is the variation within each of the three groups. Each of the three groups has a mean and a range of scores. If there were no variation within the group, each score would be the same. But they are not. Since every person in the group received the same conditions, then this variance has nothing to do with the treatment. Instead, it is a reflection of the natural variation you would expect to find in any group. This variance is called "Within Groups" variance.

The last source of variance is the variance between the groups. This variance is directly tied to the treatments. It is the evidence that there are real differences among the groups. This is called the "Between Groups" variance.

If you think about it, you can see that Between Groups variance and Within Groups variance have nothing to do with each other, and so they are independent sources of variance. Therefore, you can add them together to get the Total variance. This is a good little test to see if your computations are correct.

SS

SS is shorthand for "sum of squares." Sums of squares are the actual numerical values that the variances are based upon. They are simply the measure of differences of each score from its relevant mean. Since these totals are always zero because of the balance of scores above and below the mean, then the squares of these differences are used.

For the Total condition, the sum of squares is the sum of the squared differences between each score and the mean for the entire distribution. For the Within

Groups condition, it is the sum of the squared differences between each score in its treatment group and that group mean, taken across all groups. For the Between Groups condition, it is the sum of the squared differences between each group mean and the mean for the entire distribution. Since these sources are independent of each other, then the Between Groups SS and the Within Groups SS should add together to equal the Total SS.

df

df is shorthand for "degrees of freedom." The notion of "degrees of freedom" is actually a very profound notion; it is the reflection of the amount of potential change within any given set of data. In most cases, though, it can be found rather simply. It is one less than the target group. For the Total condition, it is one less than the total of all scores in the distribution. In this case, Total $df = (30 - 1)$ or $df = 29$. For the Within Groups condition, it is one less than the total within each group, taken across all groups. In this case, Within Groups $df = (10 - 1)$ times 3 groups, or $df = 3(10 - 1)$ or $df = 3 \times 9$ or $df = 27$. For the Between Groups condition, it is one less than the total number of groups. In this case, Between Groups $df = (3 - 1)$ or $df = 2$.

As was the case with SSs, dfs are also additive. In this case, $2 + 27 = 29$.

MS

MS is shorthand for "mean squares." The whole point of doing an ANOVA is to compare the amount of variance Between Groups to the amount of variance Within Groups.

At this point, it is time to change language in a more general direction. In this example, "Between Groups" is the specific way to talk about the more general idea of Treatment variance. This is because, in this case, the treatment is found by looking at the differences between groups. In more complicated designs, there might be more than one treatment, or the treatment might be defined in more complex terms. The basic idea of Treatment variance is still sound, however.

In this example, you looked at Within Groups variance. Since there is no systematic or explainable reason for the members within each group to differ from one another, you can consider this variance to be Error variance. Again, in more complex designs, Error variance will often be defined in complicated ways. Again, however, the basic idea will be the same.

In short, you are interested in comparing Treatment to Error. One of the best ways to do that is to create a ratio of the two. In order to have a ratio, though, you need to be able to compare terms on common ground. Consider the current example. If you tried to compare the Between Groups SS to the Within Groups SS (or, as you now know, the Treatment SS to the Error SS) directly, this would be an imbalanced comparison. The Error SS is based on 27 of the total 29 degrees of freedom, while the Treatment SS is based on only 2 of the total 29 degrees of freedom. That is, the Error SS is much larger but it addresses most of the degrees of freedom available to account for change.

To even things out, you create MSs. The MS is simply each SS divided by its associated df. This puts the two measures of variance, Treatment and Error, on the same footing and allows you to compare them directly.

F

F is the name for the ratio between the Treatment *MS* and the Error *MS*. It is called *F* in honor of Sir Ronald Fisher, one of the early pioneers of statistics in research design.

In this case, there is only one *F* ratio computed. In more complex designs, there might be a number of *F* ratios computed, to address various sorts of Treatments. No matter how complex any design might be, however, each *F* ratio is simply the ratio of one Treatment source of variance to one Error source of variance.

Significance

Finally, you have to know what a given *F* ratio means. The larger the value of *F,* the higher the ratio of Treatment to Error variance. This means that any given variance you might find would be more likely to be due to the Treatment rather than naturally occurring things that cause scores to be different from one person to the other.

Another way to look at this is to consider the *F* ratio as the answer to the following question: Is there at least one treatment condition that is different from the rest, or are they all about the same? If the *F* ratio is significant, the answer to this question is "yes." Otherwise, you cannot assume anything. You have no way of knowing why none of these conditions differed from any of the others. All you know is that nothing really was found out in this test.

How do you decide if an *F* ratio is significant or not? The simple answer to this question is to go to an *F* table. An *F* table is a series of precalculated values for the *F* ratio at critical levels of probability. As stated before, the most common critical values are $p < .05$ and $p < .01$. These are well-accepted standards in the field for levels of probability that indicate real differences. Any decent statistics book has a copy of the *F* table in it. Computer programs like SAS and SPSS will also compute the exact probability of any given *F* ratio. Notice that you also cannot assume that all the treatment conditions are different from each other. You can only assume that at least one (and maybe more) stands out from the rest.

In this case, the *F* ratio would be reported as $F(2,27) = 86.58$, $p < .01$. From an *F* table, you can see that the critical *F* ratio for 2 and 27 degrees of freedom at the level of $p < .01$ is 5.49. That is, the Treatment variance must be at least 5.49 times greater than the Error variance in order for the results to be significant with these many degrees of freedom and at the $p < .01$ level. As you can see, the actual Treatment variance is 86.58 times greater than the Error variance. Since 86.58 exceeds 5.49 (it does not matter by how much; 5.50 would work just as well), then these results are significant.

This is what you now know about the results of this study—Of the three treatment groups, namely protein snacks, carbohydrate snacks, and fruit snacks, at least one of them is different from the others. This is a step in the right direction, but Miro now has to show which (or how many) of these groups are different from each other. In fact, she only has to show that the protein group is better than the other two, but if there are other differences they are usually reported as well.

In order to determine which groups are actually different, you need to do what is called a post hoc analysis. *Post hoc* is Latin for "after the fact." There are a number of post hoc analyses and tests that can be done. The most common, especially for a simple design like this one, is to compare each mean to each of the other means.

The first step in comparing means to each other is to look at the actual differences among the means. Table 10.8 organizes these differences.

Table 10.8   Differences Among Means

Variable	Protein	Carbs	Fruit
Protein	—	1.23	2.63
Carbs	—	—	1.40

As you can see from the differences, scores in the protein snack condition seem to be higher than scores in the carbohydrate snack condition, and scores in the carbohydrate snack condition seem to be higher than scores in the fruit snack condition (it also makes sense that scores in the protein snack condition are higher than scores in the fruit snack condition, and the numbers bear that out as well).

There are a number of tests that can be used to see if these apparent differences are significant. One of the commonest and easiest to use tests for comparing means to each other is the Tukey test. This test adjusts the differences among means in terms of the amount of variation they have in common, and then these adjusted means are compared to critical values for significance in a probability table. This is a different table than the one used for determining critical values for *F* ratios.

In this case, you need to compute two critical values—one for comparing means that rank next to each other, and one for comparing means that are separated by two ranking positions. That is, you need a critical value for comparing ranks one and two and then ranks two and three, and a separate critical value for comparing ranks one and three.

When the means are ranked like these means are (from Protein to Carbohydrates to Fruit), the critical values depend on how many ranks are between any given two means. For the Protein-Carbohydrate mean comparisons and the Carbohydrate-Fruit mean comparisons there is only one rank between them (first to second and second to third); for the Protein-Fruit mean comparison there are two ranking steps between these means (first to third).

Are the differences between each pair of means significant? To find this out, you first need to create an index that you can use to adjust the difference values that you find from the table of critical difference values. This index is created by using the *MS* error (which in this case is the *MS* Within Groups) adjusted for group size. You then take the square root of this value to get your index, and you use this new value to adjust the table of variance. In this study, the square root of the *MS* error adjusted for group size is 0.1966. From a table of critical values, you find the following critical values for each comparison. For a comparison of means that rank side by side with each other, where the *MS* error has at least 60 degrees of freedom (the *MS* error in this study has 87 degrees of freedom, so it qualifies), and at a probability level of $p < .01$, the critical value is 3.76. When you are comparing means that span two ranks, as in first and third, then the critical value under the same conditions is 4.28. All you need to do is then multiply each critical value by the index for this study to get the critical differences between means for the data in this study.

When you actually compute the difference values, you find that means one and two, and means two and three, needs to be 0.74 or greater. For means one and three, that actual difference needs to be 0.94 or greater. In fact, all mean differences exceed their actual critical values. To illustrate this in an easy to read fashion, you can redo Table 10.8. Table 10.9 is the revised version of Table 10.8. Significant comparisons are now marked with an asterisk, and the necessary computational values are also listed.

Table 10.9 Revised Table of Differences Among Means

Variable	Protein	Carbs	Fruit
Protein	—	1.23*	2.63*
Carbs	—	—	1.40*

$\sqrt{(MS\ error/n)}$ = 0.1966. df = 87. *p < .01.

At this point, all the key points of the study have been tested and the results of those tests have been reported. In this training article, tables were used to present ANOVA and post hoc mean comparisons data. In nearly all cases nowadays in actual articles, these results would not be presented in table form. More often than not, only the *F* ratios and the actual comparison values would be presented. Usually (but not always) the *MS* error will be presented as well. From the *F* ratio, degrees of freedom, and the *MS* error you can compute backwards and put together tables if you wish to do that. By not using tables for ANOVA data, authors and editors can save a lot of preparation time and space.

Looking for Patterns and Making Predictions

Qualitative studies often organize and explore information. The same is true of quantitative studies that focus on description and exploration. This fact is illustrated by the training article by Chagall. Chagall is looking at the way variables might be grouped in helping to understand possible intervention strategies for youthful offenders. She starts by looking at the descriptive statistics of these variables. These statistics have been organized in Table 10.10.

Table 10.10 Means and Standard Deviations for Variables

Variable	Mean	SD
Peer Support	3.63	1.45
Missed Homework	9.33	6.42
Victim Awareness	3.97	1.50
Part Time Work	10.27	5.08
Positive Drug Testing	3.27	2.02
GPA	2.00	0.47

N = 30

Table 1 in the article "Critical Factors for Understanding Male Juvenile Offenders: Developing an Empirically Based Model" in Appendix D

Tables are a useful and economical way to display findings. They also allow the reader to look at overall patterns of findings. The table above allows you to look at a summary of her distribution of youthful offenders. The statement ($N = 30$) tells you that there are 30 youthful offenders in the study.

What does the average offender look like? That is where the means come in. From this table, you can see that the average offender has below average peer support, failed to turn in about 9 homework assignments the first semester, shows below average awareness of his impact on his victims, works about 10 hours per week, failed his drug test on 3 days over the past semester, and has a C average in school.

What is the likely range of behaviors you might expect from these offenders? Here is where you can use the standard deviation. As a rule of thumb, moving 1 standard deviation below the mean and 1 standard deviation above the mean will give you a range of what might be considered average for this distribution. When you do this for this table, you get the following ranges:

- Peer Support ranges from 1.91 to 5.08. This range runs from very low peer support to average peer support. In this case, average support is about the best you could expect to find.
- Missed Homework ranges from 2.91 to 15.75. In other words, you could expect a low of 3 missed homework assignments to a high of 15 missed assignments for the average offender.
- Victim Awareness ranges from 2.47 to 5.47. This pattern is very similar to that of peer support. You could expect anything from very low awareness to average awareness at best.
- Part Time Work ranges from 5.19 to 15.35 hours. That is, you could expect these offenders to be working, on the average, anywhere from 5 to 15 hours a week.
- Positive Drug Testing ranges from 1.25 to 5.29 positive daily tests. In other words, you could expect these offenders to test positive, over the course of a semester, anywhere from 1 to 5 times.
- GPA ranges from 1.53 to 2.47. Therefore, you might expect their grades to range from a D+ average to a C+ average.

These findings are quite interesting and informative in themselves, but Chagall wants to take the process even further. Are these variables in some way related to each other? If they are, then this can influence the ways that they are addressed in terms of intervention.

The way to explore whether or not variables are related is to correlate them with each other. In Table 10.11, Chagall correlates each variable with every other variable.

There are three things to remember about correlations in general. First of all, they are descriptive. That is, they describe possible relationships, but they do not explain them. If you want to explain *why*, for example, drug testing and homework are related, you need to do further research. But knowing that there is a possible relationship in the first place is a valuable piece of information, so correlational research can be very important.

Second, you need to realize that these correlations describe *possible* relationships. That is, a correlation is a probability statement. Correlations are indexes, and

Table 10.11 Variable Correlations

	Peer	Homework	Victim	Work	Drugs	GPA
Peer	—	–0.59*	0.14	0.05	–0.19	0.33
Homework	–0.59*	—	–0.28	–0.64*	0.59*	–0.83*
Victim	0.14	–0.28	—	0.06	0.160	.20
Work	0.05	–0.64*	0.06	—	–0.51*	0.75*
Drugs	–0.19	0.59*	0.16	–0.51*	—	0.63*
GPA	0.33	–0.83*	0.200	.75	–0.63*	—

* $p < .01$.

Table 2 in the article "Critical Factors for Understanding Male Juvenile Offenders: Developing an Empirically Based Model" in Appendix D

so they range, in absolute terms, from zero to one. A zero tells you that the probability that these variables are related are vanishingly small, and a one tells you that it is very likely indeed that they are related.

What do you do with correlations between zero and one? There are two useful things you can do. First of all, you can compare the probability of the correlation with some standard. Consider, say, a correlation of +0.60. Here you can ask a simple question: is this correlation high enough to be indicating a real relationship, or is it really no better than a correlation of zero? Nowadays, researchers usually answer this question by referring to a table of values. These tables are based on the number of cases in the sample being tested, and the standard that is being used. Two standards are the most common, and they are represented in tables and reports in the following ways:

$$p < .05$$

$$p < .01$$

The first standard says that there is a 5% likelihood that a correlation of this size (say, +0.60) is not significantly different from a correlation of zero. Otherwise, it is safe to say that there really is a relationship between these two variables. The second standard tightens that likelihood to a 1% chance of falsely reporting a significant relationship. In tables and in articles, an asterisk (*) is used to mark those correlations which match or exceed the standard being used.

The next thing you can do to help understand what a correlation might be telling you is to look at the amount of common variance between the two variables being correlated. This is an easy task to perform. All you have to do is to square the actual correlation coefficient, and that will tell you the percentage of common variance. For instance, in our example of +0.60, this correlation indicates that these two variables seem to share 36% common variance. That is, 36% of the variance in one variable can be explained by the variance patterns of the other variable.

The third key point to remember is that a correlation is a *directional index*. That is, while a correlation ranges in absolute terms from zero to one, it also ranges in directional terms from –1 to +1. You can see that zero is right in the middle between –1 and +1. As you move away from zero, in either direction, the likelihood that there is a relation increases. The nature of the relationship is different, however, depending on the direction that you move. As you move toward –1, you are describing an *inverse* relationship. That is, as one variable goes up, the other goes down and vice versa. As you move toward +1, you are describing a *direct* relationship. As one variable goes up, the other goes up, and as one variable goes down, the other goes down.

Now it is time to interpret the correlations found in Table 10.11. You can do this one variable at a time. First of all, you can eliminate all correlations that do not meet the standard of the article. This means discarding all correlations that are not marked by an asterisk (*). Then, you indicate whether or not this relationship is a direct or an inverse relationship. Finally, you can report what percentage of variance these variables share:

- *Peer Support*: As Peer Support increases, Missed Homework assignments decrease. These two variables share 35% variance in common.
- *Missed Homework*: In addition to the previously described relationship with Peer Support, there is also a direct relationship with Positive Drug Testing where they share 35% of the variance in common. There are also two more significant relationships. Higher levels of Missed Homework is related to lower hours of Work (41% common variance) and lower GPA (69% common variance).
- *Victim Awareness*: None of the other variables related to this variable.
- *Work*: There is the previously described inverse relationship with Missed Homework. In addition, as number of Work hours increase, incidents of Positive Drug Testing decrease (25% common variance), and GPA increases (56% common variance).
- *Positive Drug Testing*: In addition to a previously described direct relationship with Missed Homework and an inverse relationship with hours of Work, as incidents of Positive Drug Testing increase, GPA goes down (40% common variance).
- *GPA*: Inverse relationships to Missed Homework and Positive Drug Testing have already been described.

When you look at these findings, there seems to be a pattern to these various significant correlations. In order to try to pin down these patterns, Chagall proceeded with a factor analysis. The key assumption of factor analysis is that patterns among correlations indicate the presence of higher order relationships that encompass a number of variables together as factors. Conceptually, the idea is to try to plot these correlations as if they were points in space. In order to make sure these correlations cluster together, the axes of the variables are rotated to minimize distances between variables. The mathematical computations needed to do this are so involved and tedious that no one can really do it by hand. Therefore, all factor analyses are done by computer.

In the simplest form of factor analysis, which is the one used here, these clusters are called "principal components." Chagall performs a factor analysis on these data, which is reported in Table 10.12. Chagall was able to find two components, or factors, in these data. By convention, the first factor reported is the strongest, or the one that accounts for the most variance (this will be demonstrated in Table 10.13).

There are two principal ways to extract information from this table. First of all, there are the correlations within each component (or factor). These correlations

Table 10.12 Component Matrix

Variable	Component 1	Component 2	Communality
Peer	0.49	0.51	0.50
Homework	−0.94	−0.19	0.92
Victim	0.21	0.80	0.68
Work	0.78	−0.29	0.69
Drugs	−0.73	0.45	0.74
GPA	0.93	−0.05	0.87

Table 3 in the article "Critical Factors for Understanding Male Juvenile Offenders: Developing an Empirically Based Model" in Appendix D

are between the variable in question and the rest of the component. The higher the correlation, regardless of whether it is positive or negative, the stronger the case for including that variable when describing the component as a whole. For component 1, Homework, GPA, Work, and Drugs have the highest correlations, and so have the best case for being included. For component 2, Victim by far has the highest correlation, followed by much weaker correlations (and cases) for Peer and Drugs.

The next key piece of information is the communality of each variable. This measures the degree to which the variable "belongs" to one component or another. In this case, since there are only two components, it suggests whether the variable should be assigned to one component or the other, or neither. Homework and GPA clearly "belong" in component 1, Victim clearly "belongs" in component 2, and Peer seems split between the two.

While inclusion and belonging are often related, that need not be the case. It is possible to have a variable that ought to be included in each factor, but does not really "belong" to either. With these data, Peer is operating in this way to some degree.

Once Chagall has identified these components statistically, she needs to label them conceptually. There is no standard formula for this. It requires a certain degree of creative and intuitive thought from the researcher. Here is how Chagall labeled her factors:

> In the case of the first component, the key positive variables are GPA and part time employment, and the key negative indicators are missed homework and positive drug testing. The key dynamics here appear to be academic effort and responsible behavior, with the academic aspect being the strongest. So we can label this factor as "adopting a responsible student role" factor. This involves doing your homework, keeping your grades up, getting extra money via part time work, and staying off drugs. This is by far the most powerful factor, data wise.
>
> The second significant factor was less clear cut. Its major input was victim awareness, and there was a significant contribution from peer support (peer support was also involved in the first factor as well). So we might label this factor as "social awareness." In this case, the person is aware of the impact of negative behaviors of others, and turns to positive peer interactions for support.

Chagall has now identified, labeled, and described two key factors from her data. She goes on to justify their existence and use:

Between them, these two factors seemed to capture the major contributions of all six variables collected in this study.

This last point is supported by the data in Table 10.13.

Table 10.13 Total Variance Explained

| Component | Extraction Sums of Squares Loadings | | |
	Total	% of Variance	Cumulative %
1	3.185	3.02	53.02
2	1.212	0.20	73.22

Table 4 in the article "Critical Factors for Understanding Male Juvenile Offenders: Developing an Empirically Based Model" in Appendix D

Table 10.13 looks at the comparative usefulness of each component. First of all, totals are reported for each component. "Total" in this case is shorthand for "total sums of squares used (or extracted) in order to create each factor." These totals lay out the basic roots of the equations used to generate the best possible set of factors for the data, and they are important as sources for understanding the amount of variance actually accounted for by the factor analysis. The results that are most useful to the literate consumer, however, are found in the next two columns, where the percentage of variance that each component explains and the cumulative variances are reported. In this case, 73% of all variance is accounted for by using these two components. The first component by itself addresses over half of the variance, and the second component adds another 20%.

In summary, factor analysis is used for two main purposes. First of all, it allows the researcher to reduce a whole collection of variables into a smaller number of more abstract and comprehensive factors. In this case, there was a reduction from six variables to two factors. Then, factor analysis allows the researcher to look for structure within the data. In this case, the structures involved a major factor dealing with being a good and responsible student, and a lesser factor that dealt with being aware of social aspects of such people as victims and, to a lesser extent, peers.

Final Thoughts About Statistics and Results

At this point, we have examined four basic types of quantitative results and findings. As you read more complex articles, you will be exposed to different combinations and extensions of these ideas. For example, researchers often create complex ANOVA designs, and even conduct tests looking at more than one dependent variable at a time (these are called multivariate analyses). Simple correlations can be replaced with multiple and partial and part correlations, and specialized correlations such as point biserial correlations are sometimes used. Factor analysis models are expanded into path analysis models, structural equation models, and hierarchical linear models. And these are only the tip of the iceberg—as personal computers become more powerful, our ability to compute complex statistics at our desktops also expands.

In the face of all this growth in inferential and analytic tools, we need to remember that most of these complex designs are rooted in the simple notions of description, comparison, pattern finding, hypothesis testing, model building, and prediction. If we keep these basic ideas front and center, we should be able to understand at least the broad outlines and general directions of even the most complex sets of statistical tests.

Our Emerging Literacy Orientation

More than anything else, novice readers of educational research are uncomfortable with quantitative results and findings. How often have we skimmed through the details of the analyses and findings, only to skip to the end and see what the researchers say about them in plain English?

Research literacy depends on us being able to linger within the results, be they qualitative or quantitative. As we have seen, most of these quantitative tests are based on simple ideas. Do these treatments make a difference? Are these results what we might expect to find? Does this model address important issues, and allow us to predict what will happen? If we can keep these simple ideas in front of us, then it will be easier for us to build our technical literacy.

Technical literacy, especially in quantitative matters, is really based on practice. If we remember the simple ideas that ground these methods, then we can wade out farther and farther from shore without getting lost. Do not try to learn it all at once. It takes time to master any skill, but any content area, even something as complex as quantitative methods, will become clearer with authentic practice. If we are patient, and we allow ourselves the luxury of not understanding and going slow, then we will make progress faster than we might have imagined—going a step at a time.

Practice Makes Perfect

It is now time to practice some of the insights and skills you have explored in this chapter:

- First of all, there are two quantitative training articles and two quantitative real articles whose results have not been examined. Try your hand at laying out the results, using the examples in this chapter as your guide. Compare your efforts with those of your classmates.
- If none of your personally selected primary articles are quantitative, find at least one quantitative article in a field of your interest. Can you follow the results more clearly now? What are some of your remaining problems? How might you address them? Compare your efforts with those of your classmates.

Discussions and Conclusions

After researchers have presented their results, then one final task remains. Results have to be put into meaningful contexts.

There are a number of directions that researchers can take when they are exploring and explaining their results. Results can be summarized or compared with researcher predictions, and any and all discrepancies between predictions and reality can then be examined. Complex or unusual or unexpected results can be explained. Implications of the findings in relation to existing theories and practices can be discussed, and limitations of the current research can be examined as well to help put the findings into contexts. Directions for future research can also be mapped out. These are only some of the moves and efforts that can be made.

We will start by looking at examples of each of the four main discussion tasks in turn. It makes sense to start with the simplest—summarizing the main findings.

Summarizing

Sometimes, the most effective way to discuss findings is to simply summarize them. If the findings are clear-cut and easy to understand, then all the researchers need to do is to remind readers of what has happened. Also, if the research is ongoing, then researchers need to be careful about overstating their findings. Both of these considerations seem to be in play with the Davidson article. As an action research study, the results were presented as part of the ongoing narrative of the process. Therefore, at the end, there was little need to do more than summarize:

> Initial data indicate that the character education classes were quite successful. Attendance was high at the outset and was maintained throughout the program. Children did well on oral quizzes on the class material. Most importantly, behavior patterns began to change. Follow up data collection will be conducted to see if these behavioral changes persisted through the summer months, when the children were not in school together, and stayed in place the next school year.

At the very end of the Asimov article there is also a summary, in a fashion that is similar to the abstract at the very beginning. The purpose of this summary is to restate the key points and findings, and then point the reader toward the need and possible nature of future research:

> In summary, this study has uncovered and examined an existing enclave similar to those discussed at a theoretical level in the literature. This enclave operates outside of the existing school system, but that fact makes it no less formal or structured. In addition to its formal properties, this enclave also functions as a social entity, held together by a strong leader and guide. Further research needs to look for more of these sorts of enclaves, and to see if the principles manifested here are unique to this experience, or if they are necessary for educational endeavors such as these to survive and thrive.

Sometimes, the summary can be very detailed and explicit. For instance, Danili and Reid offer a very comprehensive set of six summary conclusions. They are, in order:

1. A relationship exists between working memory capacity and pupils' performance.
2. A relationship exists between extent of field dependency and chemistry scores.
3. It is possible to bring working memory and field dependency measures together.
4. It is postulated that the size of the available working memory space is a critical factor in success in learning chemistry at this stage.
5. Using teaching materials which were specifically designed to minimize the impact of limitations in working memory space increased pupil performance.
6. When re-designed materials were used in several topics, it was found that they enhanced pupil performance significantly and the impact of the new materials did not depend on any teacher effects.

Other times, the list of summary points can be more narrative in nature, as we find in Klein's article:

> Two factors were identified as principal contributors to the level of meeting effectiveness. One was the quality of prior planning and the manner in which the meeting was conducted. . . . The second was the balance in the session between the requirements for cooperative endeavour and the individual needs of each teacher. The interviews revealed the need for consideration at meetings of the manner of distribution of institutional tasks.
>
> Other criteria for productivity included (a) early and methodical planning of meetings; (b) avoidance of last minute notification unless urgent issues arise; (c) orderly, cultured and focused discussions in which all present listen to each other; and (d) generally accepted decision making procedures.

Explaining

Results do not interpret themselves. Sometimes, the chief purpose of a Discussion is to look at results carefully, and interpret and clarify them. This is clearly illustrated in the Cassatt article. He starts off by showing that the actual results are quite substantial from a statistical perspective:

> Simply completing a higher number of practice problems appeared to correlate highly with midterm scores. Roughly half of the variance in these data could be accounted for by this comparison. Given all the other possible sources of variation, from class and regional differences, to background and IQ differences among students, along with many other possibilities, this is a very powerful finding.

These findings however lead to questions of their own. Within the limitations of his method, Cassatt lays out three plausible explanations for his findings. Note that he does not choose among these possibilities. The unstated implication is that further empirical research needs to be conducted to see which of these possible explanations work the best when compared directly with each other:

> Why did simply completing these problems seem to be so highly related to higher midterm grades? Given that this was a correlational study, that answer cannot be directly inferred from these data and findings. There are a number of possibilities to consider. Here are just a few. First of all, it could be the case that the brightest students worked quicker, and so were able to both complete more problems and do better on the midterm. On the other hand, it could be the case that the extra practice and effort had a positive impact on student learning, which showed up on midterm scores. Finally, it could be the case that the more highly motivated students both did more practice problems and also tried harder on the midterms. Given that all of these students were talented, motivation might have been the key here.

In the Cassatt article, the researcher started from a position of testing the claims that practice might help test performance. In the Picasso study, however, there is no specific set of claims being tested. Picasso is instead looking for possible differences among valedictorians. Are there more males or females, or are they about the same? What are the career plans for valedictorians from differing sociocultural backgrounds, if any?

Once Picasso has her findings, though, they need to be interpreted as well. She starts by listing her most prominent findings:

> There appears to be solid evidence for differences in anticipated early career plans between Suburban and Inner City valedictorians, as well as more indirect evidence of gender differences among these groups, at least in relation to early career plans. Overall, very few of these valedictorians, in either group, plan to eschew further education and go directly to work. Furthermore, there are no gender differences between those who choose to work as opposed to those who are going on with more education.

Picasso goes on to look deeper into her findings, to see what they might mean:

> Sociocultural and gender differences are present, however, in terms of where and how these students will further their education. Very few Inner City males plan to go to college, especially when compared to Inner City females. Nearly equal numbers of Suburban males and females plan to go on to college. On the other hand, many more Inner City females plan to go to vocational school when compared to their Suburban counterparts.

As these findings are compared to each other, Picasso starts to argue for a bigger picture of matters. The picture for suburban students appears to be one of equality and a preponderance for moving on to college, while inner city students are less balanced along gender lines and seem much more likely to go on to vocational training. She has no data to explain these differences, so she speculates on possible causes. Such speculation by its very nature almost demands a call for more research:

An overall picture seems to be emerging. For Suburban valedictorians, there are nearly equal numbers of males and females. The vast majority of these Suburban valedictorians plan to go to college (23 out of 30). There appear to be no gender differences at all between Suburban male and female valedictorians. For Inner City valedictorians, another picture seems to be emerging. While overall gender differences were not significant, most of the Inner City valedictorians were female (22 out of 30). Unlike the Suburban valedictorians, who were almost all going to college, the Inner City valedictorians were pretty much evenly split between college and vocational school. There were no gender differences in this split. In summary, it seems that Inner City valedictorians are much more likely to go to vocational school than their Suburban counterparts. Possible reasons for this difference need to be explored. Some of these possible reasons might include the fact that Inner City students come from a more practical background, they might have less money available for college, or they might be more likely to be guided in a vocational direction by their school career counselors. The apparent lack of male Inner City valedictorians, even though this gender difference was not significant, is suggestive enough to warrant more extensive research to see if this is indeed the case.

In field research, findings are usually woven within a set of complex and interactive contexts. Researchers often give simple labels to these contextual concepts, in order to study and describe them. It then becomes one of the tasks of the Discussion section to "unpack" these contexts. The key concept in the Asimov article was the notion of "enclave." Asimov first studied and described one such enclave. In the final discussion, he then reflects upon what he has learned, and how it fits in and extends prior understanding:

> First, and most importantly, this study demonstrates that enclaves of learning, as predicted in the literature, can and do arise within poor neighborhoods and settings. On the surface, the enclave looks like an informal gathering between motivated students and a volunteer tutor. Upon closer inspection, however, its true nature is shown to be more formal and more complex. Students must pass an interview process in order to be allowed to join. Once they become members, they are expected to put in at least six hours a week into the meeting process. This does not include the extra time involved with reading and practice outside of the meetings. Given the increasing demands of school and community on these children, this is a remarkable investment of time for a project where they get no formal credit or recognition.

Once Asimov compares this example of an enclave with the general notion from the literature, he goes on to discuss the nature of this particular enclave in more depth:

> Another aspect of the formality of the enclave is the fact that it adheres to a set of operational rules. Perhaps the most important rule is the principle of a consensus of understanding. All participants understand that no point is finished unless everyone understands it. While this might appear to slow down the progress of the group, this is considered okay. The resulting cohesion is well worth the extra investment of time and energy, and besides, there is no

schedule to try to adhere to, anyway. The efforts and personality of Mr. Jerry is another key. Magda and the other children find it hard to imagine the enclave continuing under the direction of another person, and they worry about his health and vitality. Perhaps the strength of individuals such as Mr. Jerry is necessary to counter the milieu of powerlessness that characterizes the environments of the children who are involved.

Sometimes, explanations about cultural issues or areas of specialized knowledge are required to understand results. Klein offers an excellent illustration of just such a point:

> Consideration of the results of this study requires an understanding of the educational scene in Israel. Unlike administrative personnel, teachers do not spend the entire school day on the premises. A full time teacher spends 30 hours a week in elementary school classrooms, and 24 weekly hours in high schools. Teachers are required to be present only for scheduled periods of instruction and for another few hours dedicated to pupil guidance, consultations with parents, rotational staff tasks and teachers' meetings. Lessons are prepared in free time at home. From time to time, there are meetings during the late afternoon or evening. During the school year, two meetings are usually scheduled for intensive parent-teachers' meetings. These conferences are devoted to private discussions with parents of each child with regard to his or her achievement and methods of promoting progress.

Examining Implications

Another crucial dimension to the interpretation of findings is the task of determining and examining certain implications of the findings. These implications can take a variety of forms.

For instance, sometimes implications direct us to possible changes in current practices. This is well illustrated in the Danili and Reid article, as they make suggestions for changing instructional practices in secondary level chemistry:

> In light of these results, it is recommended that the design and delivery of school chemistry courses should take into account the predictions from information processing models derived from the psychology of learning and that such changes will bring about improved performance. This may involve changing the order of presentation and method of presentation. It may involve the careful use of appropriate analogy and models (remembering that not all analogies or models will bring about information reduction). It may mean a more careful linking of new material to previous knowledge and a deliberate effort in flagging up what is important and what is peripheral.
>
> If assessment is to be fair for all pupils, it should not unnecessarily penalize those who happen to have lower working memory spaces and those who tend to be field-dependent. Working memory space is fixed for an individual although there is some evidence that field dependency can be enhanced. This can be achieved by a small group of 'experts' looking at questions and assessing the

working memory demand. Again, it has to be stressed that this is not the same as difficulty. However, if assessment is to be fair, it must not require working memory capacities that favour some learners more than others.

Wyss calls for both practical and theoretical change in her list of implications. First, she lists some practical initiatives:

> First, the incidents discussed here highlight the desperate need for comprehensive, age-appropriate sensitivity training of all educational staff and students in the USA. Second, gender-variant people's lives must permeate all classrooms, and school libraries should be fully stocked with up-to-date writings on transgender, gender-queer, gayness, lesbianism and bisexuality. Third, suicide prevention and anti-bullying programs in schools must deal with the issues faced by LGBTQ young people. . . . Finally, on an institutional level, school boards must pass non-discrimination policies that would make it a violation of school conduct codes to harass, assault or discriminate against students and staff on the basis of actual or perceived gender identity or expression.

Then, Wyss points out a set of broader and more comprehensive theoretical goals and implications:

> My findings and the theoretical framework of 'doing gender' also indicate areas for broader cultural change. Despite mounting evidence to the contrary, most of us continue to assume that there are only two sexes and that each sex has a gender with which it is inexorably associated (West & Zimmerman, 1987). . . . In response, I am calling for a radical revisioning of gender, including the eradication of the binary sex/gender system, a move away from the assumption that there are only two sexes and two genders (Devor, 1997; Wilchins, 2002), and the elimination of all gender hierarchies and other forms of injustice (Califia, 1997).

Picasso also talks about the social implications of her findings. She reminds us that valedictorians are an important cultural resource, and that if some students appear to unfairly lack opportunities, we need to do more research to make sure this is not the case. If it turns out to be the case, then societal changes would need to be made:

> In conclusion, it is a fact that valedictorians are among the best and brightest of all our students. If valedictorians from poor areas and impoverished schools are not getting an equal chance for continued education at the highest levels, then eventually all society must suffer from this case. Therefore, it is important to continue research along these lines, to make sure we are not wasting one of our most precious resources.

Finally, James examines the implications of the research process itself. Given the recursive and reflective nature of her research study and its emergent processes, this is a quite appropriate topic for examination:

> Research is a first-hand experience for teachers that brings learning to life. This study showed me that young people interact in astonishing ways as they seek to solve the endless problems that surround them. . . . Teachers engaging in research are taking a step into the unknown, as they begin an uncertain and hazardous journey, possibly isolated from a research community.

Her final implications are intensely personal:

> This is why I believe teacher research is so important, causing a change of perspective that has so many benefits for everyone concerned. . . . As I reflect on my learning I am aware that the more I see the more there is to understand: children hold a wealth of surprises. One of the most valuable lessons for me is that I have learned to become attuned to children's play: to listen to their voices and respond to their interests and concerns.

Suggestions for the Future

Suggestions for future research are not all that common in educational research articles. However, when they are present, they often reflect areas of great importance to the researchers.

Danili and Reid make a fairly traditional sounding call for more research to be done in the area they explored in their article:

> Further work needs to be carried out to explore whether the benefits of the approach adopted here bring specific benefits to those with lower working memory spaces and those who are more field-dependent.

Cassatt finishes his article with a call for further research, which was implied in the discussion of possible explanations above. Finally, there is the realization that this study was descriptive in nature, while changes in practice in real schools should be based on causal data. Therefore, this study should be seen as opening the door for a whole program of research that can then nail down these effects in a more solid fashion. Cassatt is on solid ground here, since the tradition of moving from descriptive to causal research is a strong one in quantitative inquiry:

> In conclusion, this correlational study has shown that it is reasonable to assume that there is some relationship between practice and good grades in this sample. Further research will be needed to control some of the factors described above, as well as others, in order to see if higher practice rates has a causal impact on grades, or not.

With some forms of research, the call for more work is sometimes blurred with the nature of the research itself. This is often seen in action research, in particular. Davidson concludes with a simple statement about the nature of action research in general, and what she would like to see transpire in this study over time. Her last sentence, in particular, is an honest assessment of the possibilities:

One of the key tenets of action research is for the researcher to leave things in better shape than she found them (Bunting, 2002). At least for the school year under question, this seemed to be the case at Garfield Elementary. Time will tell, whether these changes lead to lasting change, or were only a brief bright spot in a declining social milieu.

Sometimes, suggestions for the future do not direct themselves toward more research but for a new and better vision of the future. Such a vision is offered by Wyss:

> In setting out to accomplish these goals, however, we can begin to make our schools—and our society—safe for all youth (Human Rights Watch, 2001; Safe Schools Coalition of Washington, 1995). Not only will trans and genderqueer young people then be able to learn in school instead of just trying to survive, but LGB-identified youth, sissy-acting straight boys, butch-looking heterosexual girls and teens who in other ways defy the strict gender standards of our culture will feel more secure in their own lives and will find education a much less traumatic experience.

Our Emerging Literacy Orientation

Researchers begin their articles by introducing their topics and raising some questions. They end their articles by reflecting on the answers to those questions, and by considering how these answers change our knowledge and understanding of those topics of interest.

It is important to remember that articles may end, but there are no real endings to research. In a real sense, doing empirical research is like running a middle leg in a relay race. Chances are that we did not start the process but rather picked up a direction within a field of ongoing research. Even more surely, we will not finish the race either. It may be trite and a cliché, but every answer only raises many more questions. A good discussion section brings some momentary closure and reflection to one set of questions, but in the process opens up new directions for research as well.

Practice Makes Perfect

It is now time to practice some of the insights and skills you have explored in this chapter:

- First of all, there are four training articles and four real articles whose discussions have not been examined. You can also look at the discussion section in the three or four articles you chose to examine.
- Try your hand at looking at these discussion sections. How do the researchers interpret what they found? How do they summarize? Are there problems with their findings that need to be explained? What implications do they draw? Are there suggestions for future research? Compare your results with those of your classmates.

Understanding
Mixed-Methods Articles

You should congratulate yourself at this point. You have now established that, with some work, you can read an article from its title to its discussion section. You might not be able to work out every technical or precise detail, but you do have a sense of what the researchers are trying to accomplish and why they used the methods and analyses that they did. This is quite an accomplishment, and you should be proud of yourself.

At this point, however, you might run into articles that are somewhat confusing. They appear to be qualitative, but they might cite statistical data and test hypotheses. Or they might appear to be quantitative, but they use interview data and quotes and observations to make certain points. Should you consider these articles to be qualitative or quantitative, or what?

Actually, these sorts of articles are examples of an emerging category of research articles—mixed-methods articles. In this chapter, we will look at the basics of these sorts of articles, by examining two actual mixed-methods articles (which can be found in Appendix I). Before we look at the actual articles, however, we need to make a few general points about these sorts of articles.

Mixed-Methods Articles Attempt to Combine the Advantages of Both Types of Research

The basic goal behind mixed-methods research is praiseworthy. If each type of research can give us certain kinds of knowledge and insight, would not a combination of these methods give us an even better set of findings?

In other words, the driving motivation behind mixed methods is the desire to get the whole story, as much as possible. If abstract patterns of numbers can tell us one thing about a phenomenon, what will a set of verbal descriptions tell us that we could not get from abstractions? If a compelling narrative illustrates an important point, what happens when we try to nail down the particulars of that point using objective methods?

The rallying cry for most mixed-methods advocates is the notion that the research question determines the method, and not the other way around. These supporters advise us to look at what questions we want to ask and not worry about method. Once we are clear on the question, they say, we use the best methods possible to answer that question. If it is qualitative or quantitative, then so be it. In more and more cases, though, they argue, the best method is to use both methods.

The Mixed-Methods Approach Is Still Somewhat Controversial

As with most everything, there are usually two sides to every story. The controversial side to mixed methods is the implicit assumption that all forms of research are, at heart, the same. This is far from a settled matter. For instance, look at the two chapters in this work on basic qualitative and basic quantitative literacies. From these chapters, we can see that practitioners of each method often look at the world in quite different ways. Can these worldviews be that easily reconciled, so that their methods can be mixed together readily and commonly? The answer to these questions will require much thought and practice in the field, and so for now it is probably best to keep an open mind on the extent of the role of mixed methods in educational research.

In Practice, There Are Usually Two Types of Mixed-Methods Articles

When we actually look at published mixed-methods articles, we tend to find them gravitating into one of two camps. An article is usually basically a quantitative article, with a qualitative section designed to add "flesh to the bones" of the numerical or statistical findings. We can call this a *Quantitative Enhanced by Qualitative* article. On the other hand, we might have a qualitative article that incorporates quantitative findings to drive home a point or nail down some finding more precisely. We can call this a *Qualitative Driving Quantitative* article. We will look at specific examples of each type of article in turn:

Quantitative Enhanced by Qualitative

Our first mixed-methods article is by Worrall, and it deals with building a research culture in a school. Worrall asked the following three research questions:

> Why do teachers decide to carry out classroom-based research?

> How do teachers feel about doing research?

> Why do teachers choose to further develop or neglect their skills in undertaking classroom-based research?

To answer these questions, Worrall began working with a group of six schools in the UK to get participants:

> With the assistance of the teacher research coordinators in three other partner schools, I drew up a sample of seven teachers from each school, 28 in all. . . . The sample of 28 consisted of a relatively experienced group of teachers with comparatively little experience of research. For example, of the 18 teachers who had been teaching for more than 15 years, only three of them had been actively involved in research.

Once she had identified her participants, Worrall implemented the following mixed-methods research design:

> The TRCs [teaching research coordinators] were asked to distribute a questionnaire to the selection of their colleagues who had been involved in research projects of various kinds. This was designed to establish the teachers' experience of, and general attitudes towards, research. Semi-structured interviews with 12 (three TRCs, two assistant head teachers, two heads of department, two heads of year, three mainscale teachers) of the sample then followed to generate qualitative data to illustrate the main concerns identified through the questionnaires.

> Regarding the questionnaire, Worrall reports the findings from the question "Why did you decide to carry out classroom-based research?" The results are

Table 12.1 Question: Why did you decide to carry out classroom-based research?

Reasons	No.
To generate greater understanding of specific issues in teaching and/or learning	23
To solve immediate problems	10
Effective self-directed continuing professional development	9
To regain professional control over and confidence in what happens in own classroom	9
Part of higher degree/programme giving access to promotion	8
To satisfy intellectual curiosity about issues of teaching and learning	6
To capitalise on collaboration with colleagues	5
To provide evidence and feedback on aspects of School Improvement Plan	5
As part of reflective practice	4
To promote development of teaching as evidence-based profession	4
To provide data for external researchers	3

presented in Table 12.1. Eleven choices were tabulated. The most common, with 23 responses, was "To generate greater understanding of specific issues in teaching and/or learning." The least common, with three responses, was "To provide data for external researchers."

After gathering the results of the questionnaire, Worrall then turned to semi-structured interviews in order to gather additional data. It should be noted that semi-structured interviews are very popular in mixed-methods designs. In this technique, great care is taken to make sure that each participant is asked the same set of questions. This is done for two reasons. First of all, it provides a way to emulate the same degree of consistency of response that we find when questionnaires are used. That is, we can make sure that each participant has the same data-gathering experiences. Second, semi-structured interviews can be tightly and explicitly linked to the issues that were addressed in the questionnaires. In this way, there is a bridge between the two modes of data gathering and analysis.

In the interview data we find the emergence of the qualitative side of this study, where the questionnaire results can be fleshed out. Worrall asked four basic questions—why did you get involved in research, what are your reasons for carrying out research, why do you choose to continue to do research, and why did you stop doing research? Here are a few representative answers to each question:

Why did you get involved in research?

I was living in a milieu where a lot of research was going on and [Name] in particular, you know, being an educational researcher would throw books at me and say. 'Look, what do you think of this?' So that's how I became interested.

So, because I was in a group and you had to come and share ideas and then in the end we knew we were actually trying to get something that was good enough to publish. In a way it forces and disciplines you though into finding an idea that's worth turning over and telling someone.

What are your reasons for carrying out research?

Well I think it's something that . . . I won't say 'good teachers' but any teacher who wants to do the job properly, almost inevitably does. I remember you talking about definitions of research and one idea that came to me was a willingness to think about experiences in the classroom and to answer questions, mainly why did this happen. Now it may . . . I don't now, you don't get that much chance to talk to teachers but I imagine that others might come out of the classroom and say, 'that was terrible. Why?' and for whatever reason, perfectly good reasons maybe, be distracted so they don't actually investigate. My personality is such that when I get into the situation of why did that happen and why is that happening now when it didn't happen then, it's something that bugs me until I get it sorted out.

For me it is investigating the process, furthering your education, investigating in order to reflect, gathering information.

Why do you choose to continue to do research?

It frees your thinking. . . . It refuels you . . . it's about keeping doors open, keeping ideas open, keeping things flowing.

For some colleagues, I know last year two of them said that it was the thing that they enjoyed most and I know some of their colleagues I'm working with this year on their research project are really, really enjoying it. They're excited about it. For example, one of our senior teachers spent the whole of yesterday in a library and he's worked here for over 30 years and I think it's probably the first time in those 30 years that he's actually been working, doing a normal school day in the library reading and he said, 'I can't wait to tell you.' You know, 'Have you got any free time today' and sadly I haven't but it's really exciting for somebody to have worked that long and to have that kind of enthusiasm I think that is really important. It won't necessarily affect his teaching at all but what he's interested in looking at is any social inclusion and attendance which would directly affect the way he teaches his subject but I think that also is one of the things that we're looking at when we're looking at the impact of research. There are other factors that are really, really important.

It is a lot easier to carry out research activity if there is some sort of research culture and I wonder if one could have research activity, meaningful research activity without some notion of a research . . . well, within the context of a research culture.

I think if the head wasn't interested it would be very difficult because that would then mean that they probably wouldn't give me any time. Without time, I think it would be impossible to do. Yeah, it's critical. Absolutely critical that the head is interested.

Why did you stop doing research?

It's time and getting caught up in the day-to-day things of your own life . . . when you're thinking about things that you have to do, you do the things that you absolutely have to do first.

I mentioned to one of our 'gender experts' that I was having my gender research published and she seemed surprised . . . you know, they don't sort of realise that actually what you are doing has some validity. . . . Perhaps that's partly why people don't want to get involved because they realise that the academic barrier is of suspicion and they don't feel even the smallest bit confident about trying to suggest they could do it because people are often embarrassed to say they might be doing some research because it sounds very grand.

There might be those who are so stuck in their ways, personality-wise, not just in teaching, in life generally, that even if they did read something that kind of made sense to them, they might not actually change.

Of all the kinds of mixed-methods articles, this type is most common. There seems to be a sense that qualitative findings are most useful in enriching and elaborating results gathered in more traditional quantitative ways. For one thing, the responses on the interviews could be useful in creating a more extensive questionnaire to give to a larger sample of teachers in order to get a wider picture on the topic. Perhaps there is a level of comfort in starting with well-established research methods, and using the newer and less established qualitative methods to enhance the original design and results.

Qualitative Driving Quantitative

Qualitative articles using quantitative components are much rarer. This might be due to the fact that qualitative researchers are less inclined to use quantitative methods to buttress their efforts. There are a number of possible reasons for this. On one hand, qualitative researchers might feel that it is important to expand and extend the nature of qualitative methods without "clouding the waters" with quantitative data. These researchers might also feel that nailing down aspects of the study by using quantitative methods might be premature. Finally, it might even be the case that qualitative researchers are not as comfortable using quantitative methods as quantitative researchers might be in their own use of qualitative methods. That is, since quantitative methods are often more prescribed and focused, there is more of a chance of methodological error in the application of quantitative methods than in the application of qualitative methods. Or perhaps there are reasons that go beyond these simple speculations. The result is the same—fewer qualitative researchers employ mixed-methods designs than their quantitative counterparts.

For our purposes, we will look at a mixed-methods article by Swennen et al. This research is primarily qualitative. Like many qualitative articles, it begins by laying out an explicit theoretical framework. They start by examining the nature of teacher concerns:

Research on teachers' concerns draws heavily on the work of Fuller (1969). Fuller and Bown (1975) drew a distinction between the development of concerns of teachers and those of student teachers. In the case of student teachers, they distinguished four main stages of concerns. During the first stage pre-teaching concerns are dominant. Student teachers identify with pupils, but with their teachers they do so only in their fantasies. After their first teaching experience, a radical change takes place. Idealized ideas about pupils are replaced by concerns about their own survival. Now the central question is, will I be able to manage the class? Next, student teachers develop concerns about the teaching situation: they become concerned about methods and materials and start looking for new ideas for their lessons. Still, these are concerns about their own performance as a teacher and not concerns about pupils and their learning, which is the fourth category of concerns. At this fourth stage, student teachers have an eye for pupils' social and emotional needs and they become more focused on their relationships with individual children.

As research linking concerns and teacher cognitions began to develop, alternative modes for measuring those cognitions and concerns also began to develop as well. In particular, Swennen et al. became interested in the role of images as a way to tap into these cognitions and concerns:

> Calderhead (1989), among others, considers images to be a key factor in explaining the professional development of teachers. Students enter pre-service teacher education with images about their future profession and their own role as a teacher. . . . He presents an overview of different types of images, from rather concrete to more abstract. On the highest level of abstraction, an image is a powerful metaphor with affective and moral connotations. On a lower level, we find the images of an 'ideal teacher' that students sometimes carry with them as a result of experiences with positive role models. On a still lower level are the images that student teachers have of the contents of particular lessons, for example a mathematics lesson or a physics practical.

Swennen et al. operationalized the use of images in their research by looking at drawings made by student teachers:

> We focused on drawings that student teachers made about themselves in relation to their teaching practice situation.

After developing this theoretical argument, the researchers then asked the following five explicit research questions:

1. What are the concerns of first year students at the beginning of their preparation programme?
2. What are their concerns after their first teaching practice period (in the first year)?
3. What are their concerns at the end of the first year?
4. What development in concerns, if any, occurs during the first year?
5. Can concerns be assessed in a valid and reliable way using drawings?

Three separate modes of data collection were used to measure concerns. One of the modes was quantitative, and the other two were qualitative.

The first, and the quantitative, mode used was a card sorting process:

> We developed the card sorting instrument not only as a research instrument, but also as an instrument that can be used to promote reflection by student teachers about their own concerns. The instrument is based on the Teacher

Concern Checklist developed by Fuller and Borich (1988). The original checklist consisted of 50 items and was adapted until 16 items remained. These 16 items were transferred to cards and a set of cards was made for each student. Students were asked to rank the cards from the item concerning them the most to the item concerning them the least or not at all. For each of the three measurements the mean rank number was calculated, as well as the standard deviation. The ranking scores could be compared to assess an overall change in the development of concerns (using Friedman's test). The remarks of all the students were analysed in order to gain an insight into the students' interpretations of the items.

Data for the rankings based on the card sorting instrument are reported in Table 12.2.

Table 12.2 Scores for the three measurements of the instrument 'cards'

Item	1st measure (n = 35)			2nd measure (n = 28)			3rd measure (n= 28)		
	Rank	Mean rank score	SD	Rank	Mean rank score	SD	Rank	Mean rank score	SD
1. Diagnosing pupils with learning problems	1	4.6	2.6	7	7.9	3.7	6	7.1	3.9
2. Selecting and teaching content well	2	5.2	4.0	1	4.1	3.8	2	4.8	4.1
3. Motivating pupils to learn	3	5.3	3.5	2	4.4	2.6	1	3.9	2.7
4. Adapting myself to the needs of different pupils	4	5.4	3.1	3	4.8	2.9	3	5.5	4.1
5. Becoming a good teacher	5	5.6	4.8	4	4.9	4.5	7	7.5	5.6
6. Staff collaboration	6	7.6	3.9	5	6.9	2.9	4	6.6	2.9
7. Adequately presenting all of the required materials	7	8.2	4.0	9	8.5	3.3	5	7.0	3.1
8. Whether the pupils like me or not	8	8.5	4.0	10	8.9	4.0	11	9.1	3.4
9. Being fair and impartial	9	8.8	4.5	8	8.3	4.3	10	8.5	4.0
10. Getting a favourable evaluation from my mentor	10	8.9	3.1	6	7.2	3.9	8	7.9	3.5
11. The socio-pedagogical climate	11	9.0	4.3	12	9.9	3.8	12	9.9	4.5
12. Pupils who disrupt class	12	9.7	3.8	11	9.1	3.4	9	8.3	3.8
13. Too many non-instructional duties	13	11.1	3.9	14	11.9	3.0	14	11.0	3.9
14. Too many pupils in one class	14	11.3	4.1	13	10.5	3.9	13	10.3	3.2
15. Lack of freedom to initiate innovative instruction	15	12.5	3.6	15	13.9	2.3	15	13.7	2.8
16. Inadequate teaching salaries	16	14.1	2.4	16	15.0	1.6	16	15.0	1.9

Table 2 in the article "Studying Student Teachers' Concerns, Combining Image-Based and More Traditional Research Techniques" in Appendix I

Overall, the ranking data suggests a pattern for categories:

> Of the four concern categories, the concern category 'pupils' needs concerns' scores the highest. There is a reasonable distance to the score for the second highest category, 'instructional concerns.' The category 'self concerns' appears not to score highly. The fourth category, 'overall educational concerns', scores lowest.

These findings were tested for significance:

> Using the Friedman test, we determined whether or not there were significant differences between the three measures (the fourth research question). The X^2 test gave a value of 0.66, with a corresponding P value of 0.72. This means that there were no significant differences between the results of the three measurements. The students' remarks also did not show a change over the year. However, the students made considerably fewer remarks on the forms for the second and third measurement.

Regarding the card sort data, Swennen et al. conclude:

> The main conclusion based on the analysis of the data gathered with the card sorting instrument is that there is no general overall change in the concerns of these students during their first year. . . . There are, however, indications that the students are becoming less idealistic and more realistic about teaching.

The next data-gathering method was qualitative:

> We asked the students to make a drawing of themselves in relation to the school they had been working in during their teaching practice period. A total of 64 drawings were made: 34 at the beginning of the year, a week before the teaching practice period, and 30 at the end of the year, a week after the last week of the teaching practice period. Each student received paper, (coloured) pencils and crayons. The students were free in their choice of drawing materials.

A comprehensive analysis design was then implemented:

> Analysis of the drawings proceeded in two stages. The purpose of the first stage was to develop categories of concern based on the drawings. The first author made a description of the main visual aspects. . . . On the basis of this description the similarities and differences between the drawings were determined. . . . The intention was to develop concern categories that emerged from the drawings.
> The reliability of the concern categories was assessed in the second stage. . . . During a pilot, all three authors scored the concerns in the drawings of a group of students, different from the ones being studied. . . . Finally, 28 drawings of the students involved in this study were chosen at random and scored independently by three rates with two questions to be answered: (1) is the

category of concern present in this drawing; (2) if it is, to what degree (intensity) is it present, on a scale from 1 (minimum) to 4 (maximum)?

In their analysis of the drawing data, the researchers first reported the presence of eight categories of concern across the 64 drawings:

1. Concerns about a cosy atmosphere in the classroom.
2. Concerns about pupils.
3. Concerns about maintaining discipline.
4. Concerns about the opinion of the mentor.
5. Concerns about pupils' learning.
6. Concerns about matters outside the classroom.
7. Concerns about themselves as teachers.
8. Concerns about the choice of becoming a teacher.

While many of the concern categories were similar to those found in the card sorting instrument, there were also a number of new categories that were only revealed in the drawings:

> Other of the concern categories that emerged from the drawings are different, like concerns about a cosy atmosphere in the classroom, concerns about themselves as teachers and concerns about the choice of becoming a teacher.

Results were similar to those of the card sorting instrument:

> In general, the results of the drawings, like those of the card sorting instrument, show little change in overall concerns, except for the concern about the opinion of the mentor.
> Table 12.3 shows the changes that can be seen between the first and second drawings of the student teachers. One can read from Table 12.3 that concerns about pupils, the learning of pupils, a cosy atmosphere and the opinion of the mentor are all prominent in the first drawings of student teachers, just before their first practice teaching period. The second batch still shows concerns about pupils, the learning of pupils and a cosy atmosphere, but hardly any concerns about the opinion of the mentor. It is noteworthy that the overall frequency of the concerns in the drawings diminishes.

The final data-gathering strategy involved the use of interviews:

> From the group of 37 students we selected six for semi-structured interviews. Because we wanted to interview students who had ranked the cards in accordance with the general results and students who had ranked the cards differently, we wanted to interview a minimum of three students from each group. . . . The interviews were meant to illustrate the outcomes of the analyses of the card sorting instrument and the drawings.

The following questions were used for the interviews:

Table 12.3 Percentages of presence of concern categories in the selected 28 drawings and mean scores of two raters at times 1 and 2

| Category of concerns | Measure 1 | | | | Measure 2 | | | |
| | Rater 1 | | Rater 2 | | Rater 1 | | Rater 2 | |
	%	Mean	%	Mean	%	Mean	%	Mean
1. Pupils' learning	71	1.5	79	1.6	36	1.4	43	1.5
2. Pupils	57	2.0	57	1.9	57	1.4	50	1.3
3. A cosy atmosphere	50	1.9	64	1.9	36	1.2	43	1.5
4. Opinion of mentor	43	1.8	29	2.8	7	1.0	7	1.0
5. Themselves as teachers	29	2.3	50	2.3	50	1.9	43	1.8
6. Discipline	14	a	7	a	0	a	0	
7. The choice to become a teacher	7	a	7	a	14	a	14	a
8. Matters outside the classroom	0	a	0	a	14	a	14	a

a This value could not be calculated because of too few scores.

Table 4 in the article "Studying Student Teachers' Concerns, Combining Image-Based and More Traditional Research Techniques" in Appendix I

On the ranking of the cards: (1) what strikes you about how you ranked the cards the first time; (2) what strikes you about how you ranked the cards the last time; (3) how do you explain the similarities and differences between the first and last ranking?

On the drawings of the students: (1) what strikes you about your first drawing; (2) what strikes you about your last drawing; (3) how do you explain the similarities and differences between the first and last drawing?

Interview data is not presented per se, but is incorporated to clarify specific 'results' issues with the card sorting instrument and the drawings.

In discussing their results, the researchers spent some time in describing the similarities and differences in using the more quantitative card sort method and the more qualitative drawing analysis method. First of all, they found general agreement in the findings from each method. However, the drawings were shown to give access to some concerns better than the card sort method:

Although there is general agreement about the outcomes of the analysis of the card sorting instrument and the drawings, there are some concerns that emerge more clearly from the drawings than the cards. This is particularly true of 'a cosy atmosphere in the classroom'. The students in the interviews also emphasized this issue. The students considered a good atmosphere a precondition for their own functioning and for pupil learning.

The use of drawings was also shown to have more general benefits as well:

Our results show that we found a fruitful entrance by taking drawings as a basic for measuring concerns. The validity of the drawings seems to us somewhat greater than the prefabricated card items derived from a long list of concerns. . . . Drawings help clarify factors that in other research receive less attention, especially the less conscious and less rational aspects of teacher development.

The researchers also talked about extending the method into more personalistic and narrative directions:

In our study we limited ourselves to analyses on the group level. Another line of research would be to use the card sorting instrument and the drawings as the basis for a more person-centred research approach, from a biographical perspective.

The researchers were also careful to acknowledge drawbacks and weaknesses with the use of drawings as a data-gathering tool:

Although drawings elicit responses that differ from those of more traditional, verbal research techniques, the use of drawing as a research method is not without problems. One of the problems is the ability of people to make drawings that reflect what they want to express. . . . One of the students interviewed drew a picture that was rather sober and said she did so because of her limited artistic skill. Nevertheless, most of the pictures are strong and imaginative and reflect the feelings of the students in various ways, from drawings in black and white to express anxiety to bright colours to express love for children.

In the end, Swennen et al. champion their blend of qualitative and quantitative assessment tools as a way to get at a variety of important issues in teacher education:

Finally, we think we have succeeded in developing instruments which can also be used by teacher educators with the aim of developing more understanding of their student teachers' concerns. As such, these instruments may contribute to the development of what Korthagen and Kessels (1999) call 'realistic teacher education', i.e., teacher education that builds on student teachers' actual concerns.

Our Emerging Research Literacy

At the current time, there seems to be no clear consensus on the value of mixed-methods designs. While a sizable number of educational researchers embrace the idea of bringing together all forms of empirical research under a single common rubric, there remain enough dissident voices to ensure that this topic will be debated for some time to come.

In the meantime, what should a research-literate critic do? For now, the best strategy appears to be this—approach mixed-methods articles as you would any other articles. You should be able to find a research question and an argument. The methods and analyses should lead to clear results and findings. Those findings should be interpreted with skill and care by their researchers. So long as you hold steady to the basic principles of research literacy, at least for now, mixed-methods articles should present you with no real problems.

Practice Makes Perfect

It is now time to practice some of the insights and skills you have explored in this chapter:

- First of all, can you find examples of mixed-methods articles? See if you can find at least two such articles.
- Can you categorize these articles as either primarily qualitative or primarily quantitative? Make a case for your decisions.
- Using one training quantitative article and one training qualitative article, can you redesign each article as a mixed-methods article? Share your results with your classmates.

Becoming a Personal Reviewer

As you have been working through the chapters in this book, you have been building upon and strengthening your grasp of educational research literacy. You now are in possession of the most basic and most important foundational insights and skills needed for understanding educational research articles. How well you refine and expand these basic and foundational skills is up to you. In other words, you have covered all the basic steps needed to be a consumer of educational research. From now on, your path will be that of a critic.

Here is the difference between a consumer and a critic of educational research—consumers *understand* an article and critics *engage* that article. Understanding per se is still somewhat passive and accepting. With engagement comes the added responsibility of digging deeper and holding research to higher standards.

Let us take a moment to think about the issue of standards. Researchers and journal editors alike are committed to the notion of publishing the highest quality research they can jointly produce. That is why most journal articles undergo a referee process. When an article is refereed, this means that the editors have sent the article to two or more reviewers for critical reading. These reviewers are content experts or methods experts, or both.

Good reviewers are excellent critical readers. Of course, they start with the goal of extracting and then understanding the basic information from articles. But they go beyond this consumer task by taking responsibility for evaluating articles. Are these articles clear and well written? Are their arguments plausible and logical? Are their research questions important and relevant? Are the methods used in the articles sound? Were their analyses done correctly? Do the methods and analyses really address the research questions raised? Are the discussions and conclusions warranted and valid?

The referee process is an important part of educational research. First of all, it provides a fair and equitable way to address the fact that only so many articles can be published a year in a given journal. Important journals often get ten times (or more) more submissions than they can possibly publish. Therefore, most of the articles submitted for publication have to be rejected. Editors depend upon the review process to sort through submissions and then select the relative handful of best articles that can then be published.

Referees do more than just sort articles into accept or reject piles. Even those articles which are destined to be published usually need some revision. Reviewers point out areas that need to be clarified, and even mistakes that need to be fixed. Reviewers also serve as the collective voice of the field. Are the researchers being too timid in their claims? Are they being too bold in their declarations? Are there areas that the researchers have ignored or failed to take into account in their work? Are issues raised by the researchers really important or are they trivial?

Reviewers are the front line of the voice of the field. It is their job to make sure that articles address important issues, that questions are raised in a clear manner and supported in a clear and logical fashion. It is their job to make sure that methods match questions, and that analyses are done correctly. It is their job to comment upon and evaluate discussions and conclusions. But too often, we are content to let the review process end there. There is a need for all readers to go beyond just being good consumers of research. It is our job to pick up where the official review process has left off and to ask the same sorts of questions of articles that referees have raised. We cannot expect every referee process to be perfect, or for every referee to catch every important issue. We need to realize that it is our job to be personal reviewers as well. We take the review process as we find it, and we extend our evaluation of the material based on our own areas of expertise and skills.

In this chapter, we will examine the process of becoming a personal reviewer. A good reviewer is always asking questions. There are two types of questions we need to ask as we review articles. First of all, there are questions we need to raise and the articles need to answer. Finally, there are those questions we need to ask of ourselves in order to be sure that we are capable of reading and understanding each article on its own terms:

Questions Every Article Needs to Answer

We begin with a series of key questions that every article needs to address.

Why Should I Be Interested in This Article?

No article comes with a built-in requirement that people should read it and pay attention to its issues and findings. Each and every article must make a case for its existence. An article does not have to be of interest to everyone, but it should be of interest to you. How does the article help you decide if it is of interest to you? Is the title clear? Does the abstract give you adequate guidance? Does it state its case for being worth reading in the first paragraph or two?

Does This Article State Its Problems Clearly and Succinctly?

The legendary big band leader Lawrence Welk was once asked why his music had been so popular for so many years. Welk smiled, and said that he played dance music. When you play dance music, he went on, you should not have to be Sherlock Holmes to find the beat.

The same is true for research questions. If we have to act like detectives and hunt around to find research questions, then the articles are just not being clear enough. Even if an article needs to develop a fairly complex argument to support its questions, those questions themselves should be clearly stated and clearly identified.

Is the Literature That Is Cited Relevant, Important, and Current?

As personal reviewers, we need to turn to the reference section right after we read the abstract and the opening few paragraphs. We have a sense of the goals and directions of the article—now, have the researchers done their homework? Have they grounded their work adequately within the research literature?

There are three dimensions to the well-written reference section. The first dimension is *importance*. For any field, there are some articles that are more important than others. Are these benchmark works referenced? Are they discussed properly and adequately in the body of the article?

The second dimension is *relevance*. Are the researchers not only citing important material—are they also not citing irrelevant topics or bodies of research? Sometimes, the relevance of a particular body of work might not be apparent. In that case, it is up to the researchers to make the case for relevance in the article itself. If we can find no reason for a particular article or body of work to be cited, then it should be eliminated.

The final dimension is *timeliness*. This is a problem with far too many research articles—the research that they cited is just too old. Research is an ongoing process. If a particular piece of research is, say, ten years old, then there is a good chance that there has been more research in the field that has altered the way we might look at the topic. While it is true that certain benchmark studies are timeless in a way, far more research comes with an implicit expiration date. If all of the work cited is, say, more than five years old, then this suggests that the researchers are not as current as they might be on this topic.

There is, however, one additional caveat to these guidelines. Theoretical work, by and large, has a longer "shelf life" than research findings, per se. It is not unusual for researchers to cite theoretical pieces that are ten years old, or older. This same grace period does not apply to research articles that are based on these theoretical perspectives, however. The researchers need to show that they are conversant with the latest relevant research to come out of those perspectives.

Do the Findings in This Article Address the Issues That It Raises?

Is there a match between questions raised and the methods used to answer them? Sometimes, researchers shy away from asking certain questions because the methods needed to answer them might be too complex. At the other end of the spectrum, sometimes we find researchers who are seemingly infatuated with certain complex methods, who end up making their research needlessly complicated. Both extremes are obviously to be avoided. The best way to make sure that questions and methods match up is to be as clear as possible in the planning and execution of research. As reviewers, we need to be on the lookout for these sorts of problems in research articles.

Are the Measurements and Findings of This Article Reliable?

Any decent measurement book can point you to the details of reliability. Here, we will look at the overall conceptual framework for reliability.

The key notion in reliability is accuracy. Is our measuring system or device accurate? Here is a simple example—suppose we are trying to measure the height of a building. We start by finding a yardstick, and using it to measure the height. But we need to make sure our yardstick is okay first. Is it actually a yard long? Are the feet and inches marked off correctly? Is the yardstick constant under use, or does it bend or warp or stretch or shrink as we are using it? We cannot trust our measurement of the height of the building unless we also trust our yardstick. We need to ascertain that it is a reliable measuring instrument.

In the same way, we worry about the reliability of our measures in educational research. However, the things we often measure are a lot more "slippery" than something as obvious as, say, height. Think for a moment, for example, how much harder it is to pin down something like intelligence or motivation or aptitude. We measure these things indirectly. For instance, we have tests of intelligence and aptitude, and inventories to assess motivational level.

If researchers are measuring things, then we need to see how they have addressed possible reliability issues. Do they talk about reliability directly? How have they attempted to assess reliability? One of the most common ways is to report reliability coefficients. These involve making multiple measures of the same thing, and then correlating those measures to see how close they are. Reliability coefficients ought to be very high, hopefully in excess of +0.90.

Another type of reliability measure is internal consistency. With internal consistency, we are trying to see how much any given item on a test acts like the test as a whole. If all the items are measuring in the same way, then this is good evidence of reliability. The most common measure of internal consistency is a type of correlation known as a Crochach alpha.

If you suspect that there are reliability issues with any particular article, then you need to look deeper into the technical aspects of reliability in order to see if your suspicions are correct.

Are the Measurements and Findings of This Article Valid?

Again, validity is a topic that is covered in depth in most introductory works on measurement. We will be taking a conceptual look here as well.

The idea of validity is also very simple—are the researchers actually measuring what they claim to measure? Note that we cannot have a valid measure unless we are measuring accurately in the first place. If we are not measuring accurately, then we might as well be just writing down numbers. But just because we are measuring accurately does not guarantee we are measuring what we think we are measuring. To make sure our measurements are on target, we have to pay attention to validity.

Like reliability, the targets of validity are also often measured indirectly. The best way to establish validity is to compare our measurements against some kind of standard. Some of these standards include expert judgment, other measuring devices which have proved to be valid themselves, or external criteria. Like reliability, correlations are often used to establish validity. Validity correlations tend to be lower than reliability correlations, but they should still be somewhere in the +0.70 range in order to be considered good.

If you suspect that there are validity issues with any particular article, then you need to look deeper into the technical aspects of validity in order to see if your suspicions are correct.

Are the Statistical Tests Overly Sensitive, so That They Might Be "Finding" Results That Are Not Really There?

In statistical parlance, this is known as a Type I error. People often make this idea harder than it really is, so let us take a moment to get clear on it.

We start by remembering that statistical tests are almost always designed to give us "yes" or "no" answers to our questions. But since those answers are based on probability, then they are really "probably yes" or "probably no."

The key question is this—how "probably" is "probably yes" or "probably no"? Ideally, we want to have "almost certainly and positively yes" or "almost certainly and positively no." The closer that we get to either "almost certainly and positively yes" or "almost certainly and positively no" the more *confident* we are.

As we have discussed before, $p < .05$ is a commonly agreed upon standard for acceptable probability in these cases. If we are testing at the $p < .05$ level, then we are roughly 95% correct when we decide any differences we find are real differences, and not just sampling variation. But, 95% correct can also be 5% wrong. There is always a slight chance that we are claiming to find a difference where none really exists. This is called a Type I error, or a *confidence* error. Sometimes, a Type I error is also described as a "false positive."

Since we are dealing with probabilities, we can never eliminate the chance of a Type I error once and for all. What, then, is an acceptable chance to take when measuring? Is it always $p < .05$? Or can it be lower? Or higher? Most researchers agree that $p < .05$ is as high a chance as researchers ordinarily ought to take. Type I errors are serious problems—when we claim that there is an effect where there really is none, this can mess up lots of things. It is not uncommon to see $p < .01$ or even lower when the stakes are high for mistakes. For example, if we are testing a cancer drug, we want to be really sure that it works, since lives will depend on it.

As personal reviewers, we need to decide on whether probability levels in a study are properly set to address the potential seriousness of a Type I error. We also need to check and see if there are flaws in the research design that might unintentionally increase the odds of a Type I error. The most common culprit here is the repeated use of simple probability tests. Here is an extreme case. Suppose you are looking to see if some treatment is having an effect. You measure it 20 times. One of those times, it is significant at the $p < .05$ level. Should we put any faith in that finding? Of course not. The laws of chance tell us that we should not be surprised if one of these 20 tests turned out significant. Most of the time, design errors will not be this blatant. Nonetheless, we still need to be vigilant, to make sure the designs are giving us the tests that they promise.

Are the Statistical Tests Overly Conservative, so That They Might Be Missing Results That Are Really There?

In statistical parlance, this is a Type II error. It is the other side of the coin—we are dealing with a statistical test that is telling us "Probably No" when it should be telling us "Probably Yes." It is as if the statistical test is not powerful enough to pick up what is really happening, which is why a Type II error is sometimes called a *power* error. A Type II error can also be called a "false negative."

When should we be on the lookout for a Type II error? Actually, we are less likely to see potential Type II errors in published research articles. Why is this? Because Type II errors are mainly cases of "missed significance." Rarely, if ever, will a journal publish an article where the findings were not found to be significant. This makes perfectly good sense—we have no way of knowing *why* findings were not significant. It could be that the treatment and comparison conditions are really equivalent, or it could just as likely be a case of a flawed study that did not turn up anything of note. So, while researchers have to worry about committing Type II errors, readers will usually not find any example in print.

Just about the only case where a reader might find a Type II error is this— where researchers report several significant findings, along with one or more findings that did not turn out to be significant as expected. In this case, there might actually be a Type II error in operation. The effects that did turn out to be significant may have been strong enough to turn up on the statistical "radar screen," but the non significant effects could have been too subtle or too weak to show up on the tests that were used. Sometimes, we hear researchers say that a finding "approached significance." This might also be interpreted as a possible Type II error.

How do researchers eliminate Type II errors? There are two standard approaches they can use. First of all, the researchers can lower the probability level of the test from, say, $p < .05$ to $p < .10$. This is not usually a good idea, since it immediately raises the odds of committing a Type I error. Since Type I errors are usually more serious than Type II errors—because if we do not see something once, it should likely turn up sooner or later in future research if it is really there—then this strategy often moves us in the wrong direction. A better alternative is simply to increase the sample size, if possible. The larger the sample size, the more likely we are to find even small effects. As readers, if we suspect Type II errors, then we should immediately look at the sample size and see if it should really be bigger.

How Generalizable Are the Results and Findings of This Article?

One of the key goals for researchers, and most particularly quantitative researchers, is *generalizability*. Research is generalizable if it goes beyond its little sample and deals with circumstances beyond its specific treatment conditions. There are a couple of things that can affect generalizability in quantitative work.

The first factor that can affect generalizability is the *representativeness* of the sample. Is a given sample a good "snapshot" of the population? Most of the time, there is an element of convenience to any research sample. Researchers usually, for instance, cannot afford to fly around all over the country to collect their data. But researchers also have to make sure that convenience does not lead them to inadvertently create nonrepresentative samples, either. Good personal reviewers look at descriptive and demographic data on samples, and look for evidence of representativeness in this information. Is the sample unusually old? Young? Smart? Male? Female? How well have the researchers balanced their convenience with the need for creating a representative sample?

There is another side to representativeness to consider as well. Even if the sample as a whole seems okay, there might be an *imbalance* problem at the group level. We expect a differential impact between, say, the treatment and control conditions. But how can we be sure that our groups were not "stacked" to favor our treatments? For instance, suppose we are testing a new script for door to door salespeople to use with customers. We feel that the new script will lead to more sales. To test our idea, we send out a team using the new script and a team using the old script. In order for our results to generalize, it is important that these two teams are as equivalent as possible. If all of our best salespeople are in the treatment group, for instance, how can we be sure it is not their natural skills that are leading to improved sales, instead of the new pitch? Balance across treatment groups is important, therefore, and something that a good personal reviewer considers when evaluating an article.

Is generalizability as important in qualitative research? There is some debate on this topic. On one side are researchers who say that all educational research articles, regardless of method, should be held accountable to the same general standards. For these researchers, issues such as reliability, validity, and generalizability need to be addressed by qualitative research. On the other hand are those researchers who hold that, since the goals and methods of qualitative research are so different, they need to be evaluated under their own terms.

Even when the notion of alternative evaluation criteria is raised, there are differences as well. Some researchers offer concepts that are similar to reliability, validity, and generalizability—concepts like triangulation and trustworthiness (see Denzin & Lincoln, 2000, for a number of discussions on these and related topics). Others feel we should start from scratch and develop evaluative criteria from the assumptions of the method itself (see Shank, 2006). For now, personal reviewers are probably best served by examining the evidence from all sides, and making up their own minds.

How Realistic Is This Article? Does It Deal With Conditions and Issues I Might Find in Everyday Life, or Is It Forced and Artificial?

Researchers are usually not in the business of examining trivial or esoteric or artificial situations. Instead, they most often train their gaze on the important and typical. Likewise, they also try to do their work within ordinary or naturally occurring conditions as well.

The whole idea of dealing with naturally occurring conditions appeals to the idea of *ecological validity*. Ecological validity is preserved when the conditions and circumstances of the research setting do not affect the treatments or goals of the research. That is, the research questions are tested in controlled conditions, but not controlled to the point of being overly artificial. Research goals are clearly identified and tested directly, and findings make sense when applied to real world settings.

There are numerous ways that circumstances and conditions can have a negative impact on research. Ten factors are particularly important, and deserve to be examined on their own terms:

The first two factors deal with how researchers identify, describe, and measure the *independent* and *dependent* variables. Researchers are required to identify clearly all independent variables, and to make an adequate case for the ways that they are measuring dependent variables. For instance, have the independent variables been properly operationalized? If the researchers are trying to study, say, hunger, then how are they measuring hunger? Getting clear on the independent and dependent variables is a critical part of any quantitative study.

One of the most common problems with studies is *interference*. In particular, multiple measures can interfere with each other. For example, researchers might be looking at both "the desire to please the teacher" and "hunger" as motivators in a learning task where candy is the reward. Is it not reasonable to assume that these motives might interact with each other? And if so, how could you isolate the effects of each one? Where would you draw the line between, say, the impact of hunger versus the desire to please the teacher? Would it not be better to create two simpler studies to look at each of these possible motives in isolation? In short, if a study seems to be too needlessly complex, or it attempts to answer too many questions at one time, then personal reviewers need to be alert for possible problems.

All studies take place within settings, and are conducted by researchers. These sorts of circumstances can sometimes interfere with studies in a number of ways. The most famous example is a phenomenon known as the *Hawthorne effect*. The Hawthorne effect was discovered in a study of industrial change. Researchers changed a variety of aspects of an industrial setting, looking for the relative impact of these sorts of change. What they found was that change itself, from whatever source, had an impact. That is, just the mere fact of being in a research study changed the way that the subjects went about their tasks and looked at the way they did the things they were asked to do. As a result, personal researchers need to be on the alert for the ways that researchers strive to make conditions as natural as possible for their participants.

In addition to the chronic problem of the Hawthorne effect, the presence of any sort of acute *novelty* can change the results of a study. Were there unusual events or disruptions that happened during the course of the study, and did these affect results? For instance, something as blatant as a fire drill will invalidate a research setting. What about things that are more subtle, however? Did a honking horn disrupt students for a moment on a timed test? Was the surprise of seeing herself on camera enough to cause a participant to pause or lose her train of thought? These sorts of effects are very difficult for personal reviewers to discover, but they are part of the landscape of potential problems, nonetheless.

Finally, we need to realize that research is not conducted by machines, but by people. Are the people doing the research doing the same thing in each condition? Are the subjects exposed to the same people, regardless of conditions? If not, the researchers run the risk of introducing unwanted *experimenter* effects. For example, if Jolly Joe is monitoring the experimental group, and Sourpuss Sally is doing the same for the control group, are the people affected by these radically different experimenters?

Personal reviewers should always be alert to the possible effects of circumstantial conditions. Our efforts are greatly helped by an extensive description and discussion of all research conditions and methods, so that we can be on the alert for possible sources of change that the researchers themselves might not have seen. Also, we should be alert to the presence of standardization of treatments and conditions. Any variation from those standards needs to be explained and justified, and their possible effects should have been considered by the researchers.

Finally, time can have a powerful effect on a study in a variety of ways. Time is certainly a factor in *pretest* and *posttest* designs. Each time period has its own danger zones. Is the pretest sensitizing participants to be on the lookout for a certain type of skill or body of knowledge? That is, have we put them more "on the alert" than they would be under ordinary circumstances?

For example, suppose we are looking for the effects of good manners by a teacher in math instruction. If we ask pretest questions about the manners of the teacher, then we run the risk of bringing the issue of manners into the awareness of students when ordinarily these same students would never give a conscious thought to manners when thinking about their math teacher. In a sense, researchers have to be careful about "priming the pump" and personal reviewers need to be sensitive to the possibilities of such "priming."

At the other end, sometimes the posttest has an effect of its own as well. Suppose, in the manners study from above, students are only asked about manners in a posttreatment survey. It is not unusual to suppose that students might have never thought about manners on their own, and so the posttest might really be "finishing the lesson" by bringing the topic of manners into direct awareness. If students are not asked about manners, would this awareness arise on its own? Quite possibly not. Changing awareness is probably a good thing, but in this case it could contaminate results. Researchers and personal reviewers both need to be aware of this sort of possibility, and to consider its potential impact.

Research is always conducted in time and space, and so there is always a *history* dimension to any research study. Ideally, research is conducted under ordinary times. But sometimes times are not ordinary, in ways that might affect research. Suppose, for example, researchers are interested in the effects of a peace education module on high school students. It could matter very much if these modules were conducted in peacetime vs. times of unrest and war. Researchers and personal reviewers both need to keep an eye on headlines to see how they might affect the research being conducted.

Variables are measured in time, and so we need to be aware of how the *time of measurement* might affect results in unanticipated ways. In particular, it is very important when the dependent variable is measured. If it is measured too soon after the treatments have been introduced, then there is the chance that it has not "soaked in" long enough. If too much times passes before the dependent variable is measured, then researchers are running the risk that other conditions or factors might intervene and interfere with the measurement of the treatment's effect on the dependent variable. Researchers need to determine the precise best time to measure dependent variables in order to find results, and personal reviewers need to be sensitive to this decision-making process as well, in order to judge the researchers' judgments.

Addressing the issues of generalizability and ecological validity has been a critical part of evaluating educational research for decades. The classic source of information is Campbell and Stanley (1966), which continues to be highly regarded to this day and well worth reading for any serious personal reviewer.

Does the Article Fulfill Its Potential?

This is a critical perspective that is particularly pertinent to qualitative articles. As we noted earlier, the problem with most bad qualitative research is the simple fact that it is not very good. In other words, these articles fail to live up to their potential.

In an earlier work (Shank, 2006), Shank listed seven "deadly sins" that are often pitfalls that prevent qualitative research efforts from reaching their full potential. These deadly sins are, in brief:

- *Competitiveness.* Competitiveness occurs when qualitative researchers are out to prove that their work is just as good as quantitative research—just as rigorous, just as thorough, and just as "scientific." So we often find page after page of detailed justification followed by page after page of tediously detailed data—often coded in labyrinthine and Byzantine ways. These efforts actually work against the things that qualitative research does best, and needlessly and artificially restrains qualitative researchers from doing their best work. Competitiveness can be alleviated to some degree by fostering confidence in qualitative research on its own terms.

- *Appropriation.* Appropriation occurs when researchers are less interested in the research per se and more interested in the ideological structure that supports it. For instance, it is good that researchers reject, say, racism or sexism. But it does no good to set off to do research to prove something we already believe wholeheartedly. It is much better to admit our beliefs, and then see how research can make our beliefs richer, more grounded in experience, and more sophisticated. If, by some chance, our findings go against our beliefs, then this is not the end of the world. It simply means that matters are more complex than we currently understand them. And is not this, in fact, one of the points of doing research? Appropriation can be alleviated somewhat by fostering trust in the fact that research itself will often show us the way to make things better.

- *Rigidity.* Rigidity occurs when researchers are so determined to answer a particular research question in a particular way, or to apply a particular method with total fidelity, that the overall goals for doing research end up taking second place. Qualitative research is tactical. We often do not know what to expect when we get down to details or set out in the field. We need to embrace and use ambiguity and change and surprise, not try to work it out of the equation ahead of time. Rigidity can be alleviated somewhat by always remembering that flexibility is a cardinal principle of qualitative research, and a cardinal virtue of qualitative researchers.

- *Superficiality.* Superficiality occurs when researchers renege on the promise of qualitative research to dig deeper and find things that are fresh and new and that alter the way we understand phenomena. Instead, researchers take a safe or even lazy path. And as a result, they do not tell us anything that we do not already know. We do not need, for example, qualitative research to tell us that poverty makes people desperate and unhappy, and that teachers who care about students often are the best teachers. While these beliefs are important, they are well accepted and well grounded in our culture. Good qualitative researchers often take these commonplace sorts of understandings and apply the "well but" test to them—well, but what happens when we look at them closer, or under different or unusual circumstances? Such research often enriches or even challenges our beliefs, and the educational community is often ultimately better for it. The cure for superficiality, then, is curiosity. Curiosity will naturally pull us away from superficiality and into depth.

- *Sentimentality.* Sentimentality is just another name for inauthenticity. When something is inauthentic, then it is not true to its nature. We are simply using something by manipulating it for effect, rather than looking at it on its own terms. Sometimes sentimentality is corrupt—imagine the movie producer who tells the scriptwriter to kill off the family pet in the last scene so that people can get a good cry. More often than not, sentimentality is unintentional. Researchers want to show that poverty is bad, and that racism is harmful, and that men and women should be treated equally, and so on. Fair enough, but these issues per se are not the topics of research. Creating cartoon pictures and straw men and sound bites will not further our understanding, even if it rallies people to our cause. Good qualitative research can tackle important social causes, but it needs to do so with an eye for seeing things that have never been brought to light before. The best path to the perspectives we need to see things in fresh ways is empathy. Empathy is where we understand things truly from another perspective. If we let those other perspectives lead the way, instead of trying to manipulate our readers and how they will react to what we say, then we are on far firmer ground.

- *Narcissism.* Narcissism occurs when a piece of qualitative research ends up being about the researcher. Everything is turned inward, and everything is funneled through a personal framework. We have to be careful not to confuse autobiographical work with narcissism. Some autobiographical work is wonderfully universal and reaches out to tackle great questions that reso- nate with readers. And some really apparently "objective" and "scientific" work turns out, on close inspection, to be nothing more than the researcher's opinions dressed up in the language of research. Narcissism can be allevi- ated somewhat by compassion. Compassionate researchers are never satisfied with research that is just about themselves. Compassion is always directed outwards—to the participants, to the readers, and to the field. Good research- ers are usually content to settle for fourth place, or lower.

- *Timidity.* Timidity often occurs in the final stages of qualitative research. Researchers often have more findings than they can report. Which findings should be reported, and which should be left out? Ideally, the most impor- tant findings should be presented, and things that are less important or more peripheral can be omitted. Too often, however, researchers only report those findings that they feel most sure of. This timidity is a form of protection— these are findings that no one can challenge. Too often, however, findings are safe because they are telling us things we already know. Good qualitative researchers are not afraid to state controversial or unusual findings if they are truly important. They have done the best job they can to uncover and support these findings, and they have the subsequent courage to put them out for pub- lic consumption. Courage is not the same thing as recklessness—researchers are only reporting important and well-supported findings. Courage is pres- ent when researchers know that there will be reaction and even challenge to their findings, but they need to be part of the public record and discussion, anyway.

Personal reviewers need to be alert to the negative effects of these "deadly sins" in qualitative work. We are also well served to think of ways that existing qualitative research could be improved by moving away from these "sins" and then doing our part to encourage researchers to move in more fruitful directions.

Questions Every Personal Reviewer Needs to Answer

Articles are not the only entities that need to "answer" questions. Each and every one of us, as a personal reviewer, must ask ourselves a series of questions as we read.

How Can an Understanding of the Literature Help Me Improve My Skills as a Personal Reviewer?

In most cases as well, research is built upon other research. Even in those rare cases where researchers might be heading into brand new territory, they are still aware of their own ideas and the ideas of others that are relevant to the research area. Part of doing good research is knowing what others have thought and what research efforts they have made. We can think of these earlier efforts as part of the information trail that has shaped and informed any given research project.

Do I Have Enough Content Knowledge to Understand This Article? Do I Need More Content Background? Where and How Can I Get It?

Personal reviewers never have enough content knowledge. There is always more information in the world than we can possess. It is great fun, however, to try to know as much as possible. We should never lose the zest for gaining knowledge for knowledge's sake. At the same time, we have a responsibility to get "up to speed" in areas where we need to read and understand certain areas of research that are particularly pertinent to us.

One of the fastest ways to get "up to speed" in a given content area is by using the Internet. More and more, students and researchers are turning to the Internet for quick access to content areas. Therefore, we need to say a few things about the Internet in this context.

The Internet offers many resources to the emerging critical reader of research. The Internet is timely, inexpensive, and efficient. It allows for inquiry in diverse directions. That is, researchers can follow divergent paths and directions with greater facility than ever before. Rather than wading through endless library shelves or thumbing through journal after journal, the researcher—armed only with a computer and a good search engine—can move in multiple directions with amazing ease and speed. The Internet has also created a medium of broad influence. An article, which might have only been read by a few thousand specialists in a journal, can now be read by hundreds of thousands of readers. Finally, the Internet can allow inventive readers the possibility of direct informal contact with the researchers themselves. It is no exaggeration to say that the Internet has the power to change the face of educational research in fundamental ways.

There are areas of concern with the Internet as well. Everything on the Internet was put there by someone for a purpose. Few things have been reviewed, so there is more of a chance for errors and inaccuracies. The Internet is often perceived as a lesser form of dissemination of information. As a result, it is not unlikely that some of the best research will not find its way to the Internet. In the future, that will probably change, but for now we have to be careful to seek out the best research articles that are available.

Useful guides to research on the Internet are now available, but they will always be somewhat outdated, since print lags behind online communication. Browne and Keeley (2003) provide a useful basic overview for evaluating online resources.

Another tried-and-true "trick of the trade" for improving our content knowledge is to use literature reviews to lead us to areas where we can build our skill levels. In a sense, the authors of the article have done much of the heavy lifting for us. We can follow their trail to gain access to good sources for new understanding.

The final strategy is the oldest and most fun. We need only nourish and then follow our natural curiosity. Too often, people do not nurture the curiosity we are born with. If we allow ourselves to follow our interests without worrying about its immediate value and usefulness, more often than not we learn things that will be invaluable to us later. People seem to have an instinct to learn and explore, so why not set it free? It can only help us as personal reviewers.

Do I Have the Technical Skills I Need in Order to Understand This Article?

Are the methods and tests used clear to me, and within my domain of personal knowledge? How good is my overall intuitive understanding of what this article is trying to accomplish? Where might my lack of specific personal technical expertise cause problems in understanding and evaluating this article? Where might I turn for help in gaining the technical understanding I might need?

First of all, growth in technical skills requires patience. Most of us build our technical expertise by starting with simple concrete examples and working up slowly. We need to practice our skills to make sure they are sinking in. Finally, we need to reflect and to put things together. All of these activities require time. If we try to rush through the process then all we are doing is sabotaging our own efforts. We would never do this sort of thing to students, so why should we do it to ourselves? Take the time, keep practicing, and give yourself a break. Over time, we will see dramatic gains.

Technical expertise is often too hard to learn strictly by ourselves. Therefore, good personal reviewers are always on the lookout for technical mentors. These mentors come in all sizes and shades. A very clear and practical textbook is a kind of mentor. So is the friend who has limited range, but knows his or her specialized "stuff" quite well. Former teachers are often delighted when old students seek them out for help and advice. Web sites often present complex topics at an introductory level, and provide a web of other resources as well. In short, technical experts are not in hiding. They can be found, and are often just waiting to be asked. Even if they cannot help you, more often than not they can point you in the right direction.

Technical growth is almost always enhanced when we are focused. If we have a particular reason to learn something, then we are much more likely to be able to master it. It may be a trite cliché, but necessity is often the mother of invention.

Finally, good personal reviewers are expanding their expertise along many horizons, whether they are immediately relevant or not. We need to give ourselves permission to follow our instincts and intuitions as we read and explore ideas. If we are not careful, we just might find ourselves enjoying our growth as personal reviewers.

Our Emerging Literacy Orientation

At one level, it is very comfortable to be a consumer of educational research. As consumers, we leave the task of quality control to others. We assume that all the research we get is always Grade A, and so all we need to do is learn how to read it and apply it.

As we become more skilled, however, our responsibilities increase with our powers. It is no longer enough for us to assume that each and every article comes to us without any flaws. We need to take out our detective kits, and give them a once over on our own terms. This is what it means to be a personal reviewer.

It is important for us to see that personal reviewing is not in conflict or competition with the standard reviewing process that governs the best primary research articles. It simply acknowledges the fact that each of us brings something unique to the table. We may have information that was not available to the journal reviewers.

We may be like those people who stand behind us when we are doing a crossword puzzle—we might immediately see something that has "slipped through the cracks" of reviewers who have poured carefully over the work. For whatever reasons, it is important for us to be able to give a work our own personal stamp of approval. And who knows? As we get better and better at this, someday we might be asked to review articles for potential publication. All our work in personal reviewing can only help us be that much more ready.

Practice Makes Perfect

It is now time to practice some of the insights and skills you have explored in this chapter:

- Can you think of several real-world examples of a Type I error? A Type II error? Discuss your examples with your classmates.
- You have already selected at least one quantitative and one qualitative article in a field of your interest. We will look at these articles from the perspective of a personal reviewer. For these articles, consider the following issues: Are the research questions easy to find? Are the references timely and pertinent? What are the greatest areas of strength for each article? How might each article be improved? How might you have done these studies differently?
- Look at your quantitative articles and consider the following points: How well did the researchers address issues of reliability and validity? Are there any potential problems with generalizability? Ecological validity? Discuss your thoughts with your classmates.
- Look at your qualitative articles and consider the following points: How well did the researchers address issues of reliability and validity? Are there any potential problems with generalizability? Ecological validity? Discuss your thoughts with your classmates.
- Take a look at the results and discussion for each article, and see how well integrated the articles really are. Are the results clearly linked to the research questions? What are the results telling you? Did the discussion capture everything the results seemed to say, or are there missing points? Does the article, taken as a whole, make sense to you?
- Create a personal inventory for future growth as a personal reviewer. What content areas do you need to actively pursue? What resources will you use? How can you facilitate your technical growth? What strategies and resources are best suited for you in this area?

From Consumer to Critic

We are now nearing the end of our exploration of the basic aspects of educational research literacy. We have progressed through the steps needed to start the process of becoming a consumer of educational research. We have even addressed some of the basic issues we need to address in order to function as our own personal reviewers. As we continue to read and practice these skills, we will only get better and better. We will be able to tackle harder and more complex articles with greater and greater confidence and skill. There does not seem to be any fundamental avenue left to explore. But is that true?

What About the Art and Craft of Research?

A critical reader is not just good at reading. Critical readers love reading good writing. It is not enough for an educational research article to be informative. Articles are no longer just sources of data and theory and information. In a real way, a research article is an art form. It is the vehicle that researchers use when they take one art form, namely the conduct of research, and create another art form, or the article.

Researchers are often fond of their articles as well. Sometimes, they refer to an especially good piece with the same fondness we might feel for a beloved pet. Research, and research articles, are human endeavors and so often engender genuine authentic human feelings.

Critical readers are trying to assimilate each and every relevant dimension in both the research process and the writing of articles. Critical readers know how to "unpack" articles of their content, but they also know how to respond to articles on multiple levels as well. This is true of any skilled reader. Skilled readers juggle art, craft, content, and style to the maximum benefit of each dimension.

A number of works have looked at the art and craft of research in ways that are useful to the critical reader. Here, we will only look at two of the most common and most famous.

The Elements of Style

This little book by Strunk and White (1979) has been a covert guide for many educational researchers for decades. It is true that educational researchers often turn to the MLA Guidebook or the APA Manual to handle issues of format, but it is just as likely that they will turn to Strunk and White to resolve questions of style. If you have not read this little book yet, then you should do so posthaste. In its laconic commands you will find a veritable wealth of guidance. It addresses matters of usage and grammar, but it also delves into stylistic considerations. Who can forget such compelling and wise commands like "Do not explain too much" and "Do not take shortcuts at the expense of clarity" and most importantly "Be clear." No critical reader should be without this brief and timeless guide.

The Craft of Research

This little book by Booth, Colomb, and Williams (1995) is an invaluable resource for the critical reader. Booth and his colleagues teach us about the logic of research and how it is reflected in the writing. They show us how to find an argument, and make a good one of our own. They give us a lively map of the research process, from the simple term paper to the dissertation. They help us read quickly when it is useful to us, and slowly and carefully when we need to do that. They show us how to find the beliefs that underlie the research, and how to be aware of our own beliefs. Even though this book is not aimed at the educational research literature, it is the sort of work that every critical reader of educational research can read with profit. We find ourselves more literate at the end.

A Handful of Road Maps for Critical Reading

Beyond the two invaluable style books we have considered so far, we will also look at a number of tried and true "guides" in the art of critical reading per se. None of these guides address the topic of research in general, or educational research in particular. Furthermore, we could just as easily find six different choices, and read them with great profit as well. Nonetheless, these six books have served as roadmaps for emerging critical readers for years (and in some cases, decades), and so they have established their usefulness. We will dive right in and look at a few of these classics:

How to Read a Book

This is a classic work by Mortimer Adler (a philosopher) and Charles van Doren (most famous, alas, as a contestant in a rigged TV game show in the 1950s). This book is subtitled "The Classic Guide to Intelligent Reading," and it struggles mightily to live up to that lofty goal.

Make no mistake—Mortimer Adler is the conductor of this particular train. His distinctive voice rings through loud and clear. During his long career (he lived to be nearly 100 years old), Adler wrote a number of guides like this one. He was particularly famous as an expositor of difficult philosophical ideas by using clear and concise language and argumentation, and he brings this skill into this book as well. He and his co-author attack the task of examining the reading process with great clarity, skill, and comprehensiveness.

Here is a very wise piece of advice, among many other such wise pieces, that might well have been written directly to the critical reader of educational research:

> We have said many times that the good reader makes demands on himself when he reads. He reads actively, effortly. Now we are saying something else. The books that you will want to practice your reading on, particularly your analytic reading, *must also make demands on you.* They must seem to you to be beyond your capacity. You need not fear that they really are, because there is no book that is completely out of your grasp if you apply the rules of reading to it that we have described. This does not mean that these rules will accomplish immediate miracles for you. There are certainly some books that will continue to extend you no matter how good a reader you are. Actually, these are the very books you must seek out, because they are the ones that can best help you to become an even more skillful reader. (pp. 339–340; italics theirs)

The Educated Imagination

One of the greatest and most beloved literary critics of the 20th century was Northrup Frye (1964). Frye was one of the founders of the New Criticism movement in literature. Frye was not just concerned about literature, however. He was interested in fostering literate reading in all areas. This particular work is a series of radio addresses that Frye wrote for a general audience, and so it is wonderfully accessible. Here, for instance, he is talking about the different stances that scientists and artists take toward the world, and how it makes their views both similar and different from each other:

> Science begins with the world we have to live in, accepting its data and trying to explain its laws. From there, it moves toward the imagination: it becomes a mental construct, a model of a possible way of interpreting experience. The further it moves in this direction, the more it tends to speak the language of mathematics, which is really one of the languages of the imagination, along with literature and music. Art, on the other hand, begins with the world we construct, not the world we see. It starts with the imagination, and then works toward ordinary experience: that is, it tries to make itself as convincing and recognizable as it can. You can see why we tend to think of the sciences as intellectual and the arts as emotional: one starts with the world as it is, the other with the world we want to have. (pp. 23–24)

Exercises in Style

French novelist and mathematician Raymond Queneau (1958) wrote this delightful little piece in the late 1940s, and it has stayed in print ever since. Queneau starts with a pointless anecdote about a man getting onto a bus and later showing up across town, and retells this same story in 100 different styles. Some of these styles are grammatical—passive voice instead of active voice; some are linguistic and meta-linguistic—using mathematical or medical formulations and concepts; some are cultural—retelling the episode as high opera; and finally many are delightfully unclassifiable—organizing the anecdote by sorting the words into a chart of the parts of speech. This little book is the perfect antidote for the critical reader whose vision has gone stale, and who needs a pleasant but deeply insightful jolt out of a too familiar frame of reference.

Six Memos for the Next Millennium

The greatest tragedy of this little work by Italo Calvino (1988) is the fact that there are actually only five memos. Calvino died suddenly as he was finishing this series of lectures for the Charles Eliot Norton Lecture Series at Harvard.

Calvino was a master fabulist. He told stories of empty suits of armor going into battle, of Marco Polo and Kublai Khan discussing cities that never were, and people using a Tarot deck to tell their life stories. In Calvino you find the desire to get far beneath the surface, to find the less obvious things that never see the light of day but which hold together both tales and theories of intelligibility. In this work, he explores six such hidden structures and shows us how they inform literate sensibilities. He lived to write about lightness, quickness, exactitude, visibility, and multiplicity. Alas, his lecture on consistency was never written.

These essays are lively and stretch the mind in valuably literate ways. For instance, Calvino is concerned with our obsession on being precise at the expense of being authentically human. He stakes this concern compellingly within his essay on exactitude:

> It sometimes seems to me that a pestilence has struck the human race in its most distinctive facility—that is, the use of words. It is a plague affecting language, revealing itself as a loss of cognition and immediacy, an automatism that tends to level out all expression into the most generic, anonymous, and abstract formulas, to dilute meanings, to blunt the edge of expressiveness, extinguishing the spark that shoots out from the collision of words and new circumstances.

This is certainly upping the ante for all forms of literate expression, including educational research articles.

The Limits of Interpretation

One of the most famous authors and critics of our contemporary era is the semiotician and novelist Umberto Eco (1990). Eco's model of literacy is quite complex, but his work is a constant source of reward to the careful and patient reader. For instance, here are some of his thoughts on the Model Reader:

> A text is a device conceived in order to produce its Model Reader. I repeat that this reader is not the one who makes the "only right" conjecture. A text can foresee a Model Reader entitled to try infinite conjectures. The empirical reader is only an actor who makes conjectures about the kind of Model Reader postulated by the text. Since the intention of the text is basically to produce a Model Reader able to make conjectures about it, the initiative of the Model Reader consists in figuring out a Model Author that is not the empirical one and that, at the end, coincides with the intention of the text. (pp. 58–59)

Literate readers are always eager to explore new and exciting dimensions towards being more literate, and theorists like Eco can help lead the way.

How to Read and Why

In a way, we have come full circle from Adler and van Doren with this recent book by critic and cultural advocate Harold Bloom (2000). Bloom reminds us that literacy has a long history, and that throughout its long history literacy has helped us sustain and expand our basic humanity. He makes the following case for literacy at the very outset:

> There is no single way to read well, though there is a prime reason we should read. Information is endlessly available to us; where shall wisdom be found? If

you are fortunate, you encounter a particular teacher who can help, yet finally you are alone, going on without further mediation. Reading well is one of the great pleasures that solitude can afford you, because it is, at least in my experience, the most healing of pleasures.

What Can We Say About Critical Reading as It Applies to Educational Research?

As consumers, we approach articles as sources of information. We learn how to extract that information, and put it to use. As critics, we realize that there are other dynamics as well. Here are three of the most important.

Every Article Is a Conversation

Writers do not write to us. They converse with us. Sometimes, they paint pictures with words that draw us into their realms. Other times, their writing seems like speech traveling from the page to our mental ears. Writers write for two reasons. First of all, they like to see what they can do with words. Second, they have something to say.

Every educational research article is written because its researchers have something that they wanted to say. They wanted to tell us about their studies and explorations, their puzzlements and successes, their breakthroughs and struggles. As we get to be better critical readers, we also get better at seeing how researchers go beyond merely having something to say in their articles.

Pedestrian articles have something to say, but in many cases it is either something we already knew or something we could have figured out on our own with a little bit of free time and reflection. Good articles appeal to the consumer in us—they have something to say and they make it easy for us to find it. Finally, every now and then, there is a great article. When we read a great educational research article, we realize that the researchers are not only telling us something fresh and new and important, but they are using words in ways that are worthy of admiration as well.

Lest we assume that all well-crafted educational research articles are qualitative (since word use is obviously important in qualitative articles), we should not lose sight of the fact that the history of science has been filled with people who have been both excellent scientists and great original writers. If we as critical readers become more and more aware of the conversational excellence in the best educational research articles (qualitative and quantitative), and hold these works up as models, then perhaps we can raise the critical skill level of the field as a whole.

Any Article Can Be a Dialogue

Critical readers do not just listen to authors. Critical readers talk back. They treat any piece of writing as one side of a dialogue. The reader must also contribute, and give back to the process.

How can we read back when we read educational research articles? How can we engage these works in a dialogical way? Here are three practical tips:

- *Take notes*. Reduce complex arguments to outline form. Jot down unclear or controversial points. Mark areas of agreement or disagreement. When you find an article that really speaks to you, make a copy of it and do not be afraid to mark it up. Remember, next week you will have probably forgotten that insightful point you did not get around to writing down.
- *Read it out loud*. All language is grounded in speech. Words were ultimately meant to be heard. If you are having a hard time following a point, read the words out loud. See what the researchers are trying to say to you. Sometimes, this can make a real difference. If you are struggling with statistical tests or charts of data, talk them through as well. Remember, they are trying to say something to you as well.
- *Create a dialogue*. The researchers are on one side of a matter. What is the other side? Can you put yourself on that other side, and see how others might approach the arguments, findings, and conclusions of the article? If there is any frustrated actor or playwright in you, this can be more fun than you might suppose.

As an Educational Research Article Becomes More Innovative and Experimental, Critical Aspects Become More and More Important

At last count, we are living in a postmodern world. Multiple frames of reference inform nearly every major aspect of culture. Information and news comes at us at light speed, and no one has taken much time to interpret it for us. Our contemporary repositories of information, from libraries to the Internet, make the Great Library at Alexandria look like some backwater branch library. TV, film, radio, computers, and the like allow us access to ideas and complex interactions that would have been unimagined a century ago. In this world of a million alternatives and no One Clear Choice, complexity is the order of the day.

This vector of complexity has permeated educational research as well. Action researchers around the world solve problems using virtual space. Critical theorists are reinventing not only the discourse of education, but the forms of that discourse as well. Statistical procedures of staggering complexity, which were literally not calculable by human beings 50 years ago or less, reside in statistical packages on laptop computers. In their desire to compress research and space, journals are publishing articles where two, three, and more studies are woven together in a single article.

This is the richest period in time for educational research, but it is also the hardest time to try to read and evaluate this work. We have two choices. We can either depend more and more on specialists not only to do the work but to read it for us and tell us what it means. This is a dangerous path. Research has always functioned best as a collective process. The more people who opt out of various threads and streams of work, the greater the chance that this work will cut itself off unintentionally from the Great Discussion that is the body of educational research as a whole.

The other choice is the one that this book seeks to address. We need to create more and more critical readers of educational research. At some point, perhaps there will be outlets that specialize in top level critical work. Perhaps there will be valued people in the field who do not do research but who excel at criticism and who share these profound critical insights with the rest of us. More and more, this path is looking like it will be not only useful, but a necessity.

Final Thoughts About Beauty and Truth in Educational Research

This is our final thought—educational research is not just about information. At some deep level, it is part of the overall human endeavor to discover the truth and beauty in our world and within ourselves.

We will end this chapter, and this work, with the words of someone who dedicated her life to the search for truth and beauty. Emily Dickinson had this to say about nature, and how true these words ring to critical readers everywhere, from poetry lovers to lovers of research that put us in touch with the truth in our world:

> What mystery pervades a well!
> The water lives so far,
> Like neighbor from another world
> Residing in a jar.
> The grass does not appear afraid;
> I often wonder he
> Can stand so close and look so bold
> At what is dread to me.
> Related somehow they may be,—
> The sedge stands next the sea,
> Where he is floorless, yet of fear
> No evidence gives he.
> But nature is a stranger yet;
> The ones that cite her most
> Have never passed her haunted house,
> Nor simplified her ghost.
> To pity those that know her not
> Is helped by the regret
> That those who know her, know her less
> The nearer her they get.

Our Emerging Literacy Orientation

Critical reading goes beyond the art and craft of information extraction. It raises that process to the next level by looking at educational research at a stylistic level. While most style issues in educational research are simple or straightforward, there is elegance in a well-done article. Perhaps at some point in the future we can design machines to read text and extract information. But these machines would leave behind the things that make the research process fundamentally and inescapably human. Critical readers value these fundamental aspects in all texts—from epic poetry to statistical reports.

Do not be afraid to ask the big questions. How does this research help me look at education in a different way? How does it help human beings as a whole? In fact, how does it help us be more human, and more humane? We tend to argue that education is specific and practical, but it is also much, much more. Education is a fundamental and basic human activity—as fundamental and basic as eating or sleeping or seeking shelter. Put two or three people together, and in minutes they will be educating each other.

In short, there is a big picture to educational research. Readers who are critically literate in educational research never lose sight of this big picture, even when they are happily wallowing in the methodological and stylistic details.

Practice Makes Perfect

It is now time to practice some of the insights and skills you have explored in this chapter:

- In this chapter, we have assembled a little library for the critical reader of educational research. What works would you include? What would your classmates include? Why?
- We have not developed a comprehensive definition of the concept of educational research literacy. Your final assignment is this—write one. Compare your definition with those of your classmates. Can you reach a consensus on a common definition? You are welcome to submit your definitions to the author or the publisher for possible inclusion in future editions of this work!

Article Literacy Checklist

This checklist is designed to help you remember what questions to ask as you read through each article:

Title

- ☐ Is this a description title?
- ☐ Is this an equation title?
- ☐ Is this a situation title?
- ☐ Is this a process title?
- ☐ Is this a theoretical title?
- ☐ What is the basic content of the article?
- ☐ Does the title tell me enough about the content to see if the article reflects my needs/interests?

Opening Points

☐   Does the opening of the article describe some crisis?

☐   Does the opening of the article describe some important issue?

☐   Does the opening of the article point out some gap, or lacuna, in our knowledge or understanding?

☐   Does the opening of the article suggest we need to look at this topic in more depth?

☐   Does the opening of the article call for some commitment to some action or process?

☐   Does the opening of the article merely summarize the goals or content of the article?

☐   Are both primary and secondary points covered in the opening of the article?

☐   Does the opening of the article give us a clear sense of the goals and orientations of the authors?

Abstract

☐   Does the article have an abstract?

☐   Can the abstract be decoded?

☐   Does the abstract suggest that it is worthwhile to continue reading this article?

Research Goals

☐   Does the article clearly state one or more research goals?

☐   Does the article seek to explore an area that is not well understood?

☐   Does the article seek to predict some result by manipulating and controlling important factors?

☐   Does the article seek to explain some previously unexplained setting or situation?

☐   Does the article seek to organize and interpret factors that have not previously been brought together?

Research Questions

☐   Does the article explicitly state one or more research questions?

☐   What is the research question, and can you put it into your own words?

☐   Is the research question basic, applied, or evaluative?

☐   How does the researcher plan to test or answer the research question?

Research Argument

☐   What sort of argument does the researcher make in order to support the research question?

☐   Does the argument set up the research question in a simple, linear way?

- [ ] Does the argument both set up and support the research question?
- [ ] Does the argument begin with the question and work backwards in order to set it up?
- [ ] Does the argument ground the research question in practical experience?

Literature Review

- [ ] How extensive is the literature review?
- [ ] Does the literature review cover the major studies in the area?
- [ ] Does the literature review cover classic research?
- [ ] Does the literature review focus primarily on current research?
- [ ] Can the literature review lead you to other important areas of related research?

Sample

- [ ] What sort of sample does the study use, and is sample appropriate for its goals and questions?
- [ ] Does the study use a random sample?
- [ ] Does the study use a convenience sample?
- [ ] Does the study use a stratified sample?
- [ ] Does the study use a purposive sample?
- [ ] Does the study use informants in a field setting?
- [ ] Does the study use participants in a collaborative setting?

Research Design

- [ ] What sort of research design is used, and why?
- [ ] Does the study use a descriptive design?
- [ ] Does the study use an experimental design?
- [ ] Does the study use an investigative design?
- [ ] If the study is quantitative, how does it operationalize key variables?
- [ ] If the study is qualitative, how does it detail key efforts and procedures?

Qualitative Findings and Results

- [ ] Does the study use qualitative methods? If so, how do they report their results?
- [ ] Does the study pull together various bits and pieces to form a pattern?
- [ ] Does the study use coding systems to find common themes?
- [ ] Does the study document collaborative efforts?
- [ ] Does the study seek to explain situations that have been previously poorly understood?

Quantitative Findings and Results

☐ Does the study use quantitative methods? If so, how do they report their results?

☐ Does the study seek to describe some sample or population?

☐ Does the study seek to compare one or more groups within a sample or population?

☐ Does the study seek to nail down one or more predictions?

☐ Does the study seek to test one or more hypotheses?

☐ Does the study seek to test the accuracy of some empirical or theoretical model?

Discussions and Conclusions

☐ How does the study interpret and explain its findings?

☐ Does the discussion simply summarize the main findings?

☐ Does the discussion interpret and clarify the main findings?

☐ Does the discussion address complex or perplexing or unexpected results?

☐ Does the discussion interpret complex findings from field studies?

☐ Does the discussion apply one or more theoretical frameworks toward understanding the main findings?

Summary and Technical Issues

☐ Is the article topical and interesting?

☐ Have the researchers made a case for the importance of their study?

☐ Have the researchers stated their research questions clearly?

☐ Is the cited literature clear and relevant?

☐ Have the researchers properly tested their research questions?

☐ Have the researchers made any obvious design errors?

☐ Have the researchers made any obvious statistical errors?

☐ Are any measurement tools reliable and valid?

☐ Have the researchers taken care to avoid Type I and Type II errors?

☐ Are any quantitative findings properly generalizable?

☐ Does the research address realistic issues and circumstances, or is it too artificial?

☐ Has this article helped me hone my research literacy skills?

Glossary of Key Terms

Abstract—The part of a primary research article that comes after the **Title** and before the **Introduction**. It is the job of the Abstract to provide a short review of the article, following specific rules and conventions.

Action Research—A form of **Qualitative Research** that emphasizes working with participants to bring about specific improvements.

Analysis—A systematic process of examining and/or testing **Data**. It is usually grounded in the **Research Questions**.

ANOVA—Shorthand for "analysis of variance." An **Inferential Statistics** technique designed to test if there are differences among three or more **Treatment** groups.

Applied Research—Research targeted to address specific practical issues or problems. As opposed to **Basic Research**.

Argument—A coherent set of claims to support asking a **Research Question**. These arguments can either set up the question, support the question, or both set up and support the question.

Autoethnography—A specialized form of **Ethnography** that combines ethnographic and autobiographical techniques.

Basic Research—Research conducted to advance knowledge in general, or to satisfy the curiosity of the researcher. As opposed to **Applied Research**.

Bibliography—Rarely found in **Research Articles**. A bibliography lists all sources that were useful in creating the article, whether those sources were cited or not. Most often, we find articles using a **References** section, where actually cited sources are listed.

Case Study—A type of **Qualitative Research** method where a small number of people or situations, sometimes even only one person or situation, is examined in great depth.

Central Tendency—One property of **Distributions** that is examined in **Descriptive Statistics**. Central Tendency describes the ways that scores in a distribution cluster around some middle point. Common measures of Central Tendency include the **Mode**, **Median**, and **Mean**.

Chi-Square—A statistical technique designed to compare expected and actually observed frequencies, to see if there are any differences between these two categories.

Conclusions—The part of the research article that follows the **Results**. In the conclusion, results are summarized, explained, implications are examined, and/or future research is suggested.

Confidence Error—Another name for **a Type I Error**, where the statistical test is too lenient and so the results cannot be trusted. Is also called a **False Positive**.

Constant—A measurement that never changes its value. As opposed to **Variable**.

Constructivism—A philosophical position adopted by some qualitative researchers. In its most radical form, constructivism argues that there is no inherent knowledge in the world, but that we create all knowledge. Less radical forms argue that we co-create certain kinds of knowledge in social situations.

Consumer of Research—A person who has no intention or need of becoming a researcher but who needs to know how to read and understand research reports and articles. As such people become more skilled and literate in research, they become **Research Critics**.

Convenience Sample—A type of **Sample** where **Participants** who are readily available are used. One of the weakest and least systematic types of **Samples**.

Correlation—A statistical test where two variables are compared on a pair-by-pair basis. A positive correlation indicates a strong direct relationship, a negative correlation indicates a strong inverse relationship, and a zero correlation indicates no relationship.

Critical Theory—A type of **Theory** most often found in **Qualitative Research**, where hidden **Ideologies** are uncovered and consciousness of their effects are raised.

Data—Plural of **Datum**; a collection of measurements or information used in a research study. Data that have been collected but not yet analyzed are called **Raw Data**.

Datum—A single piece of information, or a single measurement. Rarely used; most often discussed in the plural form as **Data**.

Dependent Variable—Usually found in **Experimental** or **Quasi-Experimental Designs**, the **Variable** that changes as the result of the treatment. Sometimes used in any **Quantitative Research** study that looks at the impact of different effects. As opposed to an **Independent Variable**.

Descriptive Statistics—That branch of **Statistics** that looks at **Distributions**, especially in terms of **Central Tendency** and **Dispersion**. As opposed to **Inferential Statistics**.

Determinism—The branch of scientific philosophy that says that the laws of science are absolute. Now mostly discredited and abandoned.

Discussion—The part of a **Primary Article** where **Results** and **Findings** are summarized and examined, unusual aspects are explained, implications are laid out, and possible future research is described.

Dispersion—One property of **Distributions** that is examined in **Descriptive Statistics**. Dispersion describes the ways that scores in a distribution systematically spread out from some middle point. Common measures of **Dispersion** include the **Range** and the **Standard Deviation**.

Distribution—In **Statistics**, a set of scores most often described by their **Central Tendency** and **Dispersion**. A **Distribution** can describe either a **Sample** or a **Population**.

Ecological Validity—A type of **Validity** particularly important in **Qualitative Research** where the **Data** and the research efforts are true to life and realistic.

Education—A basic aspect of human culture, where people teach and learn from each other. The formal style of education is called schooling.

Educational Research—A form of research that studies how people teach and learn in formal and informal settings.

Ethnography—A **Qualitative Research** method where researchers immerse themselves in a particular cultural setting in order to understand it better. Most often researchers use **Participant Observation** strategies to gather **Data**. Special forms of ethnography include **Autoethnography** and **Microethnography**.

Evaluation—A type of empirical activity similar to research where the evaluator seeks to determine if a set of promised or described settings or activities match the reality of the situation.

Experimental Design—A type of **Research Design** where all factors except for a treatment effect are controlled so as to isolate the impact of that treatment.

Experimenter Effects—An error in **Quantitative Research** where the experimenter himself or herself has a systematic impact on the **Participants** or process.

Factor Analysis—A particular type of model building in **Quantitative Research** where related variables are combined to create higher-order explanatory factors.

Fallibility—A principle in scientific research that states that any finding is not certain, no matter how solid the evidence so far, and could end up being proven wrong.

False Negative—Another name for a **Power Error**, where the statistical test is too stringent and so significant results cannot be identified. Is also called a **Type II Error**.

False Positive—Another name for a **Confidence Error**, where the statistical test is too lenient and so the results cannot be trusted. Is also called a **Type I Error**.

Findings—Another name for **Results**; sometimes the term **Findings** is used to describe **Results** from less controlled settings and field-oriented research.

Focus Group—A research strategy in **Qualitative Research** where six to eight **Participants** are asked a systematic number of questions to get at both individual and group understandings.

Generalizability—The ability to extend a particular set of procedures or findings to a larger group than the given set of **Participants** or conditions for a given study.

Goal—What the researcher is hoping to accomplish in the research study. Related to the **Purpose**.

Grounded Theory—A specialized form of **Qualitative Research** where the researcher starts with no preconceptions and builds **Theory** by collecting **Data** from the ground up.

Halo Effect—A source of systematic error in **Quantitative Research** where change of any kind tends to affect results in a positive way.

Hermeneutics—Literally, the art of reading and interpreting texts. Modified in **Qualitative Research** as a way of interpreting **Data** and **Patterns** of **Data** as if they were texts.

Hypothesis—In **Quantitative Research**, a claim systematically derived from the **Research Question** that is tested to see whether it is true or not.

Ideology—In **Critical Theory**, a set of unexamined but systematic beliefs that affect our behaviors without us being aware of them.

Illuminative Research Design—A type of **Qualitative Research** where the researcher is looking for new ways to understand some puzzling situation or phenomenon.

Implications—Often found in **Conclusions** sections of articles, these are discussions of what the **Findings** might mean when we look at the bigger picture.

Independent Variable—In an **Experimental Design**, the **Variable** that the researcher changes in order to create different levels of the treatment. In a **Quasi-Experimental Design**, this **Variable** is not under the strict control of the researcher, but changes in a systematic manner anyway. As opposed to a **Dependent Variable**.

Inferential Statistics—That branch of **Statistics** that looks at making decisions about whether or not two or more groups are significantly different from one another. As opposed to **Descriptive Statistics**.

Interpretation—The act of systematically looking at situations, phenomena, results, or findings in order to make sense of them.

Interpretive Research Design—A type of **Qualitative Research** where the researcher is seeking to look at some situation or phenomenon from a different type of systematic viewpoint.

Interview—A **Qualitative Research** technique where **Participants** are asked to answer questions and provide information orally. Can be either **Unstructured** or **Semi-Structured**.

Introduction—The beginning part of a research article, where the researchers lay out their **Purpose, Goals, Research Questions**, and **Arguments**.

Investigative Research Design—A type of **Qualitative Research** where the researcher is seeking to dig deeper into a situation or phenomenon in order to find something new or previously less well understood.

Literacy—Generally speaking, the ability to read. Most often used to describe the art of reading skillfully.

Literature Review—That part of an article where prior research is presented to support the **Research Argument** and shape the **Research Question**.

Material Analysis—A type of **Qualitative Research** that looks at such things as documents, records, cultural artifacts, and other products of material culture.

Mean—The measure of **Central Tendency** known as the average score. The **Mean** is an important concept in both **Descriptive** and **Inferential Statistics**.

Meaning—The central focus of **Qualitative Research**. As a researcher grasps the meaning of things, then insight and understanding follow.

Measurement—The systematic process of determining values of **Variables**.

Median—The measure of **Central Tendency** that divides the **Distribution** into two equal halves. Also called the middle score.

Methods—Another name for that part of the article that discusses **Procedures** and other logistical issues. Sometimes called **Procedures**.

Microethnography—A specialized form of **Ethnography** where the researcher conducts a narrowly focused study over a short period of time.

Mixed Methods Research—A fairly new type of research where **Qualitative** and **Quantitative Research** methods are systematically combined.

Mode—The measure of **Central Tendency** that describes the most common score.

Multiple Regression—A specialized form of **Regression** where more than one predictor **Variable** is used.

Narrative Analysis—A specialized research method in **Qualitative Research** that looks at the dynamics and characteristics of stories and story-like types of **Data**.

Nominalism—A branch of philosophy that says that complex things are built out of simple things. An important source of ideas for both science and **Quantitative Research**.

Normal Distribution—The most important type of distribution in **Educational Research**. When a **Distribution** is normal, then the **Mean** and **Standard Deviation** are related to each other in important systematic ways. It is also symmetrical, which indicates the **Variable** being measured is also systematic. Represented visually as the Normal Curve or sometimes the Bell Curve.

Null Hypothesis—The type of **Hypothesis** most often used in **Inferential Statistics**. When the **Null Hypothesis** is used, the researcher is actually testing the likelihood that the **Null Hypothesis** ought to be accepted. When that is shown to be highly unlikely, the actual **Hypothesis** is then accepted.

Objectivity—A standard of scientific research where the researcher seeks to avoid any personal bias from interfering with the research per se.

Observation—A systematic use of our senses, primarily visual, in research. Particularly important in **Qualitative Research**.

Opening—In our scheme of understanding articles, the first few sentences or the first paragraph of the article.

Operationalization—A process found in **Quantitative Research** where the meaning of concepts are defined in terms of the operations used to measure them.

Oral History—A type of specialized series of **Interviews** where one or more informants are questioned in depth about their experiences and perceptions concerning an extended period of time.

Parameter—A description of the characteristics of a **Population**.

Participant Observation—A technique in **Qualitative Research** where the researcher not only observes a particular natural setting, but gets involved in that setting to some degree.

Participants—The currently accepted term for describing people who are involved in a study. It replaces the older term **Subjects**.

Participatory Research Design—A type of **Qualitative Research** where the researcher is actually involved in the research process, usually seeking to improve matters or conditions.

Path Analysis—A specialized form of model building in **Quantitative Research**, where relations among **Variables** are lined up along some kind of meaningful time framework.

Patterns—Systematic and meaningful groupings of **Data**, most often found in **Qualitative Research**.

Peer Review—A process used in journals that publish **Primary Articles** where a submitted article is sent to two or more experts in the field for a blind evaluation (where the reviewers do not know the names of the researchers who wrote the article).

Phenomenology—A branch of philosophy that says our perceptions and our thoughts about things we experience are intermingled. In **Qualitative Research**, Phenomenological methods look at our opinions and awareness of phenomena.

Population—Another name for the entire group of people or things to be studied or measured. Most often, we draw a **Sample** from that **Population** to study instead.

Portraiture—A specialized type **of Case Study**, most often used in **Qualitative Research**, where a systematic and compelling artistically rendered picture of a **Participant** or group is rendered.

Posttest—In certain **Research Designs**, a measurement you take after the treatment that will then be compared to the **Pretest** score.

Power Error—Another name for a **Type II Error**, where the statistical test is too stringent and so significant results cannot be identified. Is also called a **False Negative**.

Pretest—In certain **Research Designs**, a measurement you take prior to the treatment that you will compare to the **Posttest** score.

Primary Article—An article written by the researchers who did the actual work, usually published in a **Peer Reviewed** journal. As opposed to a **Secondary Article**.

Probability—A mathematical principle that says that things do not have to be **Deterministic**, but only likely, in order to be systematic. Most tests used in **Inferential Statistics** are based on **Probability**.

Procedures—That part of an article where the **Methods** and other logistical aspects are described in enough detail that the research can either be **Replicated** or fully understood.

Purpose—In an article, the statement by the researchers of why they are doing the research in the first place.

Purposive Sample—A **Sample** where the members of the **Sample** are picked because of their unique characteristics. Most often found in **Qualitative Research**.

Qualitative Research—That type of empirical research that focuses on the study of **Meaning** and related phenomena in natural settings.

Quantitative Research—That type of empirical research that focuses on the task of identifying and testing basic rules and laws that underlie typical behaviors and settings.

Quasi-Experimental Design—A **Research Design** that shares most of the properties of a true **Experimental Design**, except that the **Independent Variable** cannot be strictly controlled or manipulated.

Random Sample—An important type of **Sample** in **Quantitative Research**. When a **Sample** is chosen at random, it lessens the chance for any sort of systematic distortion of that **Sample** in relation to the **Population**.

Range—The most primitive measure of **Dispersion**; it is the distance between the lowest score and the highest score.

Raw Data—Data that have been collected but not yet analyzed.

References—The part of an article where the published sources that were actually cited in the article are listed alphabetically.

Regression—A **Statistical** process where the values of a predictor **Variable** are used to help estimate the possible value of a target **Variable**.

Reliability—A **Statistical** test used to measure the accuracy of the process used to gather **Data**. Some common forms of **Reliability** include test-retest reliability, alternate forms reliability, and internal consistency.

Repeated Measures—A **Statistical Research Design** used in **Quantitative Research** where **Data** is gathered from the same **Participants** at different times. A **Pretest-Posttest** design is a simple form of repeated measures.

Replication—The ability to repeat a research process and get the same answer. Most important in **Quantitative Research**.

Representative Sample—A type of **Sample** where some effort has been made to make sure the **Sample** resembles the **Population** in one or more important ways.

Research Article—Another name for a **Primary Article**, especially where actual research has been conducted and the **Results** presented.

Research Critic—The intended end goal of the **Consumer of Research**. Research critics are active, engaged, and informed.

Research Design—The systematic plan for answering the **Research Questions**.

Research Literacy—That form of **Literacy** that allows a person to read and understand research articles in an informed and critical fashion.

Research Question—A basic question converted into a form that can be examined or tested by using research methods and procedures.

Results—That section of an article that presents the key **Data** related to the **Research Questions**. Also, the name of those **Findings**.

Rigidity—A problem in **Qualitative Research** where the researcher is too concerned with following a specific method and possibly misses a chance to find something important.

Sample—A subset of a **Population**. **Samples** can either be systematic or unsystematic.

Scientific Method—The process of observing phenomena, making predictions, testing those predictions, and modifying existing **Theory**.

Secondary Article—An article written for a lay audience, most often not written by the researchers themselves and published in more popular journals. As opposed to **Primary Article**.

Semi-Structured Interview—An **Interview** process where each **Participant** is asked the same set of questions, usually in the same order. Designed to provide consistency across participants to facilitate comparisons.

Sentimentality—A problem in **Qualitative Research** where the researcher allows his or her emotions to get in the way and obscure his or her findings.

Standard Deviation—A systematic measure of **Dispersion** that takes into account the differences of each score from the **Mean**. An important tool in both **Descriptive** and **Inferential Statistics**.

Statistics—The branch of mathematics that uses the principles of **Probability** to describe **Distributions** and test potential differences among groups. Also, a description of the characteristics of a **Sample**.

Stratified Sample—A specialized type of **Representative Sample** where key demographics in a **Population** are mirrored in the **Sample**.

Structural Equation Modeling—An advanced modeling process in **Quantitative Research** where latent variables are incorporated into the modeling process.

Subjects—Old-fashioned term to describe people in research studies. Nowadays, the term **Participants** is preferred.

Superficiality—A problem in **Qualitative Research** where the researcher settles for simple results and possibly misses a chance to find something important.

t-test—A **Statistical** test that allows the researcher to compare group **Means** to see if they are significantly different from each other or not.

Targeted Sample—Another name for a **Purposive Sample**.

Theme—A unit of **Data** organization in **Qualitative Research**. Often produced using coding strategies.

Theory—An organized body of testable claims that can be proved or disproved with research.

Timidity—A problem in **Qualitative Research** where the researcher plays it too safe and possibly misses a chance to find something important.

Title—The name of an article; often an important source of information.

Type I Error—Another name for a **Confidence Error**, where the statistical test is too lenient and so the results cannot be trusted. Is also called a **False Positive**.

Type II Error—Another name for a **Power Error**, where the statistical test is too stringent and so significant results cannot be identified. Is also called a **False Negative**.

Unstructured Interview—An **Interview** style where the researcher asks a few simple general questions to the **Participant**, and then the **Participant** is free to take the discussion in whatever direction might be useful. Most often found in **Qualitative Research**.

Validity—A measure of the authenticity of **Data**. When **Data** are valid, then we are actually measuring what we claim we are measuring. Both **Qualitative Research** and **Quantitative Research** use differing forms of validity.

Variable—A measurement that can change its value depending on conditions or treatments. As opposed to **Constant**.

References

Adler, M. J., & Van Doren, C. (1972). *How to read a book: The classic guide to intelligent reading.* New York: Simon & Schuster.

Boas, F. (1965). *The mind of primitive man.* New York: Free Press. (Original work published 1911)

Bodrova, E., Leong, D. J., & Paynter, D. E. (October, 1999). Literacy standards for preschool learners. *Educational Leadership, 57*(2), 42–46.

Bloom, H. (2000). *How to read and why.* New York: Simon & Schuster.

Bogdan, R. C., & Biklen, S. K. (1998). *Qualitative research for education: An introduction to theory and methods* (3rd ed.). Boston, MA: Allyn and Bacon.

Booth, W. C., Colomb, G. G., & Williams, J. M. (1995). *The craft of research.* Chicago, IL: University of Chicago Press.

Browne, N., & Keeley, S. (2003). *The Prentice Hall guide to evaluating online resources.* Upper Saddle River, NJ: Prentice Hall.

Calvino, I. (1988). *Six memos for the next millennium.* New York: Vintage Books.

Campbell, D. T., & Stanley, J. C. (1966). *Experimental and quasi-experimental designs for research.* Boston, MA: Houghton Mifflin.

Chambers, J. M., Cleveland, W. S., Kleiner, B., & Tukey, P. A. (1983). *Graphical methods for data analysis.* Belmont, CA: Wadsworth.

Clark, C. (2001). BIO 190—Writing an abstract. California State Polytechnic University, Pomona, http://www.csupomona.edu/~jcclark/classes/bio190/abstract.html.

Cresswell, J. W. (2002). *Educational research: Planning, conducting, and evaluating quantitative and qualitative research.* Upper Saddle River, NJ: Prentice Hall.

Crosby, A. W. (1997). *The measure of reality: Quantification and Western society, 1250–1600.* Cambridge, UK: Cambridge University Press.

Crotty, M. (1998). *The foundations of social research: Meaning and perspective in the research process.* Thousand Oaks, CA: Sage.

December, J., & Katz, S. (2003). Abstracts. Rensselaer Polytechnic Institute. Retrieved from http://www.rpi.edu/dept/llc/writecenter/web/abstracts.html.

Denzin, N. K., & Lincoln, Y. S. (1994). *Handbook of qualitative research.* Thousand Oaks, CA: Sage.

Eco, U. (1990). *The limits of interpretation.* Bloomington, IN: Indiana University Press.

REFERENCES

Eisenhart, M., & Borko, H. (1993). *Designing classroom research: Themes, issues, and struggles.* Boston, MA: Allyn and Bacon.

Ellis, C. (1995). The other side of the fence: Seeing black and white in a small Southern town. *Qualitative Inquiry, 1,* 147–167.

Evans, J. D. (1996). *Straightforward statistics for the behavioral sciences.* Pacific Grove, CA: Brooks/Cole.

Feyerabend, P. K. (1975). *Against method.* London: NLB.

Fielding, N. G., & Lee, R. M. (1998). *Computer analysis and qualitative research.* London: Sage.

Flaxman, S. G. (September, 2000). Play: An endangered species. *Instructor, 110*(2), 39–41.

Folks, J. L. (1981). *Ideas of statistics.* New York: Wiley.

Freire, P. (1983). *Pedagogy of the oppressed.* New York: Continuum. (Original work published 1968)

Frye, N. (1964). *The educated imagination.* Bloomington, IN: Indiana University Press.

Geertz, C. (1973). *The interpretation of cultures.* New York: Basic Books.

Giroux, H. (1988). *Teachers as intellectuals: Toward a critical pedagogy of learning.* South Hadley, MA: Bergin & Garvey.

Glaser, B. G. (1978). *Theoretical sensitivity.* Mill Valley, CA: The Sociology Press.

Glaser, B. G., & Strauss, A. L. (1967). *The discovery of grounded theory: Strategies for qualitative research.* Chicago: Aldine Publishing Company.

Gredler, M. E. (1999). *Classroom assessment and learning.* New York: Longman.

Habermas, J. (1971). *Knowledge and human interests.* Boston: Beacon Press.

Hammersley, M. (1990). *Reading ethnographic research: A critical guide.* New York: Longman.

Heath, S. B. (1983). *Ways with words.* Cambridge, UK: Cambridge University Press.

Hill, M. R. (1993). *Archival strategies and techniques.* Newbury Park, CA: Sage.

Hittleman, D. R., & Simon, A. J. (2002). *Interpreting educational research: An introduction for consumers of research* (3rd ed.). Upper Saddle River, NJ: Prentice Hall.

Hodder, I. (2000). The interpretation of documents and material culture. In N. K. Denzin & Y. S. Lincoln (Eds.), *Handbook of qualitative research* (2nd ed., pp. 703–716). Thousand Oaks, CA: Sage.

Hopkins, D. (2002). *A teacher's guide to classroom research* (3rd ed.). Buckingham: Open University Press.

Hubbard, R. S., & Power, B. M. (2003). *The art of classroom inquiry: A handbook for teacher researchers* (2nd ed.). Portsmouth, NH: Heinemann.

Huck, S. W. (2000). *Reading statistics and research* (3rd ed.). New York: Longman.

Jacob, E. (1987). Qualitative research traditions: A review. *Review of Educational Research, 57,* 1–50.

Kies, D. (2003). Writing an abstract. College of DuPage. Retrieved from http://papyr.com/hypertextbooks/engl_102/abstract.htm.

Kincheloe, J. L. (2002). *Teachers as researchers: Qualitative inquiry as a path to empowerment* (2nd ed.). New York: Routledge Falmer.

Kirk, R. E. (1984). *Elementary statistics* (2nd ed.). Monterey, CA: Brooks/Cole.

Kranzler, J. H. (2003). *Statistics for the terrified* (3rd ed.). Upper Saddle River, NJ: Prentice Hall.

Krathwohl, D. R. (1998). *Methods of educational and social science research: An integrated approach* (2nd ed.). New York: Longman.

Kuhn, T. (1970). *The structure of scientific revolutions* (2nd ed.). Chicago: University of Chicago Press.

Kvale, S. (1996). *InterViews: An introduction to qualitative research interviewing.* Thousand Oaks, CA: Sage.

Lakatos, I. (1978). *The methodology of scientific research programmes: Philosophical papers, Volume 1.* Cambridge: Cambridge University Press.

Lancy, D. F. (1993). *Qualitative research in education: An introduction to the major traditions.* New York: Longman.

Lather, P. (1991). *Getting smart: Feminist research and pedagogy with/in the postmodern.* New York: Routledge.

Latour, B. (1999). *Pandora's hope: Essays on the reality of science studies.* Cambridge, MA: Harvard University Press.

Lawrence-Lightfoot, S., & Davis, J. H. (1997). *The art and science of portraiture.* San Francisco, CA: Jossey-Bass Publishers.

LeCompte, M. D., & Preissle, J. (1993). *Ethnography and qualitative design in educational research* (2nd ed.). San Diego, CA: Academic Press.

Levi-Strauss, C. (1966). *The savage mind.* Chicago, IL: University of Chicago Press.

Lincoln, Y. S., & Guba, E. G. (1982). *Naturalistic inquiry.* Newbury Park, CA: Sage.

Lunneborg, C. E., & Abbott, R. D. (1983). *Elementary multivariate analysis for the behavioral sciences: Applications of basic structure.* New York: North-Holland.

Malinowski, B. (1961). *Argonauts of the Western Pacific.* New York: Dutton.

McColskey, W., & McMunn, N. (October, 2000). Strategies for dealing with high-stakes state tests. *Phi Delta Kappan, 82*(2), 115–120.

McLaren, P. (1998). *Life in schools* (3rd ed.). New York: Longman.

McMillan, J. H. (2000). *Educational research: Fundamentals for the consumer* (3rd ed.). New York: Addison Wesley Longman.

McTaggart, R. (1991). *Action research: A short modern history.* Geelong, Victoria, Australia: Deakin University Press.

Merriam. S. B. (1998). *Qualitative research and case study applications in education.* San Francisco, CA: Jossey-Bass.

Miles, M. B., & Huberman, A. M. (1994). *Qualitative data analysis* (2nd ed.). Thousand Oaks, CA: Sage.

Minium, E. W., Clarke, R. C., & Coladarci, T. (1999). *Elements of statistical reasoning* (2nd ed.). New York: Wiley.

Morgan, D. L. (1998). *The focus group guidebook.* Thousand Oaks, CA: Sage

Moustakas, C. (1994). *Phenomenological research methods.* Thousand Oaks, CA: Sage.

O'Neil, J. (September, 1996). On emotional intelligence: A conversation with Daniel Goleman. *Educational Leadership, 54*(1), 6–11.

Patton, M. Q. (2001). *Qualitative evaluation and research methods* (3rd ed.). Newbury Park, CA: Sage.

Phillips, J. L. (2000). *How to think about statistics* (6th ed.). New York: Freeman.

Polkinghorne, D. E. (1988). *Narrative knowing and the human sciences.* Albany, NY: State University of New York Press.

Queneau, R. (1958). *Exercises in style.* New York: New Directions. (Original work published 1947)

Richardson, L. (1995). Narrative and sociology. In J. Van Maanen (Ed.), *Representation in ethnography* (pp. 198–221). Thousand Oaks, CA: Sage.

Salsburg, D. (2001). *The lady tasting tea: How statistics revolutionized science in the twentieth century.* New York: Freeman.

Schatzman, L., & Strauss, A. L. (1973). *Field research: Strategies for a natural sociology.* Englewood Cliffs, NJ: Prentice-Hall.

Schumacker, R. E., & Lomax, R. O. (1996). *A beginner's guide to structural equation modeling*. Mahwah, NJ: Erlbaum.

Shank, G. D. (2006). *Qualitative research: A personal skills approach* (2nd ed.). Upper Saddle River, NJ: Prentice Hall.

Siegel, S., & Castellan, N. J., Jr. (1988). *Nonparametric statistics for the behavioral sciences* (2nd ed.). New York: McGraw-Hill.

Spindler, G. (1982). *Doing the ethnography of schooling: Educational anthropology in action*. Prospect Heights, IL: Waveland Press.

Spradley, J. P. (1979). *The ethnographic interview*. New York: Holt, Rinehart and Winston.

Spradley, J. P. (1980). *Participant observation*. New York: Holt, Rinehart and Winston.

Stake, R. E. (1995). *The art of case study research*. Thousand Oaks, CA: Sage.

Strauss, A., & Corbin, J. (1998). *Basics of qualitative research: Techniques and procedures for developing grounded theory*. Thousand Oaks, CA: Sage.

Stringer, E. (2004). *Action research in education*. Upper Saddle River, NJ: Prentice Hall.

Strunk, W., Jr., & White, E. B. (1979). *The elements of style* (3rd ed.). New York: Macmillan.

van Belle, G. (2002). *Statistical rules of thumb*. New York: Wiley.

von Glasersfeld, E. (1984). An introduction to radical constructivism. In P. Watzlawick (Ed.), *The invented reality* (pp. 17–40). New York: Norton.

Wainer, H. (1992). Understanding graphs and tables. *Educational Researcher, 21*(1), 14–23.

Weinberg, G. H., & Schumaker, J. A. (1997). *Statistics: An intuitive approach* (4th ed.). Belmont, CA: Wadsworth.

Williams, F., & Monge, P. (2001). *Reasoning with statistics: How to read quantitative research* (5th ed.). Fort Worth, TX: Harcourt.

Wink, J. (2000). *Critical pedagogy: Notes from the real world* (2nd ed.). New York: Addison Wesley Longman.

Wolcott, H. F. (1995). *The art of fieldwork*. Walnut Creek, CA: Altamira Press.

Index

Page numbers given in **boldface** type refer to tables.